Advance Praise

The destruction of the earth's environment is the human rights challenge of our time. The most devastating effects are visited on the poor, those with no involvement in creating the problem. A deep injustice. Among its many treasures, this book offers solutions that lead with equity for the benefit of all.
> —Desmond Mpilo Tutu, Archbishop
> Emeritus, Cape Town, South Africa

Carl Anthony has been ahead of the curve for decades, and, as this book makes clear, that's exactly where he remains. If you want to understand why today's intersections between environment, race, and class are so crucial, then this is the book to read. And if you want to learn how to make change, then it's the book to dog-ear and underline!
> —Bill McKibben, Cofounder, 350.org; author, *End of Nature*

The Earth, the City, and the Hidden Narrative of Race is a profound memoir that captures and grapples with some of the most critical issues of our time. Truly essential reading.
> —john a. powell, JD, Director, Haas Institute for a Fair &
> Inclusive Society; Professor of Law, African American
> & Ethnic Studies, University of California, Berkeley

No one has done more to bring forth the conjunction of cosmology, ecology, and justice than Carl Anthony. This book lights the path forward in remarkable ways. We are all in his debt.
> —Mary Evelyn Tucker, PhD, Yale University Forum on
> Religion and Ecology; coauthor, *Journey of the Universe*

Carl Anthony combines two qualities rarely found in one person. He has been an extraordinary visionary and he is a pragmatic, unflinching realist. He has been constantly ahead of his time, virtually coining the concept of environmental justice, and then brilliantly acting upon injustice throughout his life. You will find answers here to questions you may not have even considered and insights that will vividly display the roots, causes, and antidotes to our endemic racism. Most importantly, you will see the world through the eyes of one of the most wonderful men you will ever know or meet. This is a tutorial. By all means, take the class.
> —Paul Hawken, environmentalist, entrepreneur;
> author, *Drawdown: The Most Comprehensive*
> *Plan Ever Proposed to Reverse Global Warming*

Carl Anthony has devoted his life's work to finding and connecting the dots that link environment, race, cities, and justice. This new work, *The Earth, the City, and the Hidden Narrative of Race*, collects his decades of research, on-the-ground experience, collaborations with others, and lessons learned into a compendium that is at once history, analysis, and tool kit for advancing an agenda for equity and justice. Carl Anthony's wisdom, voice, and experience are gifts to activists and advocates for racial, economic, and environmental justice. Read this book, discuss its content, and take action.

—**Angela Glover Blackwell**, CEO, PolicyLink

Carl Anthony has long been a pioneer in the fields of environmental justice, urban design, and regional equity—and so, it is little surprise that he pioneers once again in offering a compelling new way to tell a powerful tale of change and transformation. Gracefully flipping between personal experience, intellectual ruminations, and play-by-play accounts of building new social movements, he offers a remarkably wise book that grips and engages you at every turn. His humble telling of his own remarkable story reminds us that a life worth lived is one that contributes to uncovering a new narrative of hope—and his evident commitment to social justice, concern for the life of the planet, and sense of the long sweep of time will inspire others to find new allies and new narratives in the struggle for sustainability.

—**Manuel Pastor**, Professor, Sociology and American Studies & Ethnicity, University of Southern California; Director, USC Program for Environmental and Regional Equity

The epic journey through what Carl Anthony calls "deep time" starts with the "flaring forth" of the Big Bang, weaves across millennia of achievements and traumas of human civilization, chronicles his own awakening in the civil rights movement and shaping the environmental justice movement, and continues to illuminate the existential challenges of our time. What he terms the "hidden narrative of race" is not so much invisible, as so finely encoded into the very essence of the human experience that it can defy human perception. We are blessed that Carl has applied his unique and magnificent cosmovision to not only reinterpret this Universe Story, but to reinspire all of our dedication to the Great Work of achieving social and environmental justice.

—**Jonathan K. London**, PhD, Director, Center for Regional Change, University of California, Davis; Chair, Community Development Graduate Group

This book maps the life of an extraordinary man. It weaves together a journey of self-discovery, a search for the roots of racial injustice, and an education in the shaping of cities. Along the way, Anthony makes the unprecedented leap of grasping the urban environment as a crucial dimension of the black experience and the struggle for liberation. Early on, Anthony realized the importance of creating a new story about people and places that could inspire struggles at every scale, from the neighborhood to the nation to the world; and what he came up with was revolutionary—a unified vision of the struggles for racial justice, equitable cities, and saving the earth.

—**Richard Walker**, PhD, Professor Emeritus, Department
of Geography, University of California, Berkeley;
author, *The Country in the City*

Carl Anthony has for many years been working on how to integrate a range of sources, from his own personal experience to the history of the universe. Now, he shares with us his carefully considered analysis of how we can transform our understandings of the earth and the cities in which we live, better achieve climate and environmental justice, and foster the full participation of people of all races in a sustainable society.

—**Lowell Gustafson**, PhD, President,
International Big History Association;
Professor, Political Science, Villanova University

I have been inspired by Carl Anthony ever since I encountered his work and, later, him in the late 1990s. *The Earth, the City, and the Hidden Narrative of Race* culminates and weaves together the interconnected strands of African American history, environmental justice, the city, and the collective revisioning of the great work of healing relationship to Earth and one another. This book contains a priceless narrative needed for any ecological and/or social justice activist, practitioner, urban planner, or scholar seeking a bigger story to restoration.

—**Jeanine M. Canty**, PhD, Professor and Chair,
Environmental Studies and Environmental/Resilient
Leadership, Naropa University

In *The Earth, the City, and the Hidden Narrative of Race*, Carl Anthony crafts a powerfully expansive evolutionary journey and vision. His is a story rooted in the transformative rethinking and revisioning of identity and place.

—**Belvie Rooks**, producer, *The House on Coco Road*

Carl Anthony's clarity and vision is here at last for us to drawn upon, and it's not a moment too soon. We've long needed a new story of race and place, and that's what *The Earth, the City, and the Hidden Narrative of Race* gives us. Hallelujah! Carl Anthony offers us a lifetime of visionary leadership and wisdom from a multiracial viewpoint, the only way we can understand our world now, much less our place in it. A must read for anyone who cares about our fragile future!

> —**China Galland**, author, *Love Cemetery:*
> *Unburying the Secret History of Slaves*

I have followed Carl Anthony's significant contribution and leadership for many years. I know him as a tireless champion of the cause of racial and environmental justice, always with a recognition of the challenge and necessity to create a world that works for all irrespective of racial, ethnic, or religious identity. This book is the story of his extraordinary life and work.

> —**David Korten**, Cofounder, *YES! Magazine;*
> author, *When Corporations Rule the World*

The Earth, the City, and the Hidden Narrative of Race is a must read, especially for young activists and academics entering the growing ranks of the ecojustice movement. This work by Carl Anthony really does give us new foundations for the great work of our time. It allows us to see the evolution of the ecojustice movement in a historical context and how elements are connected. At this crucial time, when the movement calls for stepped up action, Carl brings the hidden issues of race into the light. Thank you, Carl Anthony, for providing us with lessons learned and best practices.

> —**Joe Brooks**, Board Chair, Urban Habitat; Senior Fellow, PolicyLink;
> on behalf of the Brotherhood of Elders Network

Carl Anthony combines spirituality with hard-nosed political analysis, compassion with a rage against the racism he has encountered throughout his life, and academic rigor with grassroots organizing. He has a love for nature and for all of humanity. In this book, he connects how he sees nature being degraded and how huge swaths of humanity are being oppressed. To us, he is, more than any other person, both a man of ideas and a man of action.

> —**Gregory Galluzzo and Mary Gonzales**,
> cofounders, Gamaliel Foundation

The Earth, the City, and the Hidden Narrative of Race

The Earth, the City, and the Hidden Narrative of Race

Carl C. Anthony

New Village Press • New York City

Published in the United States by
New Village Press
bookorders@newvillagepress.net
www.newvillagepress.net

New Village Press is a public-benefit, not-for-profit publisher.

New Village Press is committed to the preservation of endangered forests globally and advancing best practices within the book and paper industries. The printing papers used in this book are recycled fiber and acid-free (Process Chlorine Free).

Original paperback ISBN 9781613320211
Publication Date: October 2017
First Edition

Library of Congress Cataloging-in-Publication Data

Names: Anthony, Carl, author.
Title: The earth, the city, and the hidden narrative of race / Carl C.
    Anthony.
Description: First edition. | New York : New Village Press, 2017. |
    Includes bibliographical references and index.
Identifiers: LCCN 2017035653 (print) | LCCN 2017036006 (ebook) |
    ISBN 9781613320228 (epub) | ISBN 9781613320211 (paperback)
Subjects: LCSH: Anthony, Carl. | Architects—United States—Biography. |
    African American architects—Biography. | Environmentalists—United
    States—Biography. | African American environmentalists—Biography. |
    Social justice. | BISAC: SOCIAL SCIENCE / Ethnic Studies / African
    American Studies. | ARCHITECTURE / Urban & Land Use Planning.
Classification: LCC NA737.A58 (ebook) | LCC NA737.A58 A2 2017
    (print) | DDC 720.92 [B] —dc23
LC record available at https://lccn.loc.gov/2017035653

Front Cover Illustration, "Bottoms Up," by Keba Armond Konte
Cover design by Lynne Elizabeth
Interior design and composition by Leigh McLellan Design
Frontispiece photograph of Carl Anthony, New York City circa 1968,
    courtesy of the author

Contents

CHAPTER 14

Laying the Groundwork for a National Movement

*For my brother, the late Lewis E. Anthony, Jr.,
and our grandchildren: Makai, Nfali, and Jasmine*

Foreword

IN 1991, FRESH OUT of law school, I arrived in San Francisco
to work with the Lawyers' Committee for Civil Rights. The police
beating of Rodney King had enraged our nation, and I immersed
myself in the subsequent movement to end police brutality. I was
working to free people from systemic forms of oppression, but I
had rarely given deep consideration to the environmental impacts
of pollution and climate change on vulnerable communities until I
was introduced to the work of Carl Anthony.

Carl had been linking issues of environmental justice to the work
of civil rights since the 1980s. His formation of the Urban Habitat
Program in 1989 was a critical development for the environmental
justice movement internationally. His leadership, locally and nationally, set the stage for so many of us who were seeking integral
solutions to the multiple issues facing our communities. The organization Green For All, my book *The Green Collar Economy*, and
so much of my work since drew inspiration from the seminal work
of Carl Anthony.

Carl Anthony has always been ahead of the curve—a rare leader
who possesses both vision and insight. Throughout his tremendous
career, Carl has drawn links between disciplines, communities, cultures, and social movements. He is capable of seeing the trail before
it has been cleared. The bridges he built between the environmental
and racial justice movements over the past forty years are the very

xvii

bedrock upon which these movements—now connected—stand today.

The Earth, the City, and the Hidden Narrative of Race offers us a rarely seen atlas of the social movements of our times. It offers a way forward for the changemakers of generations to come. Carl Anthony brings his expertise and love for architecture and urban planning—and his passion for the earth and the grandeur of the cosmos—to the conversation of racial justice and community advocacy and healing. Carl grew up in a redlined section of Philadelphia and watched his city crumble during white flight. These experiences powerfully inform his reflections on the journey of black people in America. Carl's depiction of his journey to Africa in 1970 to study architecture and culture and to search for answers about his roots is important not only for black Americans, but for all people seeking to grasp the depth and complexity of the realities we face today.

Through his multifaceted expertise, Carl Anthony has influenced many sectors—academia, philanthropy, nonprofit, business, and government. He has generously helped emerging leaders find their own voices and their own greatness. Carl's life is a model for what it means to be unafraid and to follow the path of one's own heart regardless of the tide. He set out to study that which has compelled him, and then has strategically uplifted and linked these various subjects through his life's work.

It is times like these when we need most to draw on the strength and wisdom of our elders. Carl honors the many teachers and leaders who guided his thinking throughout his journey. As people who hope to make things a little bit better for others, it is helpful to remember that we stand upon strong shoulders. Carl Anthony's book joins the literary canon of titles that illuminate the black American experience. It is also a fierce and compassionate call to action.

Carl Anthony is an unsung modern-day hero—an early adopter and creator of new paradigms. He has walked a path less chosen, and we are all better for it. Carl has written a remarkable book that lets us see into his personal journey and his life's work and offers us an impressive map of the social movements of our times.

Van Jones, Oakland, California. Spring 2017

Foreword

I T WAS CARL ANTHONY who first brought me to the historic African burial ground in New York City. The year was 2001. The Ford Foundation had selected Carl to direct the Sustainable Metropolitan Communities Initiative (SMCI) in North America, a bold program to create opportunity for disadvantaged communities. Building on our previous collaboration in the San Francisco Bay Area, Carl had invited me to join his New York team to design and implement the strategic planning, peer learning, and leadership development for this program. On the day of the SMCI dedication ceremony, Carl recommended we first visit the African burial ground site, sink our roots in, and invite the ancestors to guide us. I never suspected the life-changing impact this visit would have on the core of my being and on our work together for the next two decades.

The African burial site was discovered in 1991 as excavation began for the General Services Administration building in the lower part of Manhattan. The requisite anthropologists had been on site according to city policy, but they too were unprepared for what they found: not pottery shards or mere glass remnants, but bones—human bones. These bones were unearthed twenty-five feet below the surface, orderly and well preserved.

As they called in additional experts, what was revealed over the coming months included not only one intact skeleton of an African

American slave inside the remains of a coffin, but another and another, gradually unearthing hundreds of graves. The moist wet clay and earth composition had assisted in their preservation. Silver pendants, military buttons, and burial objects helped reconstitute the origins. Carbon dating set the year at about 1700 and an average death age at thirty-seven. African American community leaders and other concerned allies came forward to halt the destruction of this remarkable site. Although 419 bodies were initially located, as many as 20,000 free Africans and African slaves are estimated to have been buried in the 6.6-acre site.

The more I discovered, the more stunned, grief-stricken, and outraged I became by the hidden history. One quarter of early New Amsterdam had been African. Slaves had built the wall of Wall Street in 1653 to protect the Dutch from the indigenous Lenape tribe, which the Dutch settlers had nearly annihilated only days after the Pipe of Peace (or Hoboken) agreement. Yet, while enslaved Africans had borne the arduous work of building a European-style city, including its protective wall, they were excluded from the burial grounds in churchyards within the city limits. The free blacks and African slaves died segregated from the very city that was built on the backs of their stolen labor.

Experiencing all this with Carl added a further transformative dimension. We exchanged insights for our own lives and for the collaborative work ahead. The segregation, fragmentation, and spatial apartheid embedded in the land-use patterns of our twenty-first-century metropolitan regions took on deeper meaning as we uncovered this history of African slaves, buried and forgotten for centuries. Why had we not learned of this before?

Before leaving, we poured an offering of water onto the sacred ground—an expression of honor and gratitude for the many lives and history revealed here. Our journey back into the history of this place continued in our own bones as we reentered the churning sidewalks of Lower Manhattan. We rejoined present time, but we were changed. We left this place with resolve to restore our broken world.

● ● ●

Carl Anthony and I have witnessed this regenerative process over the years—with groups in our multiracial leadership development work, with organizations undergoing culture change, and with communities struggling to undertake regional equity organizing and coalition building. I have also seen this same integration occur with individuals in my practice as a psychologist. This transformative and liberatory process occurs in people who integrate their internal psychological parts, but it is equally thrilling to experience a similar revitalization in communities where a segregated neighborhood is reconnected to the streams of opportunity in their metropolitan region. Carl's book reveals that this is a continuum—our broken relationships and uncertain attachment to our own mothers and fathers, and to our extended families, create a pattern that makes it difficult to care for ourselves and for one another, and for this world we share. When individuals undergo trauma therapy and discover an inner secret, a healing can often occur, something like a numb limb that begins to wake up. There is pain at first, as the blood starts to recirculate, but the subsequent benefit it brings is usually calculated to outweigh the pain. The ability to resume using the limb and the utility it brings are obvious; however, this is not always so evident in the case of race. Carl's book forges these connections and builds these bridges.

The Earth, the City, and the Hidden Narrative of Race traces the mythic roots of spatial apartheid, a condition which has become the norm in our metropolitan regions and our national narrative. Carl Anthony challenges the absence, invisibility, or erasure of entire segments of our community, advocating instead their full participation in our democracy. He demands that concepts of sacrifice zones must end. With grounded strategies and bold invention, he insists that the limbs wake up and the body be restored, revealing the hidden narrative.

What does radical belonging mean? How do we recover parts of ourselves as we recover the history of lost peoples? And how do we simultaneously restore a lost relation to land, to place, and to time? Who is served and who is harmed by cultural amnesia and fragmentation? Carl Anthony takes up these and other questions with outrageous and courageous acumen in the pages that follow.

Throughout the journey from the first Flaring Forth to the rise of humanity in Africa and from the transatlantic slave trade to the evolution of our current social movements, Carl demonstrates that reestablishing a relationship to each of our histories is an essential healing process that connects us all to the Beloved Community.

Carl Anthony, architect, educator, and urban strategist, is one of the visionaries of the emerging climate justice movement. And his book offers a passport to this adventure, guiding us from the story of me to the story of we. As Carl travels from his roots in Philadelphia's Black Bottom, he invites us to explore our own. As Carl discovers his place within the larger community and the cosmos, he offers a framework that is liberating and unifying for diverse cultural groups, as well as for diverse parts of ourselves. His narration guides us from separation to inclusive community where none are marginalized in future planning processes and all become aware that we each matter to the whole.

I am grateful to have had the opportunity to work with Carl on the frontlines of movement building over the last two decades and for the unrelenting demand he makes to explore new horizons and expand our circles of engagement. His book is inspiration for emerging leaders (including youth), community mobilizers, faith and labor organizers, urban planners, artists, activists, and multi-racial coalitions. It is also wisdom for educators, policy experts, philanthropists, and change-makers of many varieties, field-builders, and pathfinders. As we each accompany Carl on his journey in this book, we have the opportunity to unearth lost parts of our own stories, as well as reclaim those of our communities.

Carl Anthony's book is not only an astonishing window into deep history, it is also a mirror to the present. Further, it provides a portal to an emergent future, a glimpse of a new land. As we accompany Carl on this dangerous journey, enhanced by his expert guidance and cultural humility, we have the opportunity to see with new eyes—revealing that our story (as individuals and as a species) can change, the hidden parts can be found, and wholeness rediscovered. This new possibility calls us forth to a great transformation. What better time than now?

M. Paloma Pavel, PhD, Oakland, California. Spring 2017

Introduction

WE NEED A NEW story about race and place in the United States. The civil rights movement brought forth a flow of narratives recounting valiant struggles to overcome racism and achieve social justice. Much environmental history has expressed concern for the destruction of forests, the degradation of landscapes, the uprooting and destruction of indigenous people, and the loss of species. All these concerns will continue to have force. But the experience of African Americans and other people of color has a key theme to add to the mix: the stories of the people who helped to lay the foundations of the nation despite being marginalized in an atmosphere of hostility and disrespect. Telling these stories and listening with compassion will help us heal and begin to understand that we are all, down to the core, sources of great creativity.

Conventional politics has operated as if there were a deep and unbridgeable gulf between environmentalism and social justice. Environmentalists revere and respect the natural world as a foundation for the life of future generations while social justice advocates are committed to equal opportunities for those who live in the present. When the first Earth Day happened in 1970, it was profoundly disassociated from the civil rights movement. It centered on protecting and restoring nature without acknowledging people's need for social and economic justice. The environment and people are interrelated. Both demand our attention and respect. African Americans

1

and other peoples who have labored in our cities and countryside, like all other humans, have not only a responsibility to care for planet Earth but also the right to share in its bounty.

It is clear that industrial growth is destroying life on Earth. We need a platform for all people to come together and decide to reduce our negative impact on the global biosphere. We cannot just say, "All we want is our fair share." Nor can we say, "Save the planet by any means necessary," and call the rest "collateral damage." We are all in this together, and true sustainability must include social justice along with environmental protection.

Marginalized communities—subjugated economically and racially—have firsthand experience of what it means to build sustainability in the face of hardship. This cultural and individual resilience is a resource for leadership. We need to acknowledge the leadership emerging out of the social and environmental justice movements and work to dismantle the obstacles to leadership faced by people of color. The knowledge they can bring to our planning and environmental professions is invaluable.

● ● ●

I am fortunate to have played many roles in my life, but my most deeply embedded identity is as the survivor of seven-and-a-half decades of growing up and living in racially constrained environments—first in Philadelphia, then in New York, for a summer in London, and, finally, on the West Coast in South Berkeley. Throughout my life and work, I have been seeking answers to questions about racial inequities that have troubled me since childhood and searching for ideas and disciplines to integrate the various dimensions of my personal and professional experience.

● ● ●

A class field trip to see the Better Philadelphia Exposition when I was eight years old filled me with a strong desire to become an architect and urban planner. During the following years, as I looked forward to those studies, fundamental questions were forming in my consciousness: *Who am I? Where do I belong? What is my connection to the communities I am encountering?* In a more external frame of mind I wondered: *Why do white families move out of our neighborhood as soon as families like mine move in and why do my neighborhood and my home become more run-down every year?* When I looked at the conditions surrounding me as a child, I did not realize that my city and I were not alone—these patterns of segregation and neighborhood disinvestment were prevailing throughout the country in the years of my childhood.

* * *

While I was at Columbia University in the early 1960s, I joined the emerging civil rights movement. Suddenly, I found myself in a series of struggles in which my peers were defining an agenda for a new generation. We were confronting the assumptions of the status quo and demanding the right to vote, to interstate bus travel, to be seated and served in restaurants, and to decent jobs. I wondered how architecture, the field that I was embarking upon, could respond to these demands.

I became a lifelong advocate for civil and human rights for African Americans and other communities of color in the United States. As a founding member of the Northern Student Movement, I learned a lot about community organizing, particularly how to build mutual trust and respect among the diverse groups in the community. Eventually, I found a niche for my architecture skills in the civil rights movement by coordinating the participatory planning and construction of an outdoor community space—the Harlem Neighborhood Commons.

* * *

I reflected on my situation as a college student: *the people in Harlem are black and so am I.* Out of three hundred architecture students at Columbia University, there was only one other African American. This was a time before black studies when the students were all white and didn't feel a need to study the black experience. There was no context for exploring how what we were learning might relate to the black community. Since none of my questions were being addressed by the university curriculum, I made frequent visits to Michaux's, the black bookstore in Harlem where I educated myself about the heroic struggles of Africans in the diaspora resisting racist exploitation and oppression and Africans in the homeland freeing themselves and their lands from colonialism.

Through a process of self-education, I came to feel that understanding the role of Africans as the first people—the ancestors of us all—might help to combat and even heal the damage that racism inflicts on the psyche of African Americans. In addition, it seemed that the story of human origins might help us understand our common destiny as the human species. All humans evolved from common ancestors and spent the first 170,000 years of human existence in Africa. Why, then, are people from African and African American communities today routinely looked down upon and even despised?

• • •

As I approached graduation at Columbia University Graduate School of Architecture, Planning and Preservation in 1969, my fellow students and I were planning how to use our travel grants to explore the roots of our profession. Of course, everyone was going to Europe and starting in Greece. For them, it was a well-trodden path. It was not so for me. My roots were not in Europe—*were they in Africa?* I was unsure. Nothing was marked on the map. I had already stepped out of the box to pursue training in architecture and planning. Now that I wanted to study my own roots in this field, I didn't know where to begin. I understood that what we seek to do in the present is built upon what our ancestors have done in the past, but I seemed to have no past upon which to build.

I was thinking about all this when I came across *Sticks and Stones: A Study of American Architecture and Civilization* by the great architectural theorist Lewis Mumford. Originally published in 1924, the book documents the beginning of European settlement patterns in the New World and is one of the first architectural histories ever published. Mumford (1955, 1–10) observed that people who came to the United States from Europe brought their building traditions, which provided them with a frame of reference. As a child, I had found myself in a community, but there was no sense of a shared reference point.

I suppose that everyone wants to go back to the place where their parents or ancestors came from to find their roots. At that time, though, the general feeling was that black people had no roots[1] or certainly none that were relevant to the study of architecture or city planning. Instead of going to Europe with my fellow students, I stopped there just long enough to consult their rich libraries for material on African building traditions and then I went on to explore and document those building traditions in West Africa for nine months with my friend and, at that time, partner Jean Doak. There, I faced the question: How can I understand who these people are—people I have met just recently—when I don't know who I am despite living in my own skin for thirty years? I faced a paradox: Americans saw me first as black; Africans saw me first as American. I went to Africa in search of my own history, but when I got there, I realized that I couldn't understand the things I was seeing and experiencing because I didn't understand who I was. I didn't know what vantage point to use to interpret my experience.

The work in architecture school was built upon the presumption that a usable path forward in pursuing work and projects was informed by one's history. While my roots appeared shallow, my immediate history as a member of the African American community in an age of white flight and inner-city abandonment made me ask how my professional career could serve my community. I had this question even before I entered architecture school. Throughout my school days, I experienced a growing feeling that something was missing in my studies—something about the needs of the African American community I aspired to serve and the need for support of professionals serving such communities. It seemed obvious that these topics were essential, but there was no context for them. I attended classes at Columbia, up on the hill, looking down on Harlem and seeing people living under devastating conditions. My education provided no explanation as to why and how it got that way. No one asked or talked about what should be done or why services were not being made available to the most vulnerable communities. People seemed to be ignoring what was right under our noses.

＊ ＊ ＊

By 1976, I had graduated from Columbia University, studied traditional building in West Africa, and moved to Berkeley, California, where I collaborated with some of the most innovative and creative designers and planners in the field. *Landscape* magazine published my two-part article on the architecture of the big house and the slave quarter in its bicentennial issues. I understood that my ancestors had been enslaved and that somebody had planned the places where they lived, deciding that they would live in minimal quarters distinctly different from the places where their masters resided.[2]

Whenever I had a chance, I continued reading and thinking about indigenous villages, towns, and cities in Africa; the slave trade[3] and the development of colonial cities on the Atlantic coastline; and the racialization of space in North American urban development from 1500 to the present. The future of our urban, suburban, and rural communities depends in part upon our willingness to face this terrible history and consciously make something of it. I was particularly focused on the "landscape of freedom," which I imagined as the title of a book I wanted to write about the experience of the African American freedmen during and after the Civil War. I had many questions: *What happened to my ancestors when they were emancipated? How did they live? What environments did they live in? What ideas shaped how they lived? What external circumstances continued to constrain them?*

* * *

In my years of teaching at the University of California at Berkeley, I was eager to share my thoughts and findings with my students and fellow teachers, but the nearly all-white student body and faculty had little or no interest in the historical drama of Africans and African Americans. I decided to leave the university and enter private practice.

A decade later, black studies programs emerged in colleges and universities across the nation, responding at last to the gap in awareness that I and other African American students had experienced.

* * *

In the mid-1980s, my friend and mentor Karl Linn, who had moved to California from the East Coast, introduced me to the writing of Catholic priest and cultural historian Thomas Berry.[4] Berry's insistence that humanity needs a new story excited me since I had been feeling that African Americans needed a new story—a story that is more inspiring than the horrors of the Middle Passage, slavery, and pressures of racism that seemed to intensify after emancipation.

Berry (1999) suggested that neither of mainstream culture's two dominant stories—one centering on the promise of redemption in the afterlife and the other trusting in the power of science and industry—could unify people and inspire them to engage in collective efforts to respond to the serious environmental problems that have resulted from our long practice of massive extractive industry. Berry insisted that we need to reinvent ourselves as a species within the community of life. Identifying ourselves primarily as members of nations, religions, or racial groups had proved to be a sure route to oppression and strife.

Thanks to my third-grade teacher and the assignments and field trips she organized, I had always held a fascination with history and an excitement about—and love of—nature, particularly stars and trees. Looking at the fossilized remains of trilobites and a dinosaur footprint within a short distance from my home gave me a sense of deep time and appreciation for the big story of life on Earth in which we are all connected. I now found this same excitement when I read Thomas Berry.

Deeply inspired by Berry's writings and his collaborations with evolutionary cosmologist Brian Thomas Swimme and scholar of world religions Mary Evelyn Tucker, I wanted to make their vision relevant to a larger pool of readers. In order to do this, I needed to fill in the two large gaps I had encountered in their narrative: I had found hardly any mention of cities or people of color. I felt a strong desire to correct these significant oversights and to help craft a new story that could include those elements. I hope this book will make an initial contribution and will encourage others to add their own stories. We all need to embrace and understand our own histories and identities, and we all want to feel understood by others.

Since most people today live in cities and analysts predict that the majority of residents in the United States will be people of color by 2044 (US Census Bureau 2015), efforts to expand the new story seem particularly relevant.

My search for threads in the new story found me reaching back to the very origins of the universe and then coming through humanity's origins in Africa—the emergence there of agriculture, nomadic herding, and city building that developed into a variety of thriving cultures until they started to unravel with the incursions of Portuguese fortune hunters, known in the old story as *explorers*. The story developed as I studied the slave trade, the plantation era, the gradual undermining and reversal of black rights after the Emancipation Proclamation, and the betrayals of the Black Codes and the Jim Crow laws in the South, resulting in waves of black migration to the cities of the North, where the new arrivals were exploited by greedy real estate speculators and thwarted by racist policies that kept them in ghettos and denied them loans to make necessary repairs and improvements to their property.

Finally, I studied the unfolding experiences of my father, an orphan from birth and a self-made man with many achievements; my mother and her accomplished and cultured family; and my own experience, growing up alongside my brother in racially defined black neighborhoods in Philadelphia.

Our African ancestors were uprooted from their lands, transported many thousands of miles, and forced to work without remuneration for the benefit of others. Still, the majority survived and found ways to retain their dignity and humanity. Many lived truly heroic lives. Many of their descendants now live in cities where they suffer from lack of opportunities to develop their potential.

• • •

At every juncture in my life, I realized that something big was missing. The university was supposed to prepare students to step into their roles, but there were no institutions to prepare and train people of color for a role in shaping vibrant communities. Working in the civil rights movement, I had developed unique and valuable skills, such as participatory planning, but I soon noted that while many of these skills had been developed by African Americans for use in African American communities, they were being used primarily by white people.

I felt myself being split in two. My professional architect self, with specialized knowledge, spatial intelligence, and passion for designing and planning the physical world, seemed restricted to white spaces while my civil rights and community advocate self seemed to be valued only among people of color. These two parts of me lived in separate worlds, which was painful and confusing. I found myself in a crisis. I left my architectural firm and gave up the practice of conventional urban planning. I began to search for a larger vision that could contain my whole being.

When I became active in the environmental justice movement, I sought to support the development of environmental leadership in low-income communities of color. I was prompted by my intense thinking on what the future holds for people of color. Again, the threat of being split in two loomed: Earth Island Institute, the organization whose board I had joined, was made up of white environmentalists. It was hard work to invent a new framework for lifting up the voices of people of color within that movement.

The answer that emerged during long and deep conversations with Karl Linn was the Urban Habitat Program. We developed the program within Earth Island Institute, modeling it after the community design centers (CDCs) of the 1960s and the advocacy planning work promoted by architect-lawyer Paul Davidoff. But while CDCs had been serving neighborhoods, we positioned the Urban Habitat Program at the center of San Francisco's entire metropolitan region to mobilize people in many neighborhoods. My work with Earth Island Institute and the Urban Habitat Program spawned my next twenty-five years of projects with the Sustainable Metropolitan Communities Initiative at the Ford Foundation followed by Breakthrough Communities with its focus on promoting sustainability and justice in US metropolitan regions. These projects are the first steps in building a worldwide movement organized around a new story of unified effort to heal communities harmed by racial injustice so that they can participate in repairing our damaged ecosystems and social networks.

• • •

As an architect and urban planner, I was seeking to construct a usable story based on an accurate picture of the past. I was looking for evidence that all the suffering of my people meant something, that African Americans and our African ancestors played an important role in shaping the modern world—in particular, the cities and towns in which we live. I felt inspired and empowered as I considered the development of the African American community against the backdrop of the unfolding universe and the evolution of life on planet Earth.

The new planetary narrative emerging in our time suggests new ways to think about race and new strategies and directions for thinking about, planning, designing, building, and living in cities. Placing our contemporary issues in this larger context encourages a deeper regard for the miracle of life, gratitude for the diverse species with whom we share the planet, and appreciation for the gifts of air, water, and sunlight that we have long taken for granted. Everything that we do or aim to do should be grounded in and governed by our relationship with the Earth, the cosmos, and the diversity of human and other forms of life with which we coinhabit this precious planet.

• • •

I hope that this book will inspire readers to reflect on their own stories and to share them—whether by telling them to one or many friends and family members or by writing and sharing them online or in print. Deeply respectful and compassionate listening to one another is essential to establish a foundation of trust and a sense of our common humanity.

Although this book includes notes and references, it is not intended primarily as an academic work. Some of the notes contain interesting side stories and details that expand meaning and deepen understanding. The references and additional resources are there to encourage further study and guide readers to interesting and accessible sources. I intend the book to appeal to readers of all skin colors, to young and old, to both environmental and social justice activists, and to those of a spiritual or a scientific bent. I want it to be accessible to thoughtful high school dropouts and, at the same time, engaging for serious students and scholars of history, science, and human meaning. It will take all of us to meet the challenge of re-envisioning and revising our social, economic, and environmental systems—a major effort that Thomas Berry referred to as the Great Work of our time.

Origins

THE YEAR OF 1963 was significant for the civil rights movement. In April, Martin Luther King Jr. had been arrested and jailed for protesting segregation and had written his famous "Letter from Birmingham Jail." All over the world, people's eyes were fixed on their television screens as Birmingham Commissioner of Public Safety Eugene "Bull" Connor directed firefighters and police to use fire hoses and police dogs against African American children who were peacefully seeking to integrate Kelly Ingram Park. The March on Washington for Jobs and Freedom and King's famous "I Have a Dream" speech were the most high-profile events, but there was local organizing and education going on all over, including in New York City, where I was working with the Harlem Education Project (HEP). Nevertheless, several activists took time off from their organizing, boycotts, and protests in New York to join my brother, Lewie, in taking youth from HEP on a five-hundred-mile journey to Acadia National Park in Maine to see a full eclipse of the sun.

Lewie was sixteen months older than me. Growing up, we were about the same size, so people often thought we were twins. But I knew better. He could always run faster and fight harder than me. He had a way with girls I couldn't even imagine having. He could do math problems that I didn't know how to do. I remember once when I was in second grade, he punched me because I didn't know how to do long division. For the most part, though, he looked after

13

me when we were out in the world together and did what he could to soften the situation when our dad treated me harshly.

Lewie had done coursework at Drexel Institute of Technology and Haverford College, but had not completed his degree. Still, he managed by age of twenty-five to finagle his way into a job as an assistant to Dr. Martin Schwarzschild, a famous astrophysicist, a professor at Princeton University's Institute for Advanced Studies, and a protégé of Albert Einstein. They were studying the evolution of the sun and the birth and death of stars.

Lewie came up to New York from time to time, and we enjoyed long conversations while walking. We would walk for hours—sometimes from the Lower East Side to Harlem and back. For some time, I urged Lewie to join me in New York, but he was not much interested in moving nor in the civil rights movement in general. Finally, when he learned that we had organized the tutoring program bringing students from colleges and universities throughout the region to help young people in Harlem with their studies, he agreed to come; he loved to share what he was learning about the sunspots, stars, planets, and galaxies with anyone who would listen.

As a special activity, Lewie decided to organize the field trip to Maine so kids from Harlem could view the rare and amazing phenomenon of a total solar eclipse. A total eclipse occurs when the moon passes between sun and earth, completely blocking the sun. About six times per century, a total eclipse of the sun is visible in rare locations within the United States. Lewie filled vehicles with young teenagers and adult chaperones. One was a young Stokely Carmichael,[1] who was working with HEP. On July 20, 1963, the caravan with fifty mixed-race youth from Harlem arrived at Maine's Acadia National Park after a five-hundred-mile journey. Lewie felt this would be a powerful and unforgettable experience for them. It may have been memorable as well for the New Englanders who noticed the uncommon caravan along its way.[2]

As the silhouette of the moon began to edge across the face of the sun, members of the caravan had been forewarned to look away. If you look directly at the sun during an eclipse, you will damage your eyes. The young explorers hastily mounted several homemade pinhole cameras and crude homemade filtering devices (made of exposed photographic film) to watch the remarkable event. As the eclipse began, the temperature at Acadia National Park quickly dropped by twenty to thirty degrees. The wind began to howl; the flowers in the fields closed; and the birds abruptly stopped singing. Waves of alternating shadows and light passed across the land. Then, it became "night." Stars twinkled brilliantly in the sky. A ring of fire surrounded the black disk of the moon as it passed directly over the face of the sun.

Soon, the eclipse was over. The wind ceased; the flowers opened, turning back to face the sun; and birdsong resumed.

• • •

When I was in elementary school, I skipped second grade. Because Lewie and I were so close in age, it was together that we entered the third-grade classroom of Mrs. Aikens—the teacher who would open up the world to me, inciting in me an awe and wonder many of the youth of the Harlem Education Program must have felt as they watched the moon pass over the sun with Lewie.

Every Monday afternoon, Mrs. Aikens held a science class. One of our first assignments was to collect one sample leaf from as many different trees as we could find. Each new leaf we identified was an occasion for great enthusiasm. The next step was to go out into the city and learn to identify the trees by their bark. Throughout my life, I have been able to identify many of those trees—catalpa, walnut, ash, and poplar.

Mrs. Aikens also took us to the Fels Planetarium at the Franklin Institute's Science Museum and taught us about the formation of the Earth's surface. We learned how Earth's evolution created each of the three kinds of rock—sedimentary, igneous, and metamorphic—and how some contained fossils that could give us information about creatures that lived millions of years ago. She also taught us the names of the constellations and asked us to go out and look at the sky in the middle of the night to find various stars and constellations. We learned to name all the different kinds of clouds in the sky and to recognize the approach of a storm.

She told us about the dinosaurs that once roamed the hills and valleys where we lived. She took us to places where we observed the fossil record in the rocks. We learned to distinguish between tyrannosaurus and brontosaurus, as well as other types of dinosaurs. From that time on, I have been fascinated by my physical and historical surroundings.

. . .

Throughout much of my life, as I searched and reflected on past experiences, a central question remained unanswered: Where did I fit in the scheme of things? The topic came up for me over and over as I approached early professional projects and faced the fact that few African Americans practiced in my field or were considered worthy of acknowledgement. Something had gone off track in my mission to improve living conditions for people of color in their urban environments. If this was important work for my community, where was everybody? Where, I often asked myself, do we belong in the planning of the cities we share? Gradually, I came to realize that people of color do show up at planning meetings and protests when their families and community members are exposed to life-threatening impacts of pollution. But what about those of us who don't live across the street from a toxic waste dump?

When I began reading Thomas Berry, the Catholic priest and cultural historian to whose writing Karl Linn had introduced me, I often flashed back to third grade and the feelings of gratitude, awe, wonder, and curiosity that I experienced in Mrs. Aikens's science class.

Sometime in the 1980s, Berry began a long collaboration with astrophysicist and mathematical cosmologist Brian Swimme to co-author *The Universe Story: From the Primordial Flaring Forth to the Ecozoic Era: A Celebration of the Unfolding of the Cosmos.* This was Berry's vision of a new story for our times based on scientific discovery. The story recounts our origins in the context of the dramatic birth and development of the universe and invites us to see ourselves in a profoundly new way (Swimme and Berry 1992, 241–61).

I grabbed a copy as soon as it hit the shelves. While reading it, I became energized. I could tell that the universe story had something I was missing—something, in fact, that nearly all Westernized people are missing: a sense of belonging to a vast and complex web of life and experience and an invitation to participate in its continuous unfolding. Yet, for all the awe-inspiring, encouraging, and sobering elements of the story, the perspective on human history was that of the dominant, Eurocentric culture. I felt disappointed when I found not a single word about the transatlantic slave trade and the essential role of slave labor in creating our modern scientific and technological culture. This perspective ignores the embarrassing fact that the unprecedented wealth of the societies we live in was built on the foundation of bondage and forced labor of African captives—the profits made from slavery funded the industrial revolution, the development of destructive technologies, and the extraction and burning of hydrocarbons. From the outset, slavery went absolutely hand in hand with the reckless plundering of ecosystems in the New World. The exploitation of the people and environments of the New World and human beings stolen from Africa created tremendous wealth that was the foundation of the financial power that now runs the world. People of color, particularly Africans, whose forced labors undergirded a great deal of the infrastructure of the contemporary developed world, have neither been fully enfranchised into its freedoms and comforts nor received the rewards of their labor. They have traditionally been consigned to the devastated environments left behind from exploitation and extraction processes that had, meanwhile, made others wealthy.

The absence of a narrative in which people of color are recognized for their contributions to society is dangerous because it leaves unquestioned the dominance of white people on the planet today, thus tacitly endorsing the notion of white superiority. People of color receive no credit for being an essential, although coerced, part of the development of the modern world. The technological progress that Swimme and Berry (1992) both celebrate and lament rests on the skill, labor, and courage of people of color, as well as their ingenuity and grit in surviving centuries of difficult circumstances.

The dehumanization required to enslave people rests upon the same arrogance that allows the dominators to use, abuse, and pollute Earth's living ecosystems. This dehumanization continues when the contributions of people of color are missing from the history of the modern world. Humanity cannot develop a radically new ecological conscience until we re-tell its story to include the various histories and perspectives of people of color. Attempting to solve the problem of ecosystem exploitation will never work without facing up to its companion—waste and human exploitation caused by racism.

Inside the Universe

My first inkling of being part of the universe was in the third grade when Mrs. Aikens awakened my classmates and me to the mystery of the stars in the night sky. During field trips to the Fels Planetarium at the Franklin Institute Science Museum, I became familiar with Andromeda, Orion, Ursa Major, Ursa Minor, and the Dog Star (Sirius). Later, I learned about the North Star, which served as a guide to runaway slaves on the Underground Railroad. Gazing at the stars became a symbol of reaching beyond my wildest dreams.

The idea that we have a connection to the stars has been with humanity for a long time. Tales of the escapades of Greek and Roman gods have given many stars and constellations their official and common names.[3] Of course, indigenous and non-Western peoples have their own names and stories about stars. African cultures have a rich oral tradition of star stories that rival the Greek myths. Auke Slotegraaf, editor of *Sky Guide Africa South*, compiled a sampling of these, mostly from the southern part of the continent, in his article, "African Star-Lore," published in *Monthly Notes of the Astronomical Society of Southern Africa* in 2013. As I searched for information about star myths, I stumbled upon an excellent resource guide called *Unheard Voices, Part 1: The Astronomy of Many Cultures*. The pages are easy to read, and the succinct annotations on the items listed in its carefully grouped categories are extremely helpful. Multiverse at the University of California at Berkeley, formerly the Center for Science Education, commissioned veteran astronomy and space-science educator Andrew Fraknoi of Foothill College to prepare the resource guide and now hosts the updated 2016 version online. The Multiverse tagline made me smile: Increasing Diversity in Earth and Space Science through Multicultural Education.

Discovering the developing field of archeoastronomy has been a joy. Its researchers study ancient rock etchings, paintings, and architecture of ceremonial structures that echo or record patterns and movements of stars, planets, constellations, and, not surprisingly, our sun and moon. Many of these ancient structures, built long before the origin of Western science, capture a ray of sunlight in a particular spot at sunrise or sunset on the winter or summer solstice, presumably to be witnessed and experienced in sacred ceremonies.[4] These discoveries do not surprise me. The idea that people gazing at the sky night after night wouldn't speculate on their connection with the stars and develop stories and ceremonies that celebrate their observations strikes me as shortsighted to say the least.

Scientific cosmology proved several decades ago that the human feeling that we come from the stars is based on fact. In 1980, astronomer and physicist Carl Sagan reported what is now common knowledge in the field of astrophysics:

> The nitrogen in our DNA, the calcium in our teeth, the iron in our blood, the carbon in our apple pies were made in the interiors of collapsing stars. We are made of starstuff. (Sagan 1980, 233)

Contemporary astronomy provides an explanation for how those elements got from a collapsing star to us. Around 4.6 billion years ago, our sun was born from a supernova—the gigantic cosmic explosion that occurs when a star collapses. This ancient star began as a ball of light gases, mostly hydrogen and helium. As the star grew, its gravitational pressure increased, and the star's core became a foundry for synthesizing heavier elements: oxygen, nitrogen, carbon, silicon, and more. When the star became so dense, it collapsed under its own gravity, and its implosion released the energy of four billion stars, all at once. Our entire periodic table of elements was flung into space to later coalesce into new stars and solar systems, including our sun.

Swimme and Berry's (1992) narrative in *The Universe Story* goes on to chronicle the formation of Earth with our sun, moon, oceans, landforms, the appearance of the first living cells and their replication, and the gradual evolution of plants and animals. They go on to recount the emergence of our human species, the creation of neolithic villages and later cities, scientific and technological discoveries, and, finally, mechanized industry. They describe the degradation of the environment in ancient and modern times, including the destructive activities undertaken in the name of technological progress.

Now, Swimme and Berry (1992) argue, humanity has reached a critical moment as a species. Our continued survival depends on forming a new, ecological consciousness. We have learned a lot about our power to affect change in and on our environment, but we have lost our ancient sense of awe and wonder at the world. We have lost our impulse to honor and respect our environment. Our great contemporary challenge is thus to regain a sense of awe, to form a sense of connection and belonging in Earth's living ecosystem, and to learn how to live in a way that benefits the whole ecosystem.

To think about how great and sudden an impact we humans are having on planet Earth, imagine that today is midnight on New Year's Eve and the 3.5-billion-year history of life on this planet has been compressed into the past year. The first ancestors of *Homo sapiens* to shape stones into rough tools, such as choppers and awls, appeared about six and a half hours ago. The first humans on Earth to cook their food using fire, wear animal skins for clothing, and manufacture hand axes appeared about eighteen minutes ago, and the first to live in villages, domesticate animals, and practice agriculture only appeared between ninety and forty-five seconds ago. People made things out of metal for the first time a little more than a minute ago, and the first pyramid was built in Egypt forty seconds ago. Jesus lived eighteen seconds ago, and Columbus and Cortés sailed across the Atlantic and set about pillaging the peoples and habitats they encountered less than five seconds ago. Most of the transatlantic slave trade has taken place between four seconds and a second and a half ago.[5]

In the past second, humans have invented the personal automobile, the airplane, the jet, the rocket, the nuclear bomb, and the computer. We've sent a few of us to the moon, we've peered into the far reaches of the universe from a giant telescope mounted in space, and we've sequenced the human genome. Yet, our style of living on Earth in the last five seconds is having a devastating effect on the living ecosystem of this planet. There are few signs as yet that we will change our behavior in time to avert a catastrophe of a scale encountered only once or twice in the history of life on Earth.

Thomas Berry (1999) asks us to take up what he calls the "Great Work of a people": to help repair the damage humans have caused and build relationships of care and respect with all forms of life. Our cities are embedded in and dependent on Earth's living systems—bioregions, ecosystems, watersheds, climate, and atmosphere. Many ecological writers herald such a shift in our relationship with the planet—from seeing it as an endless trove of resources to be exploited and manipulated to experiencing it as our companion on a journey through time. I was inspired by the idea that our cities could be redesigned from this new perspective, but the new paradigm of the city as a living system will elude our grasp if our vision is not truly inclusive. All our human communities with their diverse histories and cultures and their inherent worth need to be represented in this great shift. Without leadership representing all segments of society, we will end up reinstalling the separations and inequities that defined the preceding centuries, and new unsustainable cities will result.

The universe story could be big enough to contain this kind of inclusive reimagining of our relationship with the planet. The old story about how society evolved until we reached the pinnacle of industrial capitalism is disintegrating. The new story is that we are the end product of a process of 13.7 billion years in which the human journey is a small portion at the end. The new story includes the birth of our universe, the formation of Earth, the emergence of the first cell and human evolution, the rise of humanity in Africa, and the great migrations of all Earth's peoples around the globe. The new story must be truthful about our origins, our history, and the forces shaping our lives today. In it, there is room for the rich, diverse experiences of all ethnic groups.

PART ONE

My Life and Work

CHAPTER 1

Growing Up in a Dying City

I WAS BORN AT HOME in 1939 in the "Black Bottom," one of West Philadelphia's most run-down neighborhoods. Black Bottom, or simply the "Bottom," was a predominantly poor and black neighborhood built on a drained swamp. In contrast, the neighborhood where the white people lived was called the "Top." My parents, my brother Lewie, and I lived in a cold-water flat above a storefront on Cuthbert Street for the first five years of my life.

Many years later, I spoke with Anne Whiston Spirn, landscape architecture professor at the University of Pennsylvania and author of *The Language of Landscape*. She told me that in cities across the country, the poorest people—primarily blacks and immigrants—had no choice but to live in such undesirable low-lying locations. These "bottom" areas produced conditions for both criminality and the creative expression that gave birth to jazz and blues.

Mother was born Mildred Cokine.[1] Her forebears were longtime residents of South Carolina, and among her ancestors were early European settlers, rice-growing West Africans (probably Wolofs), and American Indians. Her great-uncle William Jervay (likely an anglicized form of the French name Gervais) had escaped from a plantation to join the Union army and later became a South Carolina legislator.[2] At some point, Mother's family moved north to South Philadelphia. Mother was born in 1898 in the Seventh Ward, a neighborhood that the great black intellectual W. E. B. Du Bois, then a promising young sociologist, studied and wrote about in *The Philadelphia Negro: A Social Study*. The Seventh Ward was a neighborhood beset with poverty, illness, and crime primarily due to lack of economic opportunity. So, as soon as they could, Mother's family moved to a neighborhood where the "better" class of black people lived; and this is where Mother grew up. Mother learned the art of dressmaking at her mother's knee: Granny took in clients at home, and Mother would help her. Granny raised her son and four daughters on her dressmaker's income after her husband, a carpenter, had died.

Mother was the eldest daughter; she attended William Penn High School for Girls, a prestigious, mostly black school. She was artistically gifted, and had a talent for creating sewing patterns and using them to make women's clothes. At one point, she was hired for a job as a strikebreaker—most likely without knowing it—and as she was bused to a factory, bricks were tossed at her.

Mother was light skinned enough to pass for Jewish or Puerto Rican, but never chose to do so. Two of her sisters, Ede and Ruth, lived with Granny. Her sister Ida was married, and her brother, Carl, died young. Aunt Ede used to tell Mother that she could come back home whenever she wanted, but Mother was very loyal to Dad; I don't think she ever wanted to leave him.

Mother must have been a great beauty in her youth, but she had lost all her teeth by the time I was born. I thought she was crazy when she painted over the mirrored faceplates on the electric light switches in the house we moved to on Kingsessing Avenue, but, as an adult, I understood that she couldn't bear to see the change in her features.

Mother loved to draw and paint, and she made our home into a learning center. Once, she placed a lighted candle to project a shadow of my profile and, from this, traced on paper the outline of my features and cut out the image of my silhouette. It was something I treasured. I still have two paintings that she made late in her life.

Another great treasure of mine is a small book written by Mary Jenness, a poet of the Harlem Renaissance, and published in 1936 titled *Twelve Negro Americans*. The chapter, "A Negro Cooperative

Makes Good," is about my dad's groundbreaking efforts to initiate a cooperative economic system for the benefit of low-income African Americans in Philadelphia. It consisted of a farm in Yardley, Pennsylvania, and a cooperative store in West Philadelphia.

Dad was dark skinned, brilliant, and charismatic. His mother had died giving birth to him and his father was unknown. As a young child, he sometimes stayed with his mother's brother, but other times, he was circulated through a series of orphanages and foster homes. He began to live on his own at the age of twelve.

Dad's ancestors on his mother's side included Cherokees and Seminoles who were part of the forced march to Oklahoma known as the Trail of Tears. Born Lewis Edwards, Dad researched, learned that his father's name was William Anthony, and renamed himself Lewis Anthony. He moved to Pennsylvania to attend Lincoln University[3] and worked his way through by painting and wallpapering the university dorms during the summer. During the school year, he made extra money by writing love letters for his friends. Dad loved to give speeches as well—his college friends called him Mark Anthony. He could read and write in Latin and Greek, which seems amazing to me now, but was probably not as unusual in those days when universities often required students to take Latin and Greek.

He completed his college education at Temple University. After graduating in the late 1920s, he started talking with friends about starting a cooperative store. Like many of his peers, he had held a string of odd jobs for which he was overqualified—clerk, factory hand, butler, laundry sorter, and apartment manager, to name a few. Then, while working at a coffee shop owned by Finnish immigrants, he heard them talking enthusiastically about the cooperative movement.[4] Inspired, Dad organized a group of friends for a year's study of cooperative economics, focusing on the principles worked out in 1844 by a group of weavers in Rochdale, England.

One of the co-op members, a tailor, offered the back room of his shop as a meeting place. Soon after, the co-op became a small store, which then quickly took over the entire shop. Dad was invited to give talks about the cooperative, and he became well known and well liked. Eventually, the co-op teamed up with some older folks who had savings to invest, allowing for merchandise expansion and a move to a more densely populated neighborhood. Dad served as co-op manager and sometimes slept behind the counter to save money for rent. Unemployed co-op members were happy to help with maintenance, bookkeeping, and deliveries.

During the Depression, Dad was offered the use of a farm near Philadelphia and received a grant from the Federal Emergency Relief Administration to buy farm equipment and fix up residence quarters for five families with farming experience. Dad and the five families were collective owners of the farm and grew produce for the co-op; others were co-op members who had access to the produce at low costs. During the time before my parents were married, Dad would bring food from the co-op and leave it on Granny's doorstep so Mother and her family would have something to eat. For a time after their marriage, my parents lived on a co-op farm outside of Philadelphia.

Dad loved to tell the story of how he got together with Mother. One night, he explained, he had read a passage from the Bible that seemed to suggest that the next woman he met would be the "one." It wasn't clear if Mother was the very next woman he met or if he had had to do some winnowing before she emerged as the one he would marry. It was clear, though, that they shared a strong spiritual bond. Although they didn't seem to belong to any particular denomination or congregation, they shared a moral and ethical focus that they passed on to Lewie and me.

Mother and Dad devoted themselves to us. They had great dreams for us and made sure we had a rich early childhood.

Getting By in the City

Our family had always been city folk. Granny, born in 1868, moved to Philadelphia in the decades after the Civil War. Dad arrived in Philadelphia around 1920 when he began to study at Lincoln University.

Dad loved to tell us about the tricks he had learned to get by when times were hard. I'll never forget watching him pull one of those tricks: During the years after World War II, when our family had little money, Dad bought a couple of receipt pads at the stationery store around the corner and had the stationer print the words "Lewis E. Anthony, Grocer" across the top. Then, we drove down to the Italian wharf in South Philadelphia in his red Ford panel truck and bought wholesale. He could buy cases of canned food at one third of what it would have cost if we had bought it at the local A&P grocery store. When there was no money to pay for utilities, my dad would crawl to a position at roof level and delicately connect the house to the electric power line.

Our New Neighborhood

In 1944, when I was five years old, we were finally able to purchase a home in a better neighborhood and leave the Black Bottom, which, I realized later, had been a place of shame. The Black Bottom was an area filled with run-down buildings and lots of concrete with no trees. Nevertheless, I prided myself on knowing my way around and enjoyed shopping and doing errands with my parents. Later, while I was in college in New York, urban renewal policies mostly demolished the Black Bottom.

Our new home in West Philadelphia was a beautiful three-story, semidetached Victorian house built in the 1880s with ten rooms and a small front yard. Steps led up to a front porch that overlooked the sidewalk. The neighbors with whom we shared a wall were another black family with lots of kids. Our relationship with the neighbors had ups and downs, but, for the most part, we were friends. The neighborhood was one of Philadelphia's first streetcar suburbs, but even before the installation of electric railways in the 1890s, a horse-drawn trolley service had made it an ideal location for the large homes of wealthy families and the professional elite who worked in downtown Philadelphia. Gradually, the mansions were torn down and the lots divided and developed as housing for the expanding middle class. By the time we moved in, only a few of the mansions remained.

We were one of the first black families on our block, but white families had already begun their flight to the suburbs. Blacks were migrating from the South into the inner-city neighborhoods of Northern cities, taking advantage of jobs created by the US involvement in World War II; and middle-class whites were leaving for "better" neighborhoods in the suburbs. The first few years of living in this half-white, middle-class neighborhood were exciting. Our new street had giant sycamore trees, and I was delighted by the beautiful tree-lined street and the stately houses. In autumn, on our way to and from school, we loved to kick up the brown leaves piled high on the sidewalk and hear the rustling sounds. Four doors down was Clark Park, where we used to play. It had originally been an industrial area with a creek—Mill Creek—running through it. Subsequently, the creek had been enclosed in a culvert underground and the industrial buildings removed. In the middle of the park was a huge bowl, the former creek bed, where we would play.

Living in our new neighborhood, we felt that we could share in the life of the city, which was still in its heyday. The downtown had great department stores and movie houses. We had a sense that we might finally be part of the great urban life. Ironically for us, however, city life had reached its peak shortly after we moved into our middle-class neighborhood and then began a sharp decline.

We didn't play or interact socially with the white children who remained in the neighborhood. We played exclusively with black kids, most of whose families were renters living in the two-story apartment flats on Forty-Fifth Street or in row houses on the side streets. A white family, anxious to get out before blacks moved in and "ruined the neighborhood," had sold their house to our family for about six thousand dollars.

During the war years, my dad worked at the Navy shipyard helping assemble the bulkheads that became the central structural elements of aircraft carriers. We also rented out rooms on the third floor to three young single working women, and ran the house as a bed and breakfast, serving coffee and cinnamon buns to our roomers in the mornings before the sun came up.

After the war, Dad lost his job at the shipyard, and we lost our roomers, but he was an entrepreneur and started making a living as a handyman. When I was seven and Lewie was eight, we started working alongside him—cleaning and fixing up the houses that the white people had left behind, taking out trash, and whitewashing basements. At one point, Dad got a job as a paperhanger, and I became his assistant.

Dad set up a woodshop in the basement and created a hobby room for us. We got ideas for projects from the magazine *Popular Mechanics* and the book *Fun for Boys*. I began studying magazines like *Better Homes and Gardens* and sending off for catalogs for building supplies and other similar products. I also enjoyed attending home and garden trade shows with Dad.

I had my own room. Dad was into color theory, so he wallpapered one wall and the ceiling with yellow paper with an ivy pattern and painted the other walls a deep mauve. I felt honored by the special attention and spent hours contemplating the patterns and the colors.

Learning activities continued in our new home. Mother loved to diagram sentences and enjoyed teaching me the parts of speech. I filled many notebooks with diagrammed sentences.

Attending an Integrated Elementary School

When September rolled around, our parents decided to send Lewie and me to B. B. Comegys, an integrated elementary school where only ten or twelve of the three hundred students were African American. I entered kindergarten and Lewie first grade. Every day, we walked six blocks through both black and white neighborhoods to get to school. The rest of the students were Eastern European Jews, Irish and Italian Catholics, and some white Anglo-Saxon Protestants. The black kids we knew and played with went to Woodrow Wilson, the segregated elementary school, which was only a block from our home.

I didn't interact much with the kids in my class at school, who hung out in ethnic clusters. We were never invited to their birthday parties and other activities outside of school. Every day, Mother carefully packed my metal lunch box with a sardine sandwich on whole wheat bread and a healthy drink. The other kids all had their lunches in bags—baloney sandwiches on white bread and soda pop. Although I knew that my lunch was healthier than what they were eating, I was embarrassed that it was different. I would slink away and eat alone.

Going to an integrated school was supposed to be a privilege, but it was stressful in many ways. I was learning to feel superior to the black kids I played with after school, but I still didn't belong with the white kids in my class. I wanted very much to bring the black kids from our neighborhood to my school, but I didn't have the power to make that happen. I was beginning to be aware of the invisible forces that separated the races in the neighborhoods and at school. The experience of attending an integrated school left racial scars, and the feeling of being an outsider has stayed with me all my life.

Every year during Negro History Week,[5] our dad worked with Lewie and me to prepare presentations about great African Americans to share with our classmates. At the time, I was embarrassed about doing it, but later, I came to appreciate it as good training. Now I see it as a precursor of the black studies programs that emerged in the 1960s. When I compared experiences with my friend who attended the local school for blacks, I learned that they were not taught anything about black history.

My Passion for City Planning

In third grade, Mrs. Aikens taught us about William Penn, our city's founder, and his plans for Philadelphia, which means "city of brotherly love." Penn was a Quaker who believed in peace and equality among human beings. Mrs. Aikens told us how Penn had made friends with the local indigenous people, the Lenni Lenape, and had purchased land from them, and then how he had laid out the streets between the Delaware and Schuylkill Rivers and given the north-south streets numbers and the east-west streets the names of trees, an idea unheard of in the seventeenth century. Each house was to be set out on a large plot surrounded by a generous field of open space. He divided the city into four quadrants, each having a large public park. I was powerfully impressed by the notion that you could lay out a city based on ideas and dedicated to social justice and equality. I did wonder why there were no black people in the stories of William Penn and early Philadelphia though.[6]

Mrs. Aikens later took us to see the Better Philadelphia Exhibition, a display of aerial photos and models showing what Philadelphia would look like in twenty-five years. It was designed by the famous architect Edmund Bacon, who became Philadelphia's chief city planner. It occupied two floors of a prestigious downtown department store and included a full-scale model of a street corner in South Philadelphia complete with public trash can. I was delighted by the opportunity to look into the future and deeply inspired by the aerial photos and models that allowed me to look down at the city from a God's-eye point of view.

Many elements of the exhibition excited me. The sketches, aerial photographs, and motion pictures reflected my love of drawing and other modes of visual communication. My passion in math and science and my enthusiasm for making things were satisfied by the architectural plans and elevations and the various charts, displays, and models. Going to the exhibition was like magic. Something in me clicked, and I knew I wanted to be like the people who created the exhibition. However, just as I became enthusiastic about designing and building cities, I was dimly aware that white flight to the suburbs had begun. The dominant culture was losing interest in the urban environment and focusing primarily on building racially restrictive suburbs. Gradually, the pattern of suburban sprawl and inner-city decline was becoming established.

Walking in the City

Growing up, my experience of the natural world was always linked to the human community. It was never an idyllic encounter with the untrammeled landscape of water, sky, rolling hills, forest, and mountains. I didn't have such experiences until I became an adult.

Starting in early childhood and continuing throughout my youth, I developed emotionally and formed my sense of identity through my explorations of geographic space in the city of Philadelphia and beyond. As I walked throughout the city and observed patterns in the neighborhoods, I learned about ethnic communities and about issues of race and class. It occurs to me now that my love, fascination, and obsession with cities are simultaneously the cause and the effect of my walking everywhere.

Driving while Black

Our family, like nearly all black families in the forties, fifties, and later, never went on vacations; however, when I was ten years old, Dad got the idea to take us on an overnight trip to the nation's capital. On our way there, he was arrested for speeding through a little town—Laurel, Maryland—midway between Washington, DC and Baltimore. I don't think we were really speeding. The officer, who had a thick Southern accent, didn't seem to care one way or the other about anything we said. He had the power to lock my father up, and we couldn't do anything about it. I vividly recall the sensation of being in a strange, surreal landscape. I had a vague notion that we had crossed into the South and that this was the kind of thing that was said to happen there.

Dad had often told us, "You never know what is going to happen. Things could turn weird at any time. When they do, you have to stay steady and figure things out. You gotta keep your eyes open. You gotta be able to deal." At the age of nine, I was too young to fully understand what was happening, but clearly things had turned very weird. The officer took possession of the car and took Dad away to jail, leaving my fifty-two-year-old mother and two young boys standing in the street outside the home of the justice of the peace. Such callous and pointless treatment made no sense at all.

We had just enough money for Mother to get on a bus. Lewie and I hitchhiked and met up with her in the Baltimore bus station at Travelers Aid, where we called Aunt Ede and waited for her to wire us enough money to get home. I don't recall how long Dad was in jail and don't remember hearing any stories about what it took for him to be released and regain possession of the car, but I'm sure it was difficult and expensive.

Navigating Wonder and Shadow

My first years after moving to the new house were overflowing with wonder and spontaneous learning. I was enchanted with the park, the trees, the rocks beneath my feet, and the stars above. I loved walking through the city, going to movies downtown, and exploring the department stores. Gradually, though, a shadow side began to emerge. The neighborhood was changing. Although we lived in a beautiful house, as early as 1945, our second year there, our beautiful new neighborhood had begun to deteriorate. Banks made a practice of denying loans for home improvements and repairs in our neighborhood and others that were inhabited primarily by African Americans. Likewise, city agencies reduced spending on maintenance and upkeep of public properties—such as parks, schools, and libraries—in neighborhoods like ours. By 1956, when I left home at the age of seventeen, the neighborhood had become a ghetto.

Shame

After the war ended and my father was no longer needed at the Philadelphia Navy Yard, no one except the four members of our family ever set foot in our house. Dad put so much time and energy into improving white people's houses and landscapes that he was unable to keep our house in working order, much less improve it. There were always paint buckets, brushes, ladders, and other tools in our living room and no place to sit down. The upstairs and downstairs toilets were out of commission for a long time, and we had to use the toilet at the gas station, four blocks away. Sometimes, we didn't have money to pay the electric bill and had to use candles and kerosene lamps to see after the sun went down.

"There is no Santa Claus," Dad once said to us. "You want toys? You need to make them." We did have a well-equipped workshop and books and magazines that gave us ideas for things to make. I was often proud of the things we made, but I also wondered why we couldn't just buy things the way other families did.

Sometimes, before I was school aged, he would say, "You know, I was on my own when I was your age." I didn't know quite what to make of that. I grew to believe that I didn't deserve to live in a nice house and that we didn't deserve to have the toys that other children had.

My father's response once when I showed him a toy I had made was crushing but not unusual: "You did a terrible job," he bellowed. "This is a mess. You need to have discipline and do it right." In retrospect, I realize that he was trying to make sure we developed the means to be independent. The challenge of his parentless childhood had inspired him to develop extraordinary skills and savvy that he tried to pass on to us. He was quite present and worked hard to be a good father, but he lacked the emotional foundation that a secure home environment brings. He couldn't pass down to us what he hadn't received himself.

Although whites continued to flee to the suburbs, there were small pockets of a block or two where no black families had moved in. We thought of those as white neighborhoods. The buildings on our block were actually bigger and better designed than the homes in those so-called white neighborhoods. Our three-story house, for example, was semidetached with a front porch and a small backyard while the nearby white neighborhood was composed of two-story attached row houses with porches running the length of the street. Despite the obvious differences, we thought of our neighborhood as being of lower quality because black people lived there.

Losing Hope

During the years of my later childhood and early adolescence, as whites abandoned inner-city neighborhoods and the city's industrial employment base collapsed, my parents began to lose hope for a bright future for us. Lewie and I were slated to go to Central High School, the best academic high school in the city, where graduates became doctors, lawyers, and scientists. When we graduated from Tilden Junior High School in the summer of 1952, we both scored in the top 1 percent in the citywide academic achievement tests.

Clearly, our parents wanted us to be different from the other young people in our neighborhood. They had chosen the location of our house so that when we grew up, we could walk to the University of Pennsylvania, which was less than a mile away. They had done everything they could to keep us from being caught in an educational tracking system that would isolate us from achievement in the larger society.

Why then did our dad decide to send us to Dobbins Vocational School to learn to work with our hands? Vocational school was where you sent kids who couldn't achieve academically. The most obvious explanation is that he wanted us to have the skills to work with him in a family business. He admired the success of Italians in Philadelphia's construction industry and hoped to emulate them by establishing his own company, Lewis E. Anthony & Sons.

Another factor must have been a loss of ambition and hope for us after the many disappointments he had suffered. He was a brilliant self-made man with many skills and talents, yet he had been unable to overcome the stigma of racism and fulfill his potential. This was due in part to the absence of family support that resulted from his status as an orphan. He was probably afraid that without solid vocational skills, we would be at the mercy of the social and economic forces that had crushed his own dreams and aspirations.

Attending Dobbins Vocational School

To get to Dobbins Vocational School, we had to take a bus, two trains, and another bus. The trip took about an hour. On the way, we would pass by the television station, WFIL-ABC, Channel 6, which was home to Dick Clark's *American Bandstand*. We watched *American Bandstand* every afternoon, giggling at how the show cleaned up black music, toning down its sexual content for a white audience. We never saw any black people dancing on the show.

When we enrolled at Dobbins, we were assigned a homeroom in the cabinetmaking and carpentry shop. We went to basic subjects like math, English, and history in the morning and shop in the afternoon. Our first assignment in shop was to make isometric drawings of thirty wood joints on tracing paper with a thirty-six-ty-degree triangle. I loved making drawings of tongue-and-groove, mortise-and-tenon, dovetail, and all the other wood joints.

For the first assignment, I remember making a border around the drawing a half inch from the paper's edge with a 1B pencil. For the title block in the lower right-hand corner, I filled in guidelines for lettering with a 4H pencil. I used a soft pencil for the lettering and for outlining the wood blocks and a harder pencil to fill in the details.

The teacher was evidently impressed; he sent me home with a note to my parents, suggesting that I be reassigned to architectural drafting. My dad objected, but the counselors at Dobbins prevailed. I was switched out of carpentry and cabinetmaking and assigned to the architectural drafting homeroom. The studio had about thirty students distributed evenly in tenth, eleventh, and twelfth grades. It was run by Mr. Hruslinsky, an excellent teacher and disciplinarian. I loved his class. He expected nothing but the best from us. Every semester, four or five students in the studio would win first or second prizes in regional or national competitions.

Our main activity was making copies of house plans taken from magazines we had selected. I chose split-level ranch houses from magazines like *Better Homes and Gardens*. I particularly liked futuristic-looking houses with butterfly roofs, jalousie windows, and accordion-folding doors. I loved making perspective drawings of these houses.

We also had to copy watercolor and pencil landscape sketches by accomplished practitioners. The trick was to get the work done in an hour. Although we viewed anything that wasn't modern with suspicion, I enjoyed copying drawings of the ruins of Egyptian and Greek buildings. We also made copies of drawings from Sir Banister Fletcher's classic reference book, *A History of Architecture*, first published in 1896 with updated editions coming out throughout the twentieth century.

Although Dobbins was about six miles from our house, Lewie and I would sometimes walk home, saving our transportation money to buy model airplanes. The walk took about an hour and a half and gave us an interesting tour of race and class divisions in Philadelphia's neighborhoods. First, we went through a bad neighborhood and sometimes had to go out of our way to avoid being caught by local gangs and beaten up. We passed Girard College, a forty-three-acre campus boarding school for poor, orphaned, or fatherless white boys between six and eighteen years of age. The college, although owned and operated by the city, was, nevertheless, off limits to black people.[7] After crossing the Schuylkill River, we passed through luxurious Fairmont Park and the Philadelphia Zoo. At the tip of the park, we caught a glimpse across the river of exclusive boathouses with their social and rowing clubs, which did not, we imagined, include any of us. Before reaching home, we walked through the familiar run-down neighborhood where I was born: the Black Bottom.

Leaving Home

In 1955, when I was sixteen years old and halfway through the eleventh grade, Dad decided to take Lewie and me out of school to work in the family business, doing house painting and wallpapering. Soon, Lewie had a run-in with Dad and left home. Six months later, I left too.

It started one evening when Dad told me to turn off the TV and go to bed. I resisted. He said, "As long as you are living here in my house, you will do as I say. If you are old enough to make your own decisions, you are old enough to support yourself." Feeling rebellious and sassy, I replied, "I'm a man-child."

My father didn't take to that answer. He walked me out of the room and into the hallway, repeating what he had just said. I came back with the same response. We replayed the scene several times—from the hallway to the doorway to the porch steps to the sidewalk to down the block. Finally, when I repeated my line that I was a man-child, my father said, "You are on your own," and walked away.

After that collision of our two strong wills, I never lived at home again. Later, overhearing a conversation among adults, I learned that when he had come back into the house, Dad had seemed upset as he told Mother, "Your son is gone."

I spent that night at Aunt Ede's house, borrowed fifty dollars from her, and caught a Greyhound bus the next day for a destination as far away from Philadelphia as I could imagine: the home of Dad's relatives in Enid, Oklahoma. I landed unannounced on the doorstep of Great-Uncle Lewis and Aunt Mary, who took me in. Being away from home for the first time, I experienced a wonderful sense of personal emancipation. At the same time, I was shocked and troubled by the sudden immersion in a world of blatant segregation.

First Exposure to the Segregated South

My journey on the Greyhound bus was my first exposure to the American South. Although Philadelphia was no more than a dozen miles above the Mason Dixon Line, we had learned to think of it as a Northern city. The South was indeed another country. Signs of racial segregation were everywhere: separate toilets, separate drinking fountains, separate seating areas, and separate entrances to buildings. On buses, it was generally understood that African Americans took seats starting in the back and coming forward while whites started in the front and moved backwards. I had read in the newspapers and heard stories about the culture of segregation that victimized black people, but I wasn't conditioned to such formal protocols. Early on in my time there, I boarded a bus and took a seat toward the front. Nobody said anything to me, but the tension was palpable. The bus driver didn't start driving. Then, it dawned on me: *I'm in the wrong seat.* I stood up and moved more toward the rear of the bus to make room for the white passengers who were boarding.

Here I was, late in my teenage years, finally being exposed to the formal racial protocol of the South, a protocol that presumably every African American in the South already explicitly understood. And they had to: African Americans who violated the caste system, with its elaborate restrictions on small acts like showing affection in public or expressing even the slightest disagreement with a white person, were punished with many forms of violence. The culture of segregation condoned outright murder of African American people by lynching and other means and was strengthened by denial of the right to vote.

Spending time in Oklahoma and encountering such visible racism was a jarring experience for me, but one that helped me identify the more hidden racism of the North, where there were no written-out signs, but the feeling of being in the wrong seat was all too familiar.

I stayed with my relatives in Oklahoma for about five months. I found various jobs—most memorably one at an animal hospital—and managed to save around two thousand dollars before returning to Philadelphia. I took a room in the house Aunt Ede shared with my grandmother, worked odd jobs, and attended Temple University High School part time to finish my secondary education. I applied to the University of Pennsylvania (since I had grown up just a mile away, I had always assumed I would attend), but Temple failed to forward my records as promised, and that option evaporated.

CHAPTER 2

Finding Mentors

A T THE AGE OF NINETEEN, I was the volunteer head of the youth chapter at Heritage House, an African American cultural organization. The City of Philadelphia had given us an old brownstone mansion, where we conducted our programs on African American heritage and consciousness. I thrived under the mentorship of the adults who managed the programs at Heritage House, particularly the executive director Eugene Jones, who was the first black man I met who had a PhD. One afternoon, as I looked down from the second floor into the courtyard, I noticed a short man in his midthirties, surrounded by a dozen graduate students. He was gesturing energetically, directing their attention to the features of the space, particularly to an ample locust tree shading the concrete courtyard, which was otherwise devoid of vegetation.

This was Karl Linn, a professor of landscape architecture at the University of Pennsylvania. As soon as I found an opportunity, I introduced myself. Karl reminded me of my father: both men were eloquent, intellectually gifted, and loved to work with their hands; both were also short in stature—around five feet four.

I had been an avid reader, soaking up everything I could about my chosen field of architecture and city planning in books that were written by people whom, given my class and race, I could never hope to meet. But here was Karl, a university professor in the flesh, eager to not only share ideas but also demonstrate how to put them into practice.[1] Karl became a mentor to me. He suggested books to read and introduced me to an astonishing range of artists, writers, and creative professionals, such as the visionary social critic Paul Goodman and his architect brother, Percival, who had just published the second revised edition of their classic book, *Communitas: Means of Livelihood and Ways of Life*, in which they explored ways that society and the built environment could support communal values. Their radical proposals for reorganizing Manhattan to support the development of community intrigued me. With my limited understanding of planning and architecture, their ideas seemed simple to implement, but, in hindsight, I realize that many of them were complex and challenging.

Learning to Recognize Resources with Karl Linn

Large and uncaring urban renewal projects, which were demolishing houses and devastating neighborhoods, were at their peak in 1960 when Karl took his students (all of whom were white) into the ghetto of North Philadelphia to observe and, later, to serve. Karl encouraged me to join him and his students in walking the streets of North Philadelphia, finding the potential in empty lots, back alleys, and shady backyards and looking for vacant land that could be reclaimed. We talked to street musicians, kids playing pavement games, and people sitting on stoops or on chairs on the sidewalks. Karl taught his students and me to notice the genius of inner-city neighborhood residents, who transformed stoops, sidewalks, streets, and vacant lots into extensions of their home territories.

As we walked the back alleys, Karl had his students and me make drawings of what we saw. He made me aware of the many ailanthus trees growing in people's yards, which most landscape architects saw as weeds because they didn't conform to conventional notions of street trees. Walking through the streets of North Philadelphia and looking into backyards, we could see the ways the ailanthus trees had taken over the landscape. Even as the city was being destroyed by redevelopment, the presence of life was reaffirming itself.

Not only did Karl reinforce my recognition of the destructiveness of urban renewal, but the students and I began to realize that these places, which had been thought of as waste, were actually quite beautiful and full of potential. Karl trained a whole generation of architects and planners to see beauty and utility in the city's abandoned and underutilized resources.

A New Appreciation of the Natural World

When I met Karl, I didn't much care for nature. In our family, we worked all the time. There were no vacations or camping trips.[2] As a kid, I had spent time cutting grass and doing yard work to earn spending money, but that work was boring and demeaning. It felt like the subservient roles my ancestors had played as servants and sharecroppers. Karl helped me to see nature in new ways—as an opportunity for play and inspiration and as a spiritual resource. The fascination with the natural environment I had experienced in my third-grade class with Mrs. Aikens was reawakened.

Building Neighborhood Commons

Karl and the Neighborhood Renewal Corps, the nonprofit he founded, would acquire legal control over abandoned property, enabling Karl to recruit and organize neighborhood residents, teams of volunteers, and volunteer professionals to design and build common spaces for community activities. He called these places "neighborhood commons" and the process of building them "urban barnraising," a term that recalled the traditions of Pennsylvania's early Amish and Mennonite settlers, for whom building barns was a community effort.

Karl directed volunteers to collect building materials that were being discarded by industries and suppliers, such as cable reels, concrete cylinders, tiles, railroad ties, and plants. They also rescued materials from demolished houses—marble, bricks, lumber, and more. These discarded parts were reclaimed treasures and belonged to the neighborhood, Karl asserted. They were part of a community legacy.

Karl used donated money to buy an old truck for the neighborhood gang, who became eager collectors of the marble steps left behind by urban renewal and other free resources.

At Melon Commons, Karl's pilot project, the Neighborhood Renewal Corps planted greenery and used the salvaged materials to build playgrounds for kids, an amphitheater for performances, and gathering spots for adults. Karl collaborated with a man who organized Shakespeare performances by local kids in Melon Commons. One weekend, Karl gathered the neighbors and announced: "I want each of you to come here tomorrow and bring an old dinner plate from home." People were puzzled but intrigued. The next day, neighbors came with their plates, and Karl orchestrated an incredibly dramatic event: smashing plates and using the pieces to pave the alley. The result was the most beautiful mosaic I've ever seen.

To bureaucrats in the development agencies, the neighborhood was considered blighted, but Karl encouraged the ongoing celebration of what people had. Watching the project take shape gave me the idea that you could design and build beautiful, uplifting places and provide amenities to underserved people.

Karl and I were an odd pair—a tall, lanky young African American and a short, intense Jewish refugee with a thick German accent. In a sense, we were the very embodiment of discarded parts. Our dialogues during long walks through inner-city Philadelphia laid the foundation for a lifelong friendship and a series of creative collaborations. I had no way of knowing then that Karl's ideas, practice, and the force of his personality would shape my life and work as an architect, urban planner, civil rights worker, and environmental justice activist for the next fifty years. In the work and wisdom Karl shared with me, he taught me the value of discarded elements, both materially and metaphorically. There were people, stories, and communities that the dominant culture had wrongfully discarded. Building neighborhood commons with Karl was my first taste of the deep spiritual and psychological transformation that comes with asserting the value of the discarded.

A Social Agenda in Architecture

After World War II, the nation's decaying cities were spawning new developments outside their boundaries: suburbs accessible only by car. Although Karl had been very successful at designing landscapes of affluence for wealthy clients in suburban and urban settings, he had found this work unsatisfying. The subdivisions where he had worked were designed around the automobile and devoid of outdoor spaces for social interaction. Designing landscapes for increasingly affluent clients had gradually undermined his sense of social relevance.

While growing up and working with my dad as a house painter, all our clients were white. Many were suburban residents, moving into neighborhoods where no blacks could live, such as the communities along Philadelphia's Main Line rail line. I had become critical of a suburban lifestyle built around racial discrimination.

I was impressed that Karl had turned his back on a successful career working for rich and powerful clients to teach and work with students in inner-city communities. During those years, he was on the forefront of a current, gaining strength in the fields of architecture and planning, and committed to improving the lives of poor and working people. Karl was running something that he called a "community design" studio at the University of Pennsylvania; its purpose was to provide design service to disenfranchised communities while teaching the students to grapple with real-world problems. These studios led to important innovations in design and planning: increased citizen participation in the planning process and an acknowledgement that inner-city residents may have different needs than those of standard middle-class clients.

Karl's vision of building commons and community was very attractive to me. It brought together my interests in environmental design and the emerging civil rights movement. During the next few years in the early 1960s, Karl's students took on projects in a dozen inner-city neighborhoods in Philadelphia. With the rising interest in civil rights, Karl created the Neighborhood Renewal Corps that brought together students and volunteer professionals to provide architecture, landscape architecture, and planning services for African American and other vulnerable communities. The community design-and-build studio that Karl modeled was replicated in several other universities, such as Harvard University, Massachusetts Institute of Technology, Columbia University, Pratt Institute in Brooklyn, and University of California at Berkeley. Karl taught me to see the connections between the environment, architecture, and the quest for social justice. In some ways, he anticipated the movement for environmental justice three decades before the field even had a name. In a letter, Lewis Mumford, the great historian and philosopher of urban planning, wrote to Karl, "I can plainly see, in the work you are doing, the fresh shoots that will flower in a new age."[3]

Discovering James Baldwin

Shortly after I returned to Philadelphia following my time in Enid, Oklahoma, I came across *Notes of a Native Son*, a little book by the African American writer James Baldwin. The book, first published in 1955, contained his essays about growing up in Harlem and living as an expatriate in France, along with three critiques—two of popular books about the black experience and the other of a film about African American life.[4] I was greatly impressed by Baldwin's willingness to be critical of African Americans, himself, and American life, all in equal measure. I was grateful to have him as a model. Like me, he was grappling with issues of identity and seemed determined to maintain his authenticity. I wished to have direct contact with him, and later, I did.

Encountering Lewis Mumford

I remember clearly the time and place I first came across the writings of Lewis Mumford, who would become a huge influence in my life as I pursued professional training in architecture. At the age of twenty, I had a part-time job after school at the Witherspoon Library of the Presbyterian Historical Society in downtown Philadelphia, returning books to their proper location on the shelf. Normally,

I worked from three in the afternoon until about five, locking up when I was the last person there.

For some reason, I was drawn to a particular hardbound book with a maroon title on the spine that sat in a stack of six books on the wooden library cart. It was *The Condition of Man* by Lewis Mumford. Instead of putting the book away, I sat down to read:

> What is man? What meaning has his life? What are his origin, condition and destiny? To what extent is he a creature of forces beyond his knowledge and control, the plaything of nature and the sport of the gods? To what extent is he a creator who takes the raw materials of existence, the heat of the sun, the stones and the trees and the soil, his very body and organs, and refashions the world to which nature has bound him, so that a good part of it reflects his own image and responds to his will and his ideal? (Mumford 1944, 3)

I was riveted. Mumford's writing blew open a door in my mind, making it possible for me to think about architecture and buildings in a larger social and philosophical context. I had nurtured an aspiration to become an architect since my visit to the Better Philadelphia Exhibition with my third-grade class, but it hadn't occurred to me that there was more to the field than making pretty drawings, which I loved to do. I became so engrossed in the book that I didn't leave the library until eight o'clock that night. I decided at once that I would read everything Mumford had written.[5]

My Passion for Architectural History Ignited

Lewis Mumford wrote his first book, *The Story of Utopia*, in 1922 when he was in his twenties. This book introduced me to the notion that we can imagine new ways of organizing the places where we live to achieve more balanced and healthy lives and communities. Bringing together the dreams and schemes of utopian thinkers from Plato up to the twentieth century, Mumford enlarged my perspective on what might be possible beyond the world of our everyday lives.

I continued reading Mumford with a growing realization that a sense of history and cultural dynamics in society is integral to understanding and shaping the built environment. His *Sticks and Stones: A Study of Architecture and Civilization*, published in 1924, was, if not the first, one of the earliest books on American architectural history. In it, Mumford explores the relationship between America's building practices and its cultural trends. The final essay in the book celebrates one of the most fertile periods of American architectural history: the development of the Chicago School of Architecture. I was greatly moved to learn about the ways that the social, economic, political, and technological life of the city had shaped its buildings.

I decided that I wanted to write a book like Mumford's but about black people. However, I quickly encountered a serious problem. Mumford had documented the medieval influence on the architecture of New England, the heritage of the Renaissance on nineteenth-century American public buildings, and the influence of machine technology on the pioneers of modern American architecture. As far as I knew, there was no building enterprise (save housing projects and slums) that revealed African American aspirations for a better life. Consequently, I wondered why this was so and what there was to write about.

I wrote to Mumford expressing my appreciation for his books and asking for his advice on how I should be developing my career. I was amazed to receive a letter back from him several days later. Subsequently, we exchanged letters several times and spoke on the phone once. "Although we may not be able to meet right away," he wrote in response to my suggestion that we meet for lunch, "I'm happy to exchange correspondence with you." Although we never met face-to-face, Mumford's writings shaped the pathways of my thinking about architecture, cities, and the role of humans in creating the world we live in.

Mumford's book that engaged me most thoroughly was *The City in History: Its Origins, Its Transformations, and Its Prospects*, in which he explores the various factors that support the development of cities and argues that to find the roots of the idea of a city, we must look at the origin of the pre-human impulse toward community. The instinct of members of a species to come together has a deeply rooted biological basis as evidenced by schools of fish, flocks of birds, and so on. In forming cities, we are following a deep-seated trait that is grounded in our very being and in that of most other species.

I loved Mumford's analysis of the effects that trends, such as urban sprawl, have on society. Although he did not point to racism as the motive for white flight to the suburbs that led to diminished services and opportunities for people like my family who were confined to the inner cities, I had the impression that he was sympathetic to our plight. His assertion that cities be surrounded by greenbelts and provide easy access from residences to work, shopping, and recreation made a lot of sense to me.

Coming of Age in a Segregated City

As I approached adulthood and my awareness broadened, I realized that despite the inspiring, idealistic projections conveyed in the Better Philadelphia Exhibition, I had, in fact, grown up in a segregated city that offered little hope for my future. The Redevelopment Agency, the bureaucratic entity inspired by the Better Philadelphia Exhibition, became the chief public entity responsible for destroying the African American neighborhoods of North Philadelphia.[6] William Penn's vision of a "greene country towne," with its generous housing sites and its streets named after trees, was fading like a figment of the imagination. Despite the vitality of city life, the city itself was under stress. It was losing population as more and more people moved to the suburbs. The city was being abandoned.

Yet, there was hope on the horizon. The fierce honesty of Jimmy Baldwin's prose had planted a seed in me: the possibility that one could tell the truth about race in America without ignoring the complexity of human relations and interactions. My encounters with Karl Linn and Lewis Mumford helped to expand my understanding of my chosen career. I was moving away from architectural drafting as a purely technical and vocational skill and toward an appreciation of the potential for social reform in architecture, urban planning, and city building.

Karl Linn's creation of Melon Commons and other projects fostered my hope that leadership by architects and city planners was not a pipe dream. Lewis Mumford's writing gave me an insight that, by articulating utopian schemes and drawing upon the power of the imagination, architects, urban planners, and designers might contribute to changing the face of our cities and regions. The idea that I could work with others and begin to transform the legacy of racism into a vibrant expression of democracy inspired me.

Gradually, I pieced together the remnants of my secondary education. In 1960, I was accepted as a night school student at Columbia University School of General Studies in New York City. My plan was to complete my liberal arts studies and then enter Columbia's Graduate School of Architecture, Planning and Preservation to earn a professional degree in architecture.

CHAPTER 3

Moving to New York

I N SEPTEMBER OF 1960, I traveled from Philadelphia to New York City on the Greyhound bus. As it snaked down into the earth toward the Holland Tunnel that would take us under the Hudson River, I looked across the industrial wasteland of northern New Jersey and saw the New York City skyline in the distance. I wondered what my future role would be as an architect, helping to shape the human landscape. The multistoried buildings, resting on the granite base, offered outward evidence of the complex and dynamic organizational structure of the city. At that time, I didn't suspect that the Hudson River itself, the industrial landscape, and the geological foundation of the city, visible in the tunnel entrance, would become inspirations to me as I sought an undergirding for my future work as an architect.

Gaining a Sense of Place

My awareness of cities intensified after I moved to New York. When I arrived, I was impressed by the dramatic skyline. I soon learned that the city was shaped by not only commerce, but also the inexorable forces of nature. I learned, for instance, that while Wall Street and Midtown are built on solid stone bedrock, the area in between is not so secure. That is why the high buildings are most densely clustered in the midtown area.

The Hudson and East Rivers cut sharp currents on the west and east sides of Manhattan. The landscape just west of the Hudson is dominated by a high rock escarpment that stretches up from the river. I was impressed by this huge vertical ledge about forty stories high—the New Jersey Palisades. It seems to balance the mass of skyscrapers to the east on Manhattan.

Up around Columbia University, the natural world takes on racial meanings. The district of Harlem is on the flatlands while the university is high on the hill. In 1961, to learn more about myself, I began to make many journeys from Columbia to Harlem. These journeys would take me across the campus, down the hillside of Morningside Park, past the tenements, and through flatland streets littered with broken bottles. People eyed me with curiosity or didn't notice me at all. A transect of Manhattan geography across 116th Street tells the whole story: the campus on a high rocky outcrop—a citadel of learning and place of the highest European aspirations with stately buildings modeled on Roman and neoclassical examples—turns inward, away from the city. Walking east from the campus on 116th Street, you come to a cliff overlooking a vista of the flatlands below: Harlem, land of the blacks. Harlem's location in relation to Columbia's campus reminded me of the location of my birthplace—Black Bottom, Philadelphia—in relation to more privileged neighborhoods nearby.

I began visiting Harlem out of curiosity. I knew that I was related to the black people in Harlem, but that knowledge was not grounded in a shared culture, like that which many people get from going to church every Sunday. My parents were religious, but we never went to church. It was going to take time and effort for me to build a visceral sense of my African heritage.

This was a lonely time for me. I was away from Philadelphia, away from family and friends, and, during my classes at Columbia, away from black people. My first residence was a flat in Greenwich Village that I shared with a high school friend from Philadelphia. Later, I shared a basement with no kitchen on East Fourth Street in the Lower East Side with another friend, John Churchville. The neighborhood had been occupied primarily by Jewish immigrants. I complied when asked to turn the lights on and off at the small synagogue next door on the Sabbath, when faithful Jews were bound to refrain from work.

I got a job working in the bookbinding department in the Butler Library at Columbia University and went to school at night. I was majoring in philosophy. I was encouraged by a letter from Lewis Mumford in which he wrote that my working days and going to school at night reminded him of his own educational journey.

Joining the Civil Rights Movement

With the Supreme Court's *Brown v. Board of Education* decision in 1954, the Montgomery bus boycott in 1956, and the sit-ins and freedom rides of the early 1960s, the civil rights movement focused on racial integration and voting rights in the rural South and in its small towns and cities. In the later 1960s, the emphasis would shift to the idea of black power and building community leadership with increasing attention to civil rights issues in Northern and Western cities.

In April of 1962, John told me about a civil rights conference at Sarah Lawrence College in Bronxville, just north of Manhattan. John and I both went. The event was sponsored by the newly formed Northern Student Movement (NSM). It was an amazing experience: a predominantly white women's campus inviting young African American men and women to not only talk about race but also do something about it. It was a wonderful introduction for me to the effectiveness of direct action and the power of social movements. During the conference, I became a committed participant in the civil rights movement and have been engaged in struggles for racial justice ever since.

It was exciting to meet the students who had started the sit-ins in the South and meet and listen to keynote talks by two elders of the movement: Leon Sullivan and Bayard Rustin. I was fortunate to form a friendship with Bayard Rustin, with whom I met regularly for guidance and encouragement during my years in New York.

Conferring with others, Peter Countryman, who had founded NSM at Yale, conceived a tutorial project for Philadelphia for the summer of 1962. Many students, black and white, participated in tutoring black children in Philadelphia. Later, we decided to form a Harlem chapter of the NSM, calling it the Harlem Education Project (HEP). Our main focus would be tutoring youth. We were fortunate that Kathy Rogers, one of the founding members of the NSM, knew how to get funding.

Leon Sullivan was the other keynote speaker. His niece, Joan Cannady (later Countryman), was the graduating class president at Sarah Lawrence. Leon, a Baptist minister in Philadelphia, conducted what he called "selective patronage" campaigns with other ministers to pressure companies to stop refusing to hire qualified black workers in other than menial jobs. The members of a church, a neighborhood, and other groups would get the details at church or at a meeting, and then the whole group would boycott the company's products—standard items in the lunch pails of black workers—and reward the company with preferential purchasing when it started hiring black workers.

I was impressed by this sophisticated form of direct action and proud that it had been happening in my home town of Philadelphia. I decided to organize a campaign in Manhattan to pressure the Sealtest Milk Company to start hiring black deliverers. Later, I learned that campaigns like this had been going on in New York since the 1930s. I learned and grew from the experience. When I approached a prominent black church to ask members to participate in the campaign, they took the longest time to confer with one another about whether to let me address the congregation. Finally, they let me know that it wouldn't be appropriate since congregants might be uncomfortable with the fact that I had a beard—my fashion sense at the time, such as it was, was informed by the beatnik era. I went home, shaved, trimmed my hair, and put on a jacket and tie, and then I went back to enter my request again. It was good practice for me, but, gradually, I realized that I was more interested in working on community design projects. Eventually, we passed the campaign on to the New York branch of the Congress of Racial Equality.

The Message of Malcolm X

During one of my usual walks from Columbia through Harlem, I made my way east through the beautiful greenery and labyrinthine paths of Morningside Park with a sense of foreboding. I quickly became aware that the park was empty. Yet, I felt I was being watched while trespassing on unoccupied territory. I feared crossing an unnamed boundary that demanded a response from me. I experienced the curious state of double consciousness that W. E. B. Du Bois (1903, 8) had described in *The Souls of Black Folks*:

> One ever feels his twoness,—an American, a Negro; two souls, two thoughts, two unreconciled strivings, two warring ideals in one dark body, whose strength alone keeps it from being tossed asunder.

At the bottom of the hill, the path through the park emptied out onto flatland streets. I would hurry east on 116th Street, turning left at Lenox Avenue.[1] Along the way, I passed clumps of African American men, idle on the street and often engaged in animated argument. Passing by, I would nod my head in recognition, acknowledging that even though I was a student at Columbia, I was down with the hood. Inside, I felt superior to these men, but I also felt ashamed about feeling superior. I continued to ask myself why there weren't more black students at Columbia University.

Then, perhaps a block and a half away, as I approached 125th Street, a voice was coming through a loud speaker, echoing off the walls. "There's no such thing as a Negro. You're a black man!" It was the voice of Malcolm X. By the end of 1963, I had heard him speak many times; I would recognize his voice anywhere.

As a member of the Nation of Islam, Malcolm had changed his name from Malcolm Little to Malcolm X. He believed that the last name Little was given to his ancestors by a white slave owner after they were captured, chained, and shipped across the Atlantic Ocean. Since Malcolm did not know the names of his African ancestors, he simply chose the name X.

James Baldwin, too, had written of being forced to recognize that he was a person of unknown ancestry torn from his African roots. I took this shared experience of African Americans being cut off from our African heritage as a point of departure in my professional education. Much later, I understood it as a step in a journey that began with the emergence of Homo sapiens as the last surviving species of upright walking hominids (Oppenheimer 2003, 39).

As I approached the intersection of Lenox Avenue and 125th Street, I saw that the street had been closed off. A large temporary platform had been erected in the middle of the street. Six or seven men were seated on the platform with an American flag. Sometimes, there was a woman. "We're not Americans," Malcolm proclaimed. "We're Africans who happen to be in America. We were kidnapped and brought here from Africa against our will."

The five hundred people in the mostly black audience roared. Surrounding them were two hundred and fifty white policemen, who, I imagined, were wondering if they would get home that night. I could see the fear in their eyes, and I was frightened too.

Corresponding with James Baldwin

In 1962, I decided to drop out of the School of General Studies at Columbia for a semester to work for the civil rights movement in Harlem. Bayard Rustin gave me James Baldwin's address, and I sent him a note inviting him to an event I was organizing to support the selective patronage campaign to pressure the Sealtest Milk Company. He responded fifteen months later, apologizing for the delayed response and expressing his support for our project and a willingness to stay in touch. We exchanged a few letters, and, much later, in the late 1970s, when I was living in Berkeley, California, I was his host for a month while he was a visiting scholar in the African American Studies Department at the University of California at Berkeley.[2]

Baldwin's fierce critical intelligence and taut prose moved me as he focused on issues of identity and place, describing how language, music, painting, and architecture are cut from the same cloth—a cloth that feels somehow not rightfully his:

I brought to Shakespeare, Bach, Rembrandt, to the Stones of Paris, to the Cathedral at Chartres, and to the Empire State Building, a special attitude. These were not really my creations, they did not contain my history; I might search in them in vain forever for any reflection of myself. . . I would have to appropriate these white centuries, I would have to make them mine—I would have to accept my special attitude, my special place in this scheme—otherwise I would have no place in any scheme. (Baldwin 1955, 10)

I realized that if I wanted to be a great architect, or even a mediocre one, I needed to find a way to integrate all these perspectives into my work and being. It wouldn't be enough to master building in a technical sense. I would have to master the ethos of our time, which, it was increasingly clear to me, needed to include black people.

Baldwin's Letter to His Nephew

In the autobiographic statement in *Notes of a Native Son*, James Baldwin (1955, 10) writes about being forced to recognize himself as a kind of "bastard of the West." The icons of European and American culture did not contain his history nor provide a reflection of himself. And, yet, there was no other heritage he could hope to use.

Consider the message that the conventional mainstream story of our time sends to young African Americans trapped in the inner city. As Baldwin wrote to his fourteen-year-old nephew in 1963 on the centennial of the Emancipation Proclamation:

The heart of the matter is here, and the root of my dispute with my country. You were born where you were born and faced the future that you faced because you were black and for no other reason. The limits of your ambition were thus expected to be set forever. You were born into a society which spelled out with brutal clarity, in as many ways as possible, that you were a worthless human being. You were not expected to aspire to excellence: you were expected to make peace with mediocrity. . . .

. . . Please try to remember that what they believe, as well as what they do and cause you to endure, does not testify to your inferiority, but to their inhumanity and fear. . . .

. . . The really terrible thing, old buddy, is that you must accept them, and I mean that very seriously. You must accept them and accept them with love, for these innocent people have no other hope. They are in effect still trapped in a history that they do not understand and until they understand it, they cannot be released from it. They have had to believe for many years, and for innumerable reasons, that black men are inferior to white men.[3]

This text settled deep within and has stayed with me throughout the rest of my life. The power of Baldwin's clear and amazingly compassionate perspective guided and animated my efforts then and now. It is an underpinning for my purpose in writing about what I call the "hidden narrative of race." It became clear to me that all people, not only African Americans, need to understand the largely unacknowledged story of black people—a story that stretches back to the beginning of time and includes the achievements of African cultures and civilizations over millennia.

My Involvement in Civil Rights Struggles

By the early 1960s, both law and social custom had relegated black people to a separate and inferior legal status, especially blacks living in Southern and border states. Denied the right to vote and barred from public facilities, our people were subjected to routine insults and deadly violence by whites—private citizens as well as public officials. We could not expect justice from the courts.

African American protests against these conditions were at long last very much in the news, and the prominence of these struggles affected me deeply. I experienced an emerging sense of empowerment. Suddenly, I felt that I could expect to be treated as a whole person. Though most public attention focused on the Southern states, I was all too aware of the inequities in the cities of the North.

As I became personally engaged in the emerging civil rights movement, I sought to synthesize two streams of learning: from what I was gleaning from my classes at school and from my growing involvement in civil rights activism.

Cultural and Political Inspirations

During the time that I was immersing myself in Mumford's books, I was also discovering a new generation of African American writers. During the early 1960s, I came in contact with a vibrant, emerging African American literary tradition influenced by the civil rights movement. Lorraine Hansberry, Richard Wright, Ralph Ellison, Harold Cruse, LeRoi Jones (later known as Amiri Baraka), and especially James Baldwin were the most prominent. I was inspired by these writers and felt that they would influence my practice of architecture in the same way that the transcendentalists, such as Emerson, Thoreau, and Whitman, affected the architects and builders of the twentieth century as Lewis Mumford described in *The Golden Day*.

Jones published *The Blues People: Negro Music in White America* in 1963, which describes the reinvention of American music—spirituals, blues, jazz, and bebop—out of the harsh conditions of the rural South and life in the coldwater flats, nightclubs, and speakeasies in the industrial cities, like Chicago, Detroit, Philadelphia, and St. Louis. I was fascinated by this and recognized it as part of the hidden history I was struggling to discover and revive.

Civil rights news was on the front page of every newspaper around that time. We were living in exciting times. I pondered how, as an architect, I could contribute to this explosion of creativity. This was in the background of my thoughts and dreams throughout the sixties while I was studying architecture at Columbia and trying to connect city planning to the struggle for human rights and social justice. Most of the political action of the national civil rights movement was still focused on the South, but many of the most prominent people in the movement were in and out of New York on a regular basis. As a student activist, I got to meet many of them.

Given the anger and frustration I saw every day in Harlem, I figured that the arc of the movement would soon swing to the North, and I wanted to be ready. The NSM, in which I was active, had been raising money and arranging speaking engagements for students from the South. Besides boycotts of companies who refused to hire African American employees, activists organized rent strikes against unscrupulous landlords in Harlem who milked their properties for profits without concern for tenants' rights.

Michaux's Bookstore

At some point, I discovered the West End Bar on Broadway near 114th Street where beer, food, and lively conversation drew a constant stream of students and faculty. I went there after classes almost every day to listen, learn, and exchange ideas. Further up toward the Bronx on 125th Street and Seventh Avenue was Lewis Michaux's African National Memorial Bookstore. This Harlem institution was a hotbed of information regarding all things African and African American. I went there often to soak up the rich expressions of black culture and be fortified by the way they challenged the dominant culture. The store was crowded with people, books, pamphlets, flyers, and framed portraits (photos and paintings) of African American luminaries. The front exterior wall was papered with large signs: "The House of Common Sense," "Home of Proper Propaganda," "World History Book Outlet on Two Billion African and Non-White Peoples," "Repatriation Headquarters Back to Africa Movement,"[4] and smaller signs promoting particular books or causes.

At Michaux's bookstore, I encountered a great number of particularly formative works, including *100 Amazing Facts About the Negro With Complete Proof: A Short Cut to the World History of the Negro* by the highly successful self-taught Jamaican American historian Joel Augustus Rogers. Another eye-opener was *The Mis-Education of the Negro* by historian Carter Woodson. Woodson (1933) gave many examples of how black students are taught to distrust their abilities and discount their value. Taught with a curriculum designed for whites that black students find neither relevant nor useful, they end up with only a superficial knowledge and a strong sense of inferiority. Maybe this was why, even though it was sometimes hard to separate Rogers's (1934) rhetorical bravado from historical fact, his books moved me so. Woodson's (1933) points resonated deeply with me as I was still being mis-educated in many of the ways he described.

My miseducation was also reduced by another book: *Stolen Legacy: Greek Philosophy Is Stolen Egyptian Philosophy* by Professor George G. M. James. James (1954) takes readers through a detailed process of reviewing known facts about ancient Greek history and shows that many traditional stories about Greeks as originators of philosophy, art, and the sciences are impossible and likely derived from Egyptian learning and culture, which, therefore, provided the basis for the achievements of Western civilization. Whether or how the knowledge was stolen, though, is a question that seemed less pressing to me than coming to terms with the effects of the Atlantic slave trade.

Much later, in 1967, *The Crisis of the Negro Intellectual: A Historical Analysis of the Failure of Black Leadership* by Harold Cruse gave me a lot to think about. Cruse laid out analysis of the activism that had taken place in the 1930s and how it had laid the groundwork for the civil rights movement of the 1960s. While reading the book, I reflected on how little we remember about the successful boycotts they organized and the flowering of artistic expression they shared. Many of his observations gave me clues to better understand things about our communities and our struggles that were not being documented and, thus, would be lost to history.[5]

Learning about Ancient African History

It must have been at Michaux's bookstore that I came across the writing of self-educated British journalist Basil Davidson who, in 1951, began decades of research and writing aimed at correcting prevailing racist misconceptions about Africa and its history. After centuries of misinformation, people tended to think of Africa as an uncivilized land with no history prior to contact with Portuguese explorers in the fifteenth century. This assumption bolstered the idea that people of African origin were inferior to people with European ancestry and that they were less intelligent, less cultured, and even less human. European invaders used this blatant fabrication as their excuse for enslaving African people, colonizing their lands, and exploiting their natural resources.

The Davidson book that I first encountered was *The Lost Cities of Africa*. I was fascinated by the way he wove together observations and accounts by explorers, scientists, merchants, soldiers, and kings and combined them with archeological evidence and climate history to trace the development of the ancient kingdoms and empires of sub-Saharan Africa.[6] Where firm evidence could not be found, Davidson (1970) speculated about what might be reasonable to believe. For example, during the millennia between five and ten thousand years ago, when, according to scientists, the Sahara was a green and fertile land, there are faint traces of humans who were planting fields and raising animals. One can only wonder about cities buried beneath those sands.

The idea that ancient Africans had developed cities was a radical new concept for me. I spent hours and days rereading Davidson and trying to come to terms with the facts and possibilities he was presenting. At that time, the academic discipline of history was based exclusively on Eurocentric perspectives. Greece was considered to be the fountainhead of civilization. There seemed to be a consensus among my professors and fellow students that any scholarship centered on the African experience was not worth studying. My participation in anything Afrocentric would have made me academically suspect, and I wasn't ready to go out on that limb. I kept my thoughts and interests to myself and continued reading and thinking about these new ideas throughout my years at Columbia.

Family Changes

In 1961, Dad suffered a brain hemorrhage at the age of 59. He was in a coma for four days before Mother finally called her sister, Ede. She thought he was sleeping and would eventually wake up. He was taken to the hospital and remained in the coma for a few days before he died. We were all able to be there with him, and that felt good. Lewie and I had both had some reconciliation with him before his death, but I wish there had been more. The memorial service at the funeral home was not as well attended as I expected, and only a handful of friends came to the graveside.

Lewie and I had to sell the several properties our dad had purchased as there was no way we could keep up the mortgages. We just broke even on the deals so there was no money left for Mother. She lived in Philadelphia with Ede for a few months after Dad died. She was in good health, but she was lonely. I was in my first year at Columbia, and Lewie was working at Princeton. We rented a house that was halfway between Princeton and Columbia, and Mother moved in with us. We decided that would be the easiest way to deal with our new situation. The arrangement lasted for about a year. I was very comfortable living with Lewie and Mother, but commuting was stressful. I worked as a night janitor at Columbia and was taking four courses during the days. For several days in a row, I would work all night, sleep on a couch on campus for a few hours, and then go straight to my classes without returning to New Jersey. The travel and switching between train and subway was tiring and time consuming. Eventually, Mother moved back to Philadelphia, and I moved to Manhattan's Lower East Side.

Meeting Jean

I met Jean Doak briefly during my trip with John in the early spring of 1962 to the then all-white Connecticut College for Women,[7] where we had been invited to talk about life as an African American man in the United States. I described a world the students had not known. Afterward, I exchanged letters with Joanne, Jean's friend. I described the planned Sealtest Milk Company boycott and our need for staff. Wanting to work on the boycott, Jean took the bus from New Jersey to New York early that summer and found us in the basement on East Fourth Street beyond Avenue C. The absence of a kitchen and the night visits by rats were a shock to her. An Antioch student who was doing her three-month work requirement and living near us invited Jean to share her apartment. She did not find a role in the boycott and instead got a nine-to-five job to save money for the next year at college. Later that summer, we were raising funds to start up HEP, the civil rights group that I had cofounded with several other students as part of NSM. Jean ended up working at HEP and abandoned her plan to return to college.

Jean was quiet and reserved. She didn't talk a lot. In that way, she reminded me of my mother, whose calm demeanor was a counterpoint to my father's dominant personality. I thought Jean just needed to be drawn out, and I liked being able to do that. I liked that she was a rebel even though she was shy. I liked that she challenged conventions. She didn't want to get married. She didn't want to change her name. I admired her spirit of independence. It made me feel good to be connected with someone who was also rebelling. Although I was very active in the public arena, *I* was actually a loner deeper down. Being with Jean helped me feel less isolated.

Beside civil rights work, Jean and I shared an interest in drawing. After hearing so much from me related to architecture, she began to consider it as a possible career. We had interests in common and were both reluctant to be alone, so the transition to being together was easy. We became a couple toward summer's end.

Jean had a broader sense of geographic entitlement than I did despite her insistence that she had not traveled much. My territory consisted of the Lower East Side, Greenwich Village, and uptown near Columbia in Harlem and Morningside Heights. In these neighborhoods, I felt more or less welcome. I could go other places, but, in those situations, I often felt like an interloper.

I did not trust that the whole continent belonged to me as Jean and other white people I knew seemed to feel. I was wary of wandering too far from a black neighborhood. I felt that most of Manhattan, to say nothing of the suburbs, was hostile territory.

Joining the Community Design Movement

In 1962, I was among the early adopters of the community design movement, a social movement that sought to link architecture and urban and community planning with civil rights. This involved finding a site, engaging nearby residents in the planning process, and designing a shared space where youth, families, and seniors could come together to celebrate community life. My model was the neighborhood commons projects that Karl Linn was orchestrating in collaboration with neighborhood residents, volunteer teams, students, and volunteer professionals. The idea behind commons was to foster the development of a new kind of extended family living based not on blood but on friendship, mutual aid, and intergenerational support. This work is documented and illustrated in Karl's 2007 book, *Building Commons and Community*.

Karl was a champion of people's access to commons at a time when the concept of commons was lost on most Americans. In our modern society, most land-use decisions are privatized, which tends to privilege people with more money and resources and marginalize everyone else. In most indigenous, traditional, or rural societies, people have a direct capacity to come together and decide what is needed for the common good—a grazing field for sheep or cattle, a pump for water, a market space, and so on. Most people believe that air and water are common assets, but these beliefs are being challenged by neoliberal economic theorists and corporate interests.[8]

Creating a Neighborhood Commons in Harlem

With my parallel interests in urban planning and the civil rights movement, I went to work for the Architects' Renewal Committee in Harlem, which aided community groups. I involved myself in a practical project that would improve the neighborhood by surveying all the vacant land in Harlem. This was our first community design project. We surveyed 150 blocks of central and west Harlem. In collaboration with Karl Linn and members of HEP, I selected a site at 148th Street and Bradhurst Avenue to build a neighborhood commons. It took an enormous effort to clear the lot of trash, rats, mattresses, and broken appliances. A neighbor borrowed from his workplace an earth-moving vehicle, which saved us days of unpleasant work. In the summer of 1963, we moved our HEP storefront into a building adjacent to the site.

The two vacant lots formed an entrance to the commons, which included all the backyards in the city block bounded by 147th and

148th Streets, Bradhurst Avenue, and Eighth Avenue. With volunteer architects, we developed a plan for the site, cleared out the back-yards, and implemented the first phase of the project: the building of a large barbecue pit. Several big community celebrations were held in the commons, and the tutoring program continued in one of the basements. Children also met their tutors at various churches.

Lewie moved into an apartment on the block and operated a basement laboratory that engaged local kids in science and technology projects and experiments. They were building things I didn't quite understand from parts donated by computer companies, probably data processing systems. He was impressed with their ingenuity when he discovered that some of the kids were raising pigeons on the roofs of their buildings and training them to carry messages.

Through my apprenticeship with Karl in Philadelphia, I had learned about traditions of participatory design. This approach to professional services emphasized engaging all the stakeholders in the design of a building project. I thought that this would be the right approach for planning and developing community space in inner-city communities.

By late 1963, I had two years of experience under my belt working in the Harlem civil rights movement. Through this experience, I had gained some understanding of the history of African American people and our struggles for identity and inclusion in the mainstream of American life.

Partnering with Jean

In the summer of 1962, a casual relationship I had been in ended, which opened the way for deepening my connection with Jean. She had rented an apartment on St. Mark's Place in the East Village—sharing the cost with her father who came to Manhattan about once a month. He stopped coming after he chanced to meet me there. Up to his dying day, he refused to meet me or even discuss my existence. After that, Jean and I shared the apartment until a cheaper space became available.

Jean was committed to civil rights, and a lot of the things we did together were in the context of the movement. That gave our relationship a foundation. We were on the same wavelength in challenging the dominant culture's restrictions on African Americans and interracial relationships.

She gradually developed an interest in architecture. In 1964, I completed my requirements at Columbia in the College of General Studies and arranged to enter the graduate program in architecture. She started to apply to the Cooper Union, but was not admitted until the fall of 1966.[9]

Jean longed to travel, especially outside the United States. Being with her broadened my horizons. In October and November of 1963, we pooled our savings and traveled by bus to Mexico City accompanied by a fifty-pound bag of books I was reading. We continued on to San Miguel de Allende, a charming small town between Mexico City and Guadalajara. Emerging from a long bus ride, having just entered Mexico, the absence of the white antagonism toward blacks was palpable. We had been forced off the bus and challenged by a burly Texas Ranger a while before we had crossed the border.

In the end of the 1964–65 school year, Jean read an article in the *New York Times* about two recent architecture graduates who were building fanciful vacation homes near a hamlet in Vermont. They wanted workers, and Jean suggested we go up there and stay for the summer. I went along with the plan. They hired me, introduced Jean to a summer employer, and our Vermont summer commenced. We brought Mother up to the rambling farmhouse we rented. The place had long been uncared for. We had to run a new water line to the house from a new spring. At the construction site, young men were playing around with dynamite to create sites for houses. There were not a lot of drawings; they seemed to be creating the rooms as they went along. At best, the scene could be described as "white men at play."

Looking back, I realize that Jean and I were living in a kind of bubble. Being in an interracial relationship was quite unusual at the time. Jean always felt tense when we were together in white Midtown Manhattan. Jean's parents were bitterly separated and neither was in favor of our relationship nor accepted me as a family member. I tried not to take it personally, but I think the nonacceptance positioned me in a kind of perpetual limbo.

In retrospect, my expectations seem hopelessly idealistic and naïve. I had imagined that Jean's parents would be not only accepting of me but also accomplished to the degree that they would be mentors to me as I was moving into the world. To my chagrin, her mother was irritated and her father was tight-lipped and in denial about our relationship. Reluctantly, Jean's mother let me stay the night as we departed for Mexico. Her father had left the family a year before we met and never entered the picture again after that chance encounter at Jean's apartment on St. Mark's Place. There was nothing in their splintered family that I could grab onto, and I felt cut off from the sense of nourishment that I had imagined would come from having an alternate set of parents to help me navigate the world.

Mother and my aunts accepted Jean warily. Lewie was somewhat distant with her.

Jean had a married older sister. She and her husband visited New York in 1964 in part to convince us to separate. The husband wanted to talk me out of the relationship. I was impressed by the fact that he was older than me and decided I'd try to be nice, but the situation seemed odd. He took me to a bar and tried to explain why it would be a good thing if I didn't see Jean anymore. He had the attitude of an older relative cautioning me about the choices I was making. "This is a tough road," he advised. "You have to think about your children. They would have a hard time." I stuffed down my immediate reaction, which was, "Of course, my children are going to have a hard time. They'll have a hard time, like I did, just being in the world. So, what?" He was saying that it would be hard for my kids if they were not white, but I wasn't going to be having white kids in any case. So, he didn't have a compelling argument.

More troubling for me than the disapproval from Jean's relatives was the ambivalence with which many African American women perceived us. This put a cloud on our relationship. The general feeling among many black women was that there were only so many men who had not been damaged by the horrible system of racism and to see the handful of ones who were potential partners go off and get involved with white women felt like a slap in the face. It wasn't meant to be like that, but I could understand how it felt.[10]

Civil Rights in the News

The year of 1963 was a landmark year for the civil rights movement, and I was glad to be active in it. That spring, the world watched Birmingham, Alabama, on television as Sheriff Bull Connor directed his police to turn high-pressure fire hoses on and mount police dogs against African American children attempting to integrate Kelly Ingram Park. Martin Luther King Jr. was arrested for participating in a nonviolent protest and wrote his famous "Letter from Birmingham Jail." Medgar Evers, the outspoken field secretary of the National Association for the Advancement of Colored People, was assassinated.

On August 28, 1963, President John F. Kennedy watched on television at the White House as 250,000 people gathered on the Washington Mall for the March on Washington for Jobs and Freedom, where they heard Martin Luther King Jr. deliver his famous "I Have a Dream" speech. On Sunday, September 15, the Sixteenth Street Baptist Church in Birmingham was bombed, killing four young girls. These events marked a turning point in the struggle for civil rights and contributed to the support for the passage of the Civil Rights Act of 1964. In November of 1963, President Kennedy was shot to death in Dallas, Texas.

Poised on the Racial Divide

By 1964, I had completed the liberal arts requirements for entry into the professional program in architecture at Columbia University. When I went back to my classes that January, I was reminded how much I hated being the only black person in my class; I was surrounded again by white people who seemed determined to avoid talking about race. It seemed there were no black students, no black faculty, and no subject matter addressing the racial divide in our society that condemned blacks to live in horrible conditions in segregated neighborhoods.

I was disturbed by the reality that when I was around white folks, they seldom talked about race; whereas, when I was with black folks, we talked about it all the time. The situations we faced every day were shaped and determined by race, so racial issues weighed heavily on our minds. We needed to share our observations and experiences to better understand how we were navigating the challenging terrain. I wanted to write a book about this—one that could be assigned reading for everyone.

CHAPTER 4

Columbia School of Architecture

JOINING THE CIVIL RIGHTS movement had changed my life. As I began professional studies in architecture and planning, I wanted to know how the planning and design of cities could support the struggle for racial justice. In 1964, many of my friends decided to travel to the South to join Freedom Summer, a voter registration campaign in Mississippi led by the Student Nonviolent Coordinating Committee (SNCC) and a coalition of civil rights organizations. I was drawn to and impressed by this campaign which, in addition to voter registration, set up dozens of Freedom Schools, Freedom Houses, and community centers in small towns throughout the South to aid local black people.

As for me, I wanted to support the development of such helpful institutions in the inner cities of the North, so I decided to stay in New York and focus on the architecture program at Columbia University.

Professors and Curriculum

Teaching at Columbia's architecture school was centered on the design studio. The first-year studio under the leadership of Peter Pragnell was a powerful and positive experience. Influenced by a design movement in Europe called Team 10, Pragnell was interested in the social factors that shape the design of buildings. He brought to our design studio the world-famous architect Aldo van Eyck, who delivered an amazing two-hour lecture about the Dogon people, an ethnic group in Mali who live in beautifully designed mud, thatch, and stone dwellings along and near the cliffs of Bandiagara.

Our project-based learning began with designing a summer camp for twenty-four people. Next, we were instructed to find an existing English town and produce a detailed map that demonstrated how people's needs were met by the built environment. The town I chose was an agricultural settlement of fifty houses clustered around the main road. Another assignment was to do a photo essay in the city organized around a theme. I chose the theme of barriers. I noticed and photographed many walls, signs, and signals showing where not to go—restricting traffic, parking, and access to grassy lawns, for example. For a paper analyzing mechanical systems, I studied the Richards Medical Center in Philadelphia designed by Louis Kahn. For an assignment to produce working drawings and models, I chose the Carpenter Center for the Visual Arts at Harvard University by Le Corbusier.

I did well in the course, and at the end of the first year, Professor Pragnell arranged for me to get a summer job working for the firm of Patrick Desalles in the outskirts of London. Finding a place to live proved challenging. After visiting many agents without success, I realized that "no coloreds" was on the index cards they searched. I slept in the park a few nights. Finally, I got a bed in a shared flat in Islington. One of my neighbors was an infamous neo-Nazi.

While I was abroad, I visited, at Mr. Pragnell's suggestion, the architecture of Peter and Alison Smithson in England, Aldo van Eyck in the Netherlands, Le Corbusier in France, Antonio Gaudí in Spain, and a few others. Each of these architects in their own ways had tried to manifest a more humane approach to architectural design than was seen in the mainstream.

Van Eyck and the Smithsons were leading members of Team 10, a social movement of younger architects who were breaking away from the Congrèes International d'Architecture Moderne (CAIM). They were rebelling against the faceless and soulless architecture that was springing up everywhere. They tried to introduce elements of humanism into their designs. Van Eyck, for example, installed mirrors at various levels and in unusual places in the Municipal Orphanage in Amsterdam to give the children opportunities to explore and make discoveries in their environment. I appreciated that he was inspired by indigenous building traditions in America and Africa, and I was intrigued by his idea that a city should function in a unified manner like a house and that a house should function in an expansive way like a tiny city.

Le Corbusier, who was the leading architect of the twentieth century, designed buildings that were spiritually moving, such as the chapel of Notre Dame du Haut (Our Lady of the Heights) on a hill above the village of Ronchamp. The thick curved walls and roof give the impression of a massive piece of sculpture. I also visited the building he designed for the convent of Saint Mary of La Tourette. It is much larger than the chapel and contains bedrooms, study halls, a library, dining hall, kitchen, and a church. His designs are very modern, but also draw on nature and on human needs. He took the symbols of modern life and incorporated them into his designs to create a new vocabulary of modern architecture that was used by many.

Antonio Gaudíi's designs were clearly inspired by nature—organic forms that are curvilinear and flowing with lots of color and decoration, reflecting and responding to the human spirit in profound ways. I was grateful to spend time taking in the work of all these great architects who wanted to accommodate and address the needs of ordinary people while creating architectural innovations.

From the Studio to the Streets

The studio is a metaphor for the specialized training of the architect, including the physical environment in which he or she works. An inspiring studio space often features high ceilings and skylights and is shared by twelve to twenty students. Beautiful objects are located strategically throughout the space, such as plaster casts of Renaissance sculptures, Greek urns, and columns from European buildings, all intended to stimulate the muse.

The studio is led by a master architect who acts as a coach, giving frequent crits (short for critiques) at each student's drafting table.

The master architect also simulates the role of the client. Lectures and other coursework are subordinate to the studio experience. Students are given a design problem to work on for several months and spend most of their time in the studio at their drafting table. At the end of the semester, they present their work to a jury.

I call the real world where low-income families live "the streets." The physical environment where poor people live, work, and play often reflects a lack of care. Liquor stores abound, but there are few places where you can get fresh food. Buildings are boarded up and covered with graffiti. Overflowing trash containers, unclaimed automobiles, abandoned refrigerators, and broken furniture are everywhere.

Toward the end of my experience at Columbia, the conflicts of the real world intruded on the curriculum. I experienced a clash of cultures between the architecture planning studio and the streets of the city. The studio emphasized thoughtful, creative problem solving in which the practitioner controls all the variables. In the streets, life was different. In 1967, the nation experienced violent, race-related civil insurrections. Significant areas in many cities had gone up in flames. In 1968, Martin Luther King Jr. was murdered. Upon learning of the assassination, I was enraged. Eventually, when I could no longer contain my emotions, I went out to join the crowds in the streets.

The Kerner Commission, appointed by President Lyndon B. Johnson to investigate the causes of the riots, referred to the two Americas: rich white people and poor black people. Real-world, city-building processes are shaped by the conflicting interests of public officials, financial institutions, real estate developers, community groups, and civic organizations. Often, there is no single client or decision maker. African Americans and other communities of color find themselves at a disadvantage in dealing with more powerful groups in society, and the racism inherent in real-world dynamics tends to marginalize them even further.

It became clear to me that the city is shaped by the restless migrations of people and sometimes by forces for social change. The city was losing people and jobs to the suburbs. Inner-city decline and suburban sprawl went on unabated. The political landscape was turbulent. I found no one to talk to about these things during the years I was a student at Columbia's Graduate School of Architecture, Planning and Preservation, situated in Avery Hall, an acropolis perched on Morningside Heights.

At that time, there were no African American architecture students in any of my classes, and only a handful in the school as a whole. Until 1968, when Max Bond joined the faculty, there were no African American members of the architecture teaching staff. No coursework discussed the legacy of racism in the built environment or explored prospects for community development to address structural inequality of opportunity.

In 1968, social change demonstrations came to Columbia. Protesting a bungled planning process to construct a gymnasium in a park shared by residents of Harlem, African American students and residents of Harlem occupied Hamilton Hall, the university administration building. In sympathy, white students occupied other campus buildings to protest the university's complicity in the Vietnam War. The university was shut down for a month, and the president was fired. At one point, the black students occupying Hamilton Hall held a press conference and invited Stokely Carmichael and H. Rap Brown to speak. I happened to be passing by and, when I stopped to speak with Stokely, I was swept into the building with the crowd and captured on film that was aired on the television newscasts. To tell the truth, I was not very excited about the protests, but I was glad that the gymnasium was not built on that poorly sited location. As I was older than most other students and had been working in civil rights campaigns for six years, protest movements were not new and exciting to me, and I was somewhat detached from the actions.

I focused on increasing the numbers of African American and Puerto Rican faculty members and students. We not only pressured the administration but also did outreach to the historically black colleges in the South. I made a recruiting journey, funded through Columbia's School of Architecture, to several black colleges to let students know they were welcome to apply for admission. A significant number applied and were accepted. As a result of our efforts,

Columbia is among the leading universities whose graduating African American architecture students became licensed architects.[1]

Experimental Professional Projects

While I was an architecture student, I had opportunities to undertake several professional projects. The projects were experimental in nature and helped broaden and deepen my understanding of architecture and the role that building design can play in meeting people's needs.

The school was in disarray during those years since there was no permanent chairman of the architecture department. I managed my courses reasonably, but dropped out for a semester to complete a design/build of a Vermont artist residence. I also designed an odd triangle-plan house to the owners' specifications in East Hampton, and designed and built another innovative vacation home for a family on Block Island with a team that included fellow students Mark Hawkins and James Piccone, with Karl Linn deftly altering the landscaping. I had long been interested in Buckminster Fuller's thinking and work with geodesic domes, so I was excited when we bought two geodesic dome kits and erected them to form the new vacation home, converting some of the triangular panels into window openings.[2] We connected the two domes via a boardwalk elevated five feet above ground.

In August of 1968, Jean and I used the money earned on the geodesic dome construction to travel to Cuba with a group of architects and planners organized by Chester Hartman. Chester became a lifelong colleague and friend—an urban planning professional with a commitment to social justice.[3] On the visit, we documented the planning and architecture of revolutionary Cuba; ten years had passed since the ouster of Cuban dictator Fulgencio Batista. The elegant architecture of the Cuban National Ballet School particularly impressed me with its gentle vaulted ceilings that spanned large spaces—an ancient Catalan technique. The ceiling structure was composed of four or five layers of thin brick tiles with staggered mortar joints. The building has recently been restored.

In the summer of 1966, Jean and I traveled to southeast Turkey for a three-month dig at the little town of Samsat with Nemrud Dagh Excavations, directed by archeologist Theresa Goell. It was a very small group with a small budget, but we appreciated the chance to be in a faraway place. My main duty was to survey. I bought a book on surveying just before departing New York and trained myself during the journey. We all had to wait a full month in Ankara before being granted permission to go to our site. Once a fortified city, Samsat had become a small village in the near-denuded landscape of Adıyaman Province on the banks of the upper Euphrates River. Theresa entertained us with stories about her youth as a Marxist– Leninist in the 1920s and 1930s and the irony of being lectured to about "standing up to capitalist pigs" by some Black Panthers she was renting an apartment to in New York.

Being in Samsat was quite an adventure. At the top of a high hill of layered construction (the former fortified castle) was fourteenth-century material; and nine feet down was Roman era. On one occasion, I nearly died of sunstroke when I worked sunup to midday in full sun at 120°F despite Theresa's warning to quit by ten o'clock in the morning.

Later, Teresa disappeared for several weeks with a colleague to ride a traditional raft—with floatation provided by inflated sheepskins—on rapids in the Euphrates to demonstrate that it could have been done long ago. I was concerned because she had lost hearing years before and with it, a sense of balance. As she was unreachable during this absence and had left me in charge of the local digging crew (nearly all the able-bodied men of the village), we had to pray she knew what she was doing. Everywhere we wandered in the village, there were things created by people of the past—Roman stone sarcophagi used as water troughs, inscribed rocks built into house walls, and pot shards and coins underfoot. The excavation turned up fifty crates of finds—mostly pots—that ended up in the basement of a local museum.

During our time in Turkey, I felt no hostility toward me as a black man. They related to me primarily as an American.

My Experience at Columbia: A Mixed Bag

I decided early on to become an architect because it seemed to be mostly about art and beauty. Later, I found out that it was also about justice because the environment people grow up in largely determines their chances for success in life. My primary goal was to develop and learn how to use professional skills to improve the quality of life for African Americans living in cities. I wanted to learn how to plan, design, and construct buildings that would serve the needs of clients, fit into the fabric of the city, and improve the quality of life for people who lived in low-income communities of color. The defining challenge of my professional and political education during the 1960s was my quest to integrate the studio culture of architecture and urban planning with my experiences in the civil rights movement. I confronted the great challenge of fusing elitist architecture and urban planning methodologies with bottom-up direct action civil rights organizing strategies.

It became inescapably clear that our society is fractured primarily along lines of race and class, but also by gender, age, and differing perspectives about society's relationship to the natural world. The lack of consideration within my profession of these realities and their implications weighed heavily upon me.

In my decision to be an architect, I had gradually, over the years, shifted my attention away from nature to artifacts made and arranged by human beings. In my quest for racial justice, I came to see the city in terms of black and white: the abandoned part being neighborhoods where black people lived and the sprawling part being the suburbs where the white people lived. I had inherited the legacy of oppression, and I struggled mightily against it.

The architect learns to picture a reality that does not yet exist and envision a possible design solution to a physical problem, including the necessary steps to make this design a reality. In my training, matters of political power or access to economic resources were not addressed. The curriculum centered on the design of individual buildings for individual or institutional clients with power and resources.

It eventually dawned on me that if I were to have any chance of achieving my modest original goals, my work needed to incorporate some path for addressing the societal fractures that made it so hard for people of color from low-income communities to shape their physical environments to reflect their highest aspirations. So, I determined to shape my education about building in two ways: by planning and designing physical structures for community use and by building and organizing institutions, networks, and strategies to overcome the legacy of racism and make social change possible.

The civil rights movement was about ensuring that politically marginalized populations could gain access to political and economic power and resources. As Martin Luther King Jr. (1964, 67) wrote in April 1963 in his letter from the Birmingham Jail:

> Nonviolent direct action seeks to create such a crisis and foster such a tension that a community which has consciously refused to negotiate is forced to confront the issue. It seeks so to dramatize the issue that it can no longer be ignored.

Political Leadership in Architecture

In my final year at Columbia University, I grew interested in the urban design work being undertaken by Mayor John Lindsay's administration in New York City. Our studio assignment was to produce designs for a new state office building in New York City. Civil rights leaders Wyatt Tee Walker and Bayard Rustin had visited New York State Governor Nelson Rockefeller and convinced him to move a portion of the state administrative functions into an office building in Harlem. The idea was to bring these services to a portion of the city that had not been well served, where new activity on the street could stimulate economic development. However, the project was very divisive. A small group of black students (I was the only one of us studying architecture) protested the intrusion of white people into Harlem and occupied the site, referring to it as Reclamation Site No. 1. Our studio masters seemed to have no awareness or understanding of the nature of the conflict. The situation frustrated me, and for my assignment, I chose an alternative site for an office building in the Bronx. In retrospect, I realize that the conflict could have been dealt with creatively if someone had employed conflict resolution strategies and helped the two groups listen respectfully and empathetically to each other's point of view.

Paul Davidoff, an architect and lawyer, developed a theory of "advocacy planning" that became a national model during the second half of the 1960s. He argued that there is no such thing as the public interest. Projects are developed within settings in which various actors have conflicting goals. Advocacy planning asserts that disenfranchised communities have the right to professional help in developing plans that speak to their self-interest. Projects like the placing of state administration functions in a Harlem office building need to be vetted by all concerned parties—the older generation and the younger.

As a New York senator, Robert Kennedy brought together business and community leaders to found the Bedford Stuyvesant Restoration Corporation, the first community development corporation (CDC) in the nation. It had the power to acquire land and develop property for economic development and other purposes on behalf of the community. From that point on, CDCs became widespread, making it possible to apply the idea of advocacy planning to real projects.

Wrapping Up at Columbia

In my final year at Columbia, I sought to resolve the conflict between the culture of the studio and the culture of the street through my thesis project. In 1968, the New York City Board of Estimate allocated $150,000 to plan a Harlem high school for three thousand students. This funding was to cover developing an educational concept, developing a building program, and selecting a site for the school.

I made this the focus of my thesis and developed a proposal for what I called the "Community-Controlled Harlem High School System." Instead of locating the school in a campus-like setting, I proposed breaking it up into a series of small schools, each with a different focus, sited on a corridor threading through Harlem. These new examples of urban design would revitalize Harlem neighborhoods and provide facilities, laboratories, theaters, and athletic facilities that could be used by the community after school hours and on weekends. The school system would also have satellite facilities throughout the city in television studios, medical facilities, the financial district, and the airport to facilitate the students' transition from high school to the world of work. Developing and writing the thesis helped shape my ideas about the value of creating institutions for community development.

Growing Interest in African Settlements

As I continued reading Lewis Mumford, Basil Davidson, and others, I began thinking about African settlements as a resource and model for modernity. Through Mumford's books and essays, I had developed a deep appreciation for ordinary landscapes in addition to the more conventional focus on individual buildings as monuments. For three decades, Mumford had educated the public to think about the history of the built environment as a force shaping society. By then, he was writing a regular column on architecture called the Sky Line for *New Yorker* magazine.

My early interest in African settlements was an outgrowth of my desire to understand how African Americans came to live under such terrible conditions. Many writers had described those conditions, none more eloquently than James Baldwin. In his first published essay, "The Harlem Ghetto," which was included in *Notes from a Native Son*, he wrote,

> Harlem, physically at least, has changed very little in my parents' lifetime, or in mine. Now as then the buildings are old and in desperate need of repair, the streets are crowded and dirty, there are too many human beings per square block. (Baldwin 1955, 57)

Yet, as a student of American architecture, I found within the classic literature of architecture and urban planning no mention of the disparity between white and black—neither explanation nor apology nor remedy. It was, as the song goes, "just one of those things." I had set my sights on changing the conditions under which African Americans were forced to live. In order to do so, I would have to reach beyond conventional wisdom and begin at the beginning.

I wanted to know how we could gain better control over the environments in which we lived. I reasoned that a study of traditional African environmental design would provide a baseline from which to assess how our communities had become so alienated from the housing and neighborhoods where we lived. More importantly, we would be able to figure out what to do about it.

But where, exactly, was the beginning?

My interest in origins led me to a book by Sibyl Moholy-Nagy, *Native Genius in Anonymous Architecture*, published in 1957. Her goal was to closely study the fundamental nature of indigenous building: the environmental context, functions, forms, and construction methods of traditional communities in Central Asia, Oceania, Africa, and North, Central, and South America—all places foreign to me. I was curious about these traditions, which lay outside the accepted canon of architectural history.

After Graduation and Next Steps

The day in 1969 when I graduated from Columbia University, I walked the three blocks home in my cap and gown. I felt sick to my stomach. When night came, I tried to sleep but couldn't. Finally, after about two or three hours, I got up, took a match, and burned my diploma. Although it had taken me nine years to get it, burning it gave me a great feeling of relief. Mother was appalled.

Columbia had taught me how to design such exquisite buildings as two-million-dollar homes and corporate office buildings, but, in the process, I became disconnected from my own values. The university sits atop a hill overlooking Harlem, where you would see men standing around fifty-five–gallon drums burning newspapers and wood trying to keep warm in winter. People had inadequate food and there were rats, roaches, and no security in their buildings.

I didn't have the foggiest idea what to do about that. The degree made me feel like a phony.

I developed another, more personal interpretation many years later when I was at a writers' retreat. A well-known writer told me that I needed to think a lot more about my childhood. Then, I remembered an incident when Dad was upset after learning that I intended to go to architecture school. "So, now you're gonna get a big head and think you're better than everybody else," he had told me. Burning my diploma, I think, was in part a response to him telling me not to get ahead of myself.

It is remarkable how much feeling still comes up in me when I think about the indoctrination I received based on the ingrained assumption that every important human development had its origins in Greece. Why was it that white students in my classes had a history and I didn't? I found myself feeling embarrassed about my curiosity about the origins of black people. I worried that my interest in Africa would not be legitimate unless I came up with some remarkable African achievement to justify my interest.

It seemed necessary to "go back to the beginning." My interest in vernacular African architecture had been stirred by Moholy-Nagy's book and further stimulated by the lecture on Dogon villages by Aldo van Eyck during my first-year architecture studio. I had been moved and intrigued by an exhibition at the Museum of Modern Art in 1964, *Architecture Without Architects*. With photographs collected, taken, and curated by Bernard Rudofsky, a brilliant independent scholar, the exhibition raised the question of whether we need architects to create high-quality environments that meet people's needs. The images of Dogon granaries, desert fortresses in Morocco, homes in hollowed-out baobab trees, high structures built of grass, huts made of decorative woven matting with vegetal roofs, and shelters, streets, and functional enclosures crafted for the lasting use of whole communities left a lasting impression.

CHAPTER 5

Journey to West Africa

YEARS BEFORE I ATTENDED Columbia University, the architecture department had received a bequest from philanthropist William Kinne to enrich students' education through travel. A significant proportion of the graduating class each year traveled over a period of several months to sites of architectural interest in Europe—the acropolis in Greece, ancient and Renaissance cities in Italy, great cathedrals in France and Germany, and buildings by famous modern architects. Although each student prepared an individual proposal, they often met in Europe. The opportunity to travel abroad together was an important bonding experience for young architects and deepened their grounding in European traditions.

I had a different plan. By then, Jean and I had been living together for seven years. We were a good team when traveling. Jean had taken leave from school and was always happy to travel as far and as long as I wished. I used the opportunity of the Kinne grant to cover most of the cost of our journey crossing Europe and ending in West Africa in the tropical zone above the equator. I studied *National Geographic* magazines and collected pictures of mud villages. We taught ourselves to drive and got licensed and bought maps, journals, cameras, film, and other travel supplies. We talked to people who had been there. We visited embassies and consulates, collected visas and documents, got the requisite vaccinations, and planned our itinerary.

My plan was to visit, study, and document cities of pre–fourteenth-century Moorish Spain and places in Morocco, Senegal, Mali, Upper Volta (renamed Burkina Faso after independence), Niger, Nigeria, Dahomey (renamed Benin), Togo, Ghana, Ivory Coast, Guinea, and Cameroon if we could get visas. We would focus on rural villages. Our itinerary included the Casamance region in the Senegal rainforest; the ancient towns of Mopti, Djenné, and Timbuktu and the Dogon villages in the cliffs of the Bandiagara Escarpment in Mali; the village of Pô in Burkina Faso (near the border of Ghana); the Gobir granaries in Sokoto and the classic towns of Hausaland, especially Kano, in northern Nigeria; and the towns and cities that grew up around the slave-trading castles and forts in Lagos, Abomey, Accra, and Gorée.

Starting the Journey

Our journey began in January of 1970. Jean and I flew to Hannover, Germany, where our new Volkswagen (VW) van awaited us. We drove to Heidelberg to meet an African scholar I had contacted, and soon after, we headed for a three-week stay in Paris, where I reviewed the huge amount of documentation on West Africa at the Musée de l'Homme. It seems the colonizers knew a lot about the colonized!

I designed and built a big plywood storage box that we could sleep on in our VW. It fit snugly into the rear of the van, but was never quite comfortable. While in France, I enjoyed taking Jean to see Le Corbusier's Convent of La Tourette and other sites designed by the great architect. In Spain, we visited the Alhambra and the major cities of the Moorish period: Toledo, Granada, and Seville. In late February, we finally drove our van onto a ferry and crossed the Strait of Gibraltar into Tangier.

We continued learning how to travel as we went along. We decided not to drive across the Sahara but to seek a freighter to carry us and the van to Dakar, the capital of Senegal. During the month that we awaited the freighter, we explored Morocco, visiting Rabat, Casablanca, and the Medina at Fez. We drove over the Atlas Mountains, camping along the way, to Agadir, Ouarzazate (where people are generally darker skinned), and Marrakech (where we witnessed a wedding that was filled with exciting drumming). We admired the use of clustered buildings to keep out blowing sand and create cooling shadows.

We headed northwest to the coastal city of Salé, where we and the VW van boarded an East German freighter bound for the port city of Dakar. During the four days at sea, we met another American couple—he, a young African American, was fleeing the draft for the Vietnam War. They traveled with us for a while in Senegal.

In Dakar, we discovered that the French were still in charge of commerce. A French authority at the port refused to allow our van off the boat even though passage had been fully paid. Perhaps, he had wanted a bribe. When the American consul ignored my polite request for assistance, I instinctively extended my arm and wiped his desktop clear. Back at the port, I entered the van, Jean hopped in, and we drove off the boat, scattering the boxes the Frenchman had stacked to block the exit.

And so began our journey by auto across sub-Saharan Africa. From Dakar, we drove across eight nations of West Africa, sometimes sleeping in the van under the stars of the West African rainforest, savannah, and desert.

A Beginner's Mind

At the heart of my decision to make the journey to Africa was the gnawing problem I had tried to solve during my final years as a student of architecture, urban design, and urban planning: in my formal education and training, there had been little or no reference to the experiences or history of Africans or African Americans in planning, shaping, designing, and living in the built environment.

I wanted to arrive at a deeper understanding of the relationship between my chosen profession and the African and African American communities that I aspired to serve. I hoped that through my travel to the villages, towns, and cities of West Africa, I would be able to achieve a kind of beginner's mind about these things. My goal was to unlearn everything I had learned at Columbia. I needed to begin again and to learn what I had not been taught in the nine years it had taken me to earn my professional degree in architecture. In short, I wanted to find my roots—as an architect, black man, and human.

I chose West Africa because most ancestors of African Americans came from this region of the continent. I was particularly drawn to the cliff dwellings of the Dogon people in Mali, whom I had heard about from Aldo van Eyck in Peter Pragnell's studio class at Columbia.

Our Itinerary

Dakar is a jumble of villages and French colonial towns, but, in general, the central city remains expensive and French while the city's periphery is home to the traditional African neighborhoods of family compounds. We went to the Island of Gorée off the coast of Senegal and visited the *Maison des Esclaves* (House of Slaves). Originally built around 1776, the building, with its gruesome dungeons, served as a holding cell for African slaves destined for plantations and workshops in the Americas and elsewhere—first by the Portuguese and then by the Dutch, French, and British in turn. I had a strange double reaction seeing such a beautiful structure while being horrified by the inhumanity of how it was used. My intention in visiting Africa was to study the traditional architecture and building methods, and I chafed at having to expose myself to the slave castles.

Next, we headed south to the Casamance in the rice-growing Guinean rainforest, the ancestral homeland of enslaved Africans who were abducted and transported to the Georgia and Carolina Sea Islands in the sixteenth and seventeenth centuries to exploit their knowledge of rice cultivation. In Enampore, a compound across the border from Guinea–Bissau, we could hear gunshots from the Guinea-Bissau War of Independence taking place at that time.

We were stopped short when we both contracted malaria. It took a month to gain strength to continue toward the Mali border. Once on the road again, we visited the holy city of Touba in Senegal, where a major Islamic celebration was being held and being attended by ten thousand people. As visitors from North America, we were ushered in past the ten thousand worshipers to meet the imam. Most of the road from then on was unrelenting washboard that eventually destroyed our shock absorbers. At the Senegal–Mali border, we paid to transport our van on the very slow freight train, but soon discovered that we would need to load it onto the designated flatcar ourselves. Luckily, helpers showed up, and we, along with some new companions we had picked up, rode inside the uninsulated van under very hot sun, emerging occasionally to pee off the edge of the moving flatcar.

After twenty-four hours, we arrived in the hottest location we visited: Bamako, the capital of Mali. Looking down on the city, it appeared inviting with full, green trees everywhere, but the trees afforded little relief from oppressive heat that continued throughout each day and night.

In mid-May in Mopti, we spent several days in a rented room on a docked ferry, which would begin to provide regular transport up and down the Niger River once the July rainy season raised the water level. The outdoors along the riverbank was a true commons: clothes were dried in the sun on the wide sloped-rock surfaces the Niger would later cover in the rainy season; women bathed and laundered at the one end and men at the other; and fish were spread to dry on other portions of the sloped riverbank. In Mopti, we sketched and photographed the Komoguel Mosque and the large residential compound of its imam, both earth structures typical to the area.

Community Participation in Building

One day, we heard music and drove toward it. We were in Mali near the city of Mopti on the bank of the Niger River. As we parked, we saw a long procession of women with calabashes on their heads, moving toward the river in rhythm to the distant music. We left the van and approached the scene. When each woman reached the river, she bent down with rhythmic movement, filled her calabash with water, put it on her head, and started back toward the central plaza. They were remudding the mosque in preparation for the rainy season.

Approaching from a distance, a long line of men carried calabashes filled with earth and moved to the rhythm of the flutes and drums. Other people were mixing the water and earth. Every stage of the process was in sync with the music. In an elaborate ritual, people were climbing up and covering the surface of the whole mosque with the mud. It was a huge mosque, so it took half the day. The mosque needed to be repaired before the start of the rainy season, and the whole village was there to make this happen. I was amazed and thought to myself: "This is something altogether different from applying for a loan at the US Department of Housing and Urban Development."

Cities of the Middle Niger

With the ferry not yet in service, we decided to leave the van in Mopti and take a small plane to the dusty, fabled city of Timbuktu instead of traveling there by Land Rover or camel. We found meditative space in the shadowy chambers of the great mosque of Djinguereber and climbed on the roof of the thirteenth-century mosque of Sankoré to watch the sun rise over the vast desert as the imam called worshippers to prayer. We made drawings and took photographs of these ancient seats of learning, which were part of the ancient Sankoré Madrasah, or the University of Sankoré.[1] Manuscripts written in Arabic and dating back as far as the tenth century had been found in the university building and translated into English. Such artifacts demonstrate the high level of civilization that existed in sub-Saharan Africa centuries before the arrival of Europeans.

Situated on the banks of the Niger River at the base of the Sahara Desert, Timbuktu has been the focus of trans-Saharan trade for more than a thousand years. As we arrived, we encountered a Tuareg man camping out on the edge of the city, coming in from his migration across the Sahara. We approached the place just outside the city where camels were gathered after bringing in their loads for market day.

We also got a taste of contemporary life. The teens we met at the social center weren't interested in showing us their monuments; they wanted to know if we knew the R&B singer Wilson Pickett and if we could show them the latest dances from the US.

We flew back to Mopti to collect the van and proceeded to Djenné. The great mosque there was a fantastic sight. On June 7, we had an appointment with the master mason of Djenné. I made notes about the earth-brick construction process, which included at least four different kinds of earth-based materials. We learned that the mason had labored five years in apprenticeship, ten years as mason, and twenty-five years as master. His approval was required for all new construction in vicinity of Djenné.

A Dogon Village

A highlight of our trip was the Bandiagara Escarpment, where the Dogon people live. From atop long sloping cliffs overlooking the desert, we made drawings and took photographs of the granaries and compounds of rugged Dogon villages carved out of the sandstone cliff faces.

The villages along the escarpment proved to be every bit as magical as I had imagined. Standing in the field below the Dogon village, far away from European influence, I could see hundreds of granaries and dozens of houses shimmering in the sun and tucked neatly into the cliff. Gradually, my eye grew accustomed to a profound order in the patterns of rock, mud, and thatch with which the village was constructed.

Each granary and compound rested on a rock foundation. The erratic jumble of sand-colored stones laid without mortar arose willy-nilly from the ground between clumps of greenery to make a solid horizontal bed for the modest buildings above. The granaries and houses were constructed of mud brick and plastered with *banco* (a smooth stucco-like compound made by fermenting mud, grain husks, and, occasionally, cow dung). If you looked closely at the surface of these buildings, you could see a fine texture, revealing the discipline with which the banco was laid in with the arc-like motion of human hands. No windows or doorways look out over the cliff, and we learned from the Dogon man who was our guide that openings were oriented away from the fields to avoid the driving rain that always came from the north.

Villagers took advantage of the landscape features by constructing their housing on the escarpment where the sun's powerful rays were cut off each afternoon at two o'clock by the cliff edge above. The relief was immediate, and people could work in comfort. The flat lands below were divided into garden plots for individual families.

Anthropomorphic Layout of Dogon Buildings

The Dogon elder Ogotemmêli, in conversations in the 1930s with the French anthropologist Marcel Griaule, explained that the layout of a Dogon village was always anthropomorphic. The village plan would take the form of an androgynous being lying on the ground with the men's council building at the head and the original family compounds at the breasts. Other functional elements like the specially constructed houses for menstruating women, blacksmith's forge, and sanctuaries and altars would be located variously at arms, hands, legs, and feet. People would enter and leave the village through a gate that represented genitals. This village-wide pattern would be repeated at a smaller scale in the compounds and individual houses. (Griaule 1965, 1–256.)[2]

You could see the anthropomorphic pattern of Dogon architecture most clearly in the layout of the houses. Every house in the village had the same plan and orientation: a courtyard entry in the south, raised beds for sleeping flanking the east and west, and kitchen with a chimney-like structure to let the smoke out through the roof in the north.

Above rock foundations, granaries rested on a floor of branches with a sealed mat to keep rodents out and contents dry. Each granary revealed the gender of its owner: a man's granaries were tall and narrow while a woman's granaries were shorter and slightly squat. The thatch roof, which covered each granary, was shaped like the woven hat that men or women wore, performing a similar function of protection from rain and hot sun.

In traditional villages, the activity of human cycles is tied to natural rhythms as materials become available seasonally. We had come to Bandiagara from Manhattan, where real estate values primarily govern the design and layout of buildings and where most apartments and offices are located by a numerical address on a rectangular grid. It was striking to be in a place that was, by contrast, so obviously and entirely constructed in the human image.

It was equally remarkable that all the materials for the buildings are gathered within a few hundred yards of the construction site. All building and building repair work begins each year after the harvest and before the rainy season. Both men and women perform the necessary tasks with an easy division of labor: men do the heavy lifting of stones and women work at lighter tasks while carrying small children on their backs. Men might also plaster the walls with fresh banco or gather millet stalks to be woven into thatch roofs. Near the desert, walls are built thicker for better regulation of the temperature. At the end of the rainy season, the cycle of planting begins again.

The Rainy Season in West Africa

We returned to Bamako for visa renewals, and then we circled back to Ouagadougou, the capital of Burkina Faso. It was an interesting place, but we stayed weeks longer than intended because the American consul wouldn't return Jean's passport. When she submitted it with a request for additional pages, the consul saw that she had visited Cuba and failed to obtain stamped reentry into the United States. He wanted to pursue legal action against her, making the simple request a big hassle.

We made our way south and east and entered the wonderful village of Pô, near the Ghanaian border, on June 28. We had missed the main time for rebuilding in March and April before the long rainy season began. The family compounds were beautifully sculptural. We photographed women rebuilding the sculptural details on homes and then adding painted decoration. We drew plans, elevations, and renderings. The homes had ingenious design features that kept occupants comfortably cool no matter how hot the temperature outdoors.

July 1 found us in Burkina Faso in rainy season. Periodically, we had to drive off the road and onto higher ground to avoid flooding. During one long drive, we failed to notice a tiny sign instructing us to leave the road and follow a path on higher ground through the woods, and, suddenly, we were stuck in nearly two-feet-deep water from the overflowed White Volta River. We had no idea how to extricate ourselves, and we had seen no villages along the way to call upon for help. Fortunately, a slender youth appeared and indicated that it was no problem. He quickly cut and gathered a big pile of branches, placed them just in front of the tires, and told us to drive out. We were always amazed at how the African people could easily solve what seemed to us like such big problems. Once, when we had stopped to help a vehicle with a flat and no inner tube, we saw that the men had gathered several smaller inner tubes to fill up the tire. We told them that it wouldn't work, but soon they were driving along the road.

After Jean's passport was finally returned without apology, we crossed the border into Niger, where there was a fine museum of traditional building types. We thoroughly enjoyed an exhibit showing many elegant styles of woven vegetable fiber.

The Nigerian Civil War had only recently ended, so we had to fight to get one-week transit visas to enter Nigeria. Proud of completing this hurdle, we crossed the Niger River at Niamey and advanced into the country. We hit the road, but within a minute, a shouting driver in a great speeding truck bore down on us in *our* lane! Forced off the road and regaining breath, the truth dawned on us: we had forgotten that Nigeria was a British colony and had a different system of driving.

Repair of our ruined shock absorbers provided an excuse to extend the visa another week. We headed to the great Islamic city of Kano, founded in the tenth century. Each home had a wall along the street, usually sculpted in bas-relief and sometimes painted. The play of sun and shadow on these surfaces was delightful to behold.

We drove south through intermittent flash floods, stopping at a university in Abeokuta. In early October of 1970, we arrived at the vast metropolis of Lagos.

As in other coastal metropolises of West Africa, economic growth in Lagos had been stimulated by the Atlantic slave trade, which had grown up around pre-colonial indigenous settlements. The coastal region was dotted with slave-trading fortresses and castles built by various European powers from the fifteenth to the nineteenth centuries. We made our way westward along the coast through Cotonou in Benin and Lomé in Togo to Accra in Ghana.

In Togo's capital city of Lomé, Jean came down with a bad case of amoebic dysentery. When she was released after a week in hospital, we sought to pay the fees, but no office wished to bill us. I suppose we were considered part of the colonizer class of government workers whose medical costs were covered.

Insights about African Architecture and Human Settlements

We observed over and over how well the traditional architecture of West Africa was adapted to its ecological context. In West Africa, there are four main zones, running from west to east, that reflect variations in temperature, seasonal rainfall, and vegetation. Each zone's traditional architecture responds to local conditions, in many ways exhibiting what Lewis Mumford called *ecological regionalism.*

The largest zone is the Sahara, a desert extending from the Atlas Mountains in Morocco and Algeria to the Senegal River. Historically, its vast dunes and extreme temperatures have formed an impenetrable barrier to all except the nomadic tribes. The nomadic tent structures of the Tuareg people and other Berber groups are often built of straight and curved saplings with supporting coverings of goatskins, light screens, and rugs that can be carried by camels and quickly assembled or dismantled.

South of the Sahara is a band of semi-arid country with intermittent vegetation of scrub and occasional small trees known as the

Sahel. Given the region's daily extreme temperature variations, the mud buildings here have thick walls to capture and hold the heat, keeping structures cool inside during the day and then reradiating the heat during night when it is quite cold. A system of flat roofs, scuppers, and cisterns capture and store the limited supply of rainwater.

Below the Sahel is the savanna, an area with a rich growth of grass and plentiful seasonal rainfall. Structures here have wattle and daub walls, which are more permeable than the mud walls in the Sahel. Moisture-resistant grass, reed, and thatch roofs carry away the rainwater.

Further south, near the coast, is the dense rainforest region. Due to the year-round heat and heavy rainfall, structures here are more like pavilions. Steep thatched roofs supported by timber structures allowed the rain to run off. Instead of walls open structures permitted the humid air to circulate throughout the buildings.

Everywhere we went, Jean and I noticed that building materials were gathered near construction sites, often within a few hundred yards. Traditional sub-Saharan villages give shape and meaning to life by relating human activity to the natural world. Building would begin each year after the harvest and before the rainy season. The buildings were exquisitely designed for practical tasks and supported a shared vision of social life. They reflected a profound spiritual orientation toward the ancestors and the natural world and reflected the social and cultural values of the people who lived there.

Reflections on Our African Travels

The months that we traveled in Africa away from urban centers were the first extended periods of time I had spent outside a city in a world dominated not by human creations but by forces of nature. In sharp contrast to our experience of industrial cities in the United States, in the West African villages we visited, both in the savanna and the rainforests, everybody—men and women, young and old—participated in the design and construction of the places where they lived. Later, I learned that when a couple gets married, the whole village participates in building a new compound for them. I was deeply moved by the carefully woven thatch roofs, the round earthen structures, and the larger-than-life granaries markedly sculpted by human hands. These buildings, constructed by people seemingly without professional training, were beautifully adapted to the available resources, the climate, and the spiritual life of the people.

It was clear that the indigenous African people had drawn from an enormous well of creativity. With few resources, they built elegant surroundings that embodied their practical, social, and spiritual needs. I began to wonder what had happened to that creativity and that sense of agency when Africans became enslaved and what restoring a viable relationship with the natural world might look like for African Americans.

The juxtaposition between Africa's many settlement types was visually spectacular: the colonial and modern cities, urban shantytowns, traditional indigenous villages, ancient Islamic towns centered upon the mosque and the market place, and slave-trading fortress towns. Yet beyond whatever insights I picked up about the marvels of vernacular architecture, I had no theory to address and comprehend the true complexity of the built environment in Africa. For the task of learning about African architecture, I had brought the tools I had honed in the architectural design studio at Columbia University; however, while these tools gave me access to many insights about spatial organization and design solutions, they failed to give me the deeper insights I sought into the ways social organization impacts human habitat.

The journey also raised important questions about my identity, as well as the historical geography of the African American community. As a black American searching in Africa for my architectural roots, I faced a certain paradox: a house in the black ghetto of North Philadelphia has more in common with a wealthy residence on Society Hill in the same city than it has with a Dogon dwelling or an Ashanti shrine house. A study of traditional African architecture carried me far away from the familiar rooms, porches, streets, and alleys of my childhood. Ironically, these intimate places that had helped form my perceptions of the world were designed and built by people who had no understanding of my community, and we appeared to have no shared social values. Nothing in my professional education prepared me to examine such paradoxes.

One could say that I was learning what James Baldwin had learned two-and-a-half decades earlier, as he described in his famous essay, "The Discovery of What It Means to Be American."[3] I learned, in short, that I was not African. A key next step in my journey would be to confront what Baldwin (1961, 17) called "the complex fate" of being an American. If I wanted to understand my roots, I would have to come to terms with the experience of slavery in America. In short, I needed to understand how Africans had become Americans.

When Jean and I were in the dungeon of the Elmina Castle, a slave-trading fortress on the coast of Ghana, I decided that I would visit and write about the old plantations of the American South. I hoped by that research to unlock the mysteries of my heritage as an African American. "My search doesn't have to make me feel proud," I thought. "It just needs to uncover what is true."

Return to the States

We crossed the Atlantic Ocean, returning to the United States from Ghana on a freighter from the Black Star Line.[4] As the ship navigated about five miles out of the Port of Philadelphia, we crossed a clear line in the ocean where a dirty oil slick began. As we approached the shore, the backyards of the tiny brick working-class row houses came into view. In contrast to the places we had visited in Africa, Philadelphia seemed old and worn.

The buildings in Africa were made with natural, biodegradable materials and repaired and renewed each year. When not repaired, they were left to decompose and be rebuilt elsewhere. If you could get a satellite to take a photograph of the same African village from the same point every six months, I imagine the village would appear to breathe.

CHAPTER 6

Unearthing the Hidden Narrative of Race

FROM ELEMENTARY SCHOOL TO college, I was taught that the most important steps in human development and evolution had taken place in Greece. Visual arts, sculpture, architecture, literature, philosophy, and drama all supposedly began in Greece. As an architectural drafting student at Dobbins Vocational High School in Philadelphia, I learned about the famous temples of the Parthenon and the Erechtheum on the Acropolis of Athens. While Egypt's pyramids and the Great Sphinx of Giza were acknowledged as important contributions, they were understood as merely setting the stage for the main action that began in Greece.

No one expressed much curiosity about human societies that had developed along the upper parts of the Nile River and beyond. It was almost as if stories about the civilizations of the Nile were off limits. Egypt was obviously an alien culture and not at all like the one we lived in. By contrast, I could see the impact of Greece in the buildings around Philadelphia where I grew up—especially in the banks, museums, schools, and universities.

I had read *Lost Cities of Africa* and *The African Past* by Basil Davidson and *Stolen Legacy: Greek Philosophy Is Stolen Egyptian Philosophy* by George G. M. James during my student years at Columbia University, but I had learned not to think so much about Egypt (or at least to keep my thoughts to myself). I understood that raising questions about ancient African civilizations would be considered intellectually suspect, so I kept my curiosity to myself.

The very concept of African urbanization may seem to be a contradiction in terms. Most images of Africa we see in the media are of wildlife, rural poverty, and genocide—rarely do we focus our attention on the African city in a coherent way.[1] People seldom realize that the African ancestors of enslaved populations in the New World frequently came from well-established villages and towns that had deep roots in the African past through extensive oral traditions. I saw evidence of this firsthand during my journeys in West Africa with Jean. African intimacy with the natural world is not evidence of a regressive culture or lack of urbanization—the villages are masterfully and sustainably grounded in the local natural environment and shaped by available resources: mud bricks, poles, branches, saplings, straw, reeds, palm leaves, and thatch.

Mainstream Western culture often overlooks the complexity, and sometimes even the presence, of African civilization, as well as the fact that the African continent is the birthplace and cradle of humanity, the home of the first human communities. All humans are descended from these common ancestors in Africa. The failure to recognize and honor the origin of our common humanity is a major element of the hidden narrative of race. During and after our trip to West Africa, I became passionate about unearthing, understanding, and interpreting this narrative. I continued to be preoccupied with what we had seen in Africa and the questions it raised about the current situation of African Americans.

The Place of Africans in Architectural History

While in Africa, I had been shocked by the slave dungeons in Dakar and Elmina and powerfully moved by the traditional village architecture. I had intended to make an exhibition about African villages using drawings and photographs Jean and I had done, but I couldn't get those slave dungeons out of my mind. Eventually I decided to shift my focus to researching the architecture of the plantation system.

The enslavement, transportation, and forced labor of Africans made possible the building of wealth in America. The story of African slavery is an essential part of American history, but it is rarely told in the manner it deserves. I did a lot of reading and visited old plantations in the South to satisfy my curiosity about the physical setup of slavery. I also hoped that this pursuit would help me gain some historical perspective on my role as a contemporary African American architect. My interest in the architecture of American slavery had begun in the mid-1960s when the civil rights movement had brought a great deal of national attention to the experience of black people and the legacy of slavery. The vibrant self-expressions of African American writers, musicians, and political leaders fascinated the white population at the time and continue to do so into the present day.

During those same years, I witnessed the central myth of modern architecture falling apart. Planners and architects were beginning to see architecture as more than industrial and technological efficiency and human environments as embodying cultural and spiritual values and reflecting a way of life. The narrow, mechanistic interpretation of architecture—characterized by the International Style—was giving way to a broader appreciation of diverse human communities with unique needs to be met.

In the late 1960s, it became fashionable among a small group of African American architects to speak of "black architecture," suggesting a way of making buildings that responded to the particular needs of black people. In the absence of concrete examples, a great deal of confusion lay beneath such talk. There were a few practicing African American architects, but their work was largely indistinguishable from that of their white counterparts. They had received their professional training in American architectural schools where no reference was made to black people, their history, their contributions, and their distinctive needs.

The marginal position of the black American architect in the Western architectural tradition was compounded by the fact that the African American intellectual tradition had no organized body of thought concerning architecture. The prevailing racist climate in environmental design institutions prohibited the introduction of African examples, and few black American visitors to Africa had the interest or courage to marvel at the ingenuity of traditional African architecture. Most of what little was published on the subject was in French.

Looking Back at Slavery in America

Memories of the depravity euphemistically referred to as the peculiar institution have produced a misplaced sentimentality for a lost world of leisure and refinement in the descendants of white slaveholders and a vacuum formed by a mixture of outrage and shame in the descendants of slaves. The momentum of the African American struggle for human rights brought information about this dark period of American history to the attention of the public, and historical studies began to illuminate the ongoing narrative of racial oppression.

Independent British journalist Basil Davidson, whose books on ancient African history had so intrigued and educated me, assembled a detailed history of the trade in *Black Mother: The Years of the African Slave Trade*, published in 1961. In the book, Davidson notes the long-term effects of moral degradation on the Europeans and others who conducted the slave trade and, more dramatically, on the African chieftains who captured and delivered slaves in exchange for the guns they needed to protect their own people from capture. Subsequently, these African leaders became dependent on other European trade goods and, thus, enmeshed in the evils of trading in other human beings.

When it was published in 1968, Winthrop Jordan's *White Over Black: American Attitudes Toward the Negro, 1550–1812* was a first step in documenting the roots of racism in America.[2] When I began researching for my essay "The Big House and the Slave Quarter," no books on American architectural history had explored the building of the American South. Specialized works, dealing with a particular state or locality, concentrated on the stylistic variations of the mansion houses, and more generalized works on national architectural history mentioned plantations in passing with an apologetic remark about slavery.

Despite the lack of acknowledgment in much work published about the period, 75 percent of the people who came to the New World between 1700 and 1760 were African slaves (Engerman and Sokoloff 2011, 22). These enslaved people were compelled to strip the forests and drain the swamps to produce land for agriculture, drive off the indigenous people who had been living there, and then plant, cultivate, and harvest the crops that made their owners wealthy. Africans created the toehold that made it possible for Europeans to settle in the New World.

The Plantation as Precursor to Industrialization

The plantation system was based on planting and harvesting five principal crops: rice, indigo, tobacco, sugar, and cotton. The plantation served as a kind of open-air factory that consumed people and laid to waste the natural environment. The plantation's finite population was relatively isolated by distance and social convention from the rest of the world, yet connected by an umbilical cord to the pulse of change throughout the Atlantic Basin. The plantation system was the prototype for industrial agriculture all over the world. Whether it was cotton, rice, or sugar, its production involved a rudimentary form of industrial agriculture. Africans were thought of as beasts and treated accordingly.[3] Forced to do the bidding of their masters, they contributed substantially to the penetration of the North American wilderness by Europeans—and, tragically, to the conquest of the land's original inhabitants.

Slavery helped set the pattern for squandering land and natural resources in North America. Blacks were kept at arm's length, confined to brutal work on the plantation, forbidden to read and write, and isolated from emerging knowledge bases in industry, shipping, banking, and finance. Although their work was essential to creating the infrastructure that supported the emergence of city life, blacks were not allowed to share in the wealth they helped create. Instead, slave labor and the wealth generated from the crops produced by slaves provided the wherewithal to expand the plantations and the surrounding village and town economies. It also contributed to the burgeoning international economy in the port cities along the Atlantic shorelines—a shipping industry based upon the capture, buying, and selling of Africans as slaves and the subsequent use of their labor to extract resources from the New World environment and transform them into assets. The need to oppress black people in order to maintain this profitable system and the struggle to resist that oppression shaped both black and white communities. The legacy of that struggle is still alive today.

African Contributions to American Architecture

For the historian of the built environment, the plantation provides an opportunity to notice and evaluate much that has been missing from the history of American architecture. The environmental psychologist can study the meanings attached to specific places in the landscape, such as the swamp, the big house, the kitchen, the slave quarters, the sugarhouse, the landing, the bayou, and the levee. For the sociologist, it offers a field in which to test assumptions about architecture, political power, class, and ethnic identity. For me as an African American architect, the plantation system is an essential element of our collective past—the missing link without which my present and future work is incomprehensible.

Black people had an enormous impact on the settlement pattern of the Old South. Indeed, the complexities and opportunities posed by their presence were major determinants of Southern regional architecture. Understanding the story requires an appreciation of the cultural baggage brought to the New World from both Europe and Africa. The Europeans brought feudal traditions of the medieval period along with emerging technologies. The geometric, authoritarian, and rigid architectural traditions of the Renaissance informed much of their thinking and practice. The African captives brought strategies of climatic adaptation that were developed in rainforest tropics, designs for compounds that accommodated extended-family living, and methods of building with mud and thatch. In the early years of importing captured Africans, slaves had to build their own living quarters, which in layout and construction were similar to the villages they had inhabited in Africa, and always used locally available materials.

The roofed, open-air front porch, or veranda, is a feature that first appeared in the Caribbean and spread northward to the southern states and up the Mississippi River. Its origins are obviously African; buildings in Europe did not have front porches. European colonial settlers moved into Africa and to the Caribbean with building types that were completely inappropriate for the tropics. Gradually, they adopted features learned from the enslaved African people to meet the challenges of the climate. To demonstrate allegiance to their European roots, the European settlers started decorating the porches of their plantation houses with Greek columns.

The amalgam of African and European traditions that emerged on Southern soil was, perhaps, unflattering to both the European and African newcomers. Nonetheless, it is an important chapter in the emergence of the architecture of the modern world.

Social Dimensions of Plantation Architecture

Historians rarely mention that ten of the first twelve presidents of the United States were slaveholders (the exceptions being the father-son duo of John Adams and John Quincy Adams). Later, Andrew Johnson and Ulysses S. Grant, the seventeenth and eighteenth presidents, brought the total number of slave-owning US presidents to twelve.[4] Although George Washington and Thomas Jefferson both expressed disapproval of slavery, their lifestyles depended on it. The architecture of Mount Vernon and Monticello, their respective prestigious tidewater plantations, intimately reflects the slave system. Both sit along rivers and creeks of the coastal plain and take advantage of rich soil for agriculture and access to waterways for trade. The pattern of land subdivision and arrangement of buildings in the landscape, the circulation between rooms of the big house, the garden, and the slave quarters, and the disparities in detailing and ornamentation all demonstrate a grappling with what people of the time referred to as the peculiar institution of slavery and its social implications.

Planters like Washington and Jefferson had scores of slaves—perhaps ten or twenty times the number of family, relatives, and guests residing on the land at any particular point in time. Yet, upon arriving, one was only aware of the mansion house and the comfort it suggested. The architects of these mansions manipulated the builder's art to create settings that reinforced the image of the planter at the pinnacle of a caste system in which poor whites were more or less irrelevant and black slaves were situated even lower.

Thomas Jefferson turned his genius toward the invention of architectural devices that would keep his slaves discreetly hidden yet available for service. He designed a rotating door with semicircular shelves on one side that allowed servants to bring in food from the kitchen without entering the dining room and being seen. To reach the upper floors, slaves had to use two tiny stairways, each unobtrusively located in the cross passageways serving the principal wings. Perhaps one of these stairways was used by Sally Hemings as she went to and from her master's bedroom.[5]

Plantation houses such as Mount Vernon and Monticello still dot the landscape in the southern US. Many serve as museums for tourists, but few visitors, as one might suspect, are black. When I showed up at Shirley Plantation on the James River in Charles City, Virginia, the owner and caretaker, who was a direct descendant of Robert E. Lee, was as surprised to see me as I was to meet him. When I arrived, he was describing the furnishings of the mansion house to an attentive audience of perhaps fifteen tourists in a rapid dialect that was barely intelligible to me. The tour concluded beneath the spectacular mansion staircase where it had begun.

When his daughter took over and greeted the new group of tourists already forming at the door of the Shirley Plantation, the owner and I had a chance to talk. He was quite pleasant. I learned from him that the domestic slaves had lived above the kitchen, which was in a separate building flanking the entry court and some distance from the big house. Presumably, the arrangement was dictated by a desire to keep the odors of cooking and the noise made by the slaves away from the main house. It certainly was inconvenient from the point of view of the serving people—particularly when, during a great rainstorm, they were required to carry food through the mud and slush from the kitchen to the big house. At this plantation, approximately two hundred field slaves slept in seven barracks three quarters of a mile from the main house.

Patterns similar to the tidewater plantations were repeated in other parts of the antebellum South. For example, sugar plantations built along the Mississippi in the nineteenth century usually had a large mansion facing the river and were flanked by the *garçonnière*, where young men of the ruling family entertained their friends, primarily via sexual adventures with enslaved concubines. Slave quarters were constructed out back in the sugar fields.

The plantation was a shared environment. Between the big house and the slave quarters were places of work and play shared by both master and slave. The extremes of penury and luxury in that shared space had deep psychic impacts on all who passed their lives within its secluded precincts. The architecture of slavery demonstrates a hunger to create an illusion of wealth, beauty, ease, and graciousness at any price in a land of harsh realities. The buildings I have been describing were known to antebellum southerners as show plantations. Most whites could not achieve this ostentatious display, which, nevertheless, set the tone for the whole region. Despite its rarity, the romantic ideal of the country gentleman came to dominate the architecture of the Old South. Not surprisingly, this grandiose architectural style is reflected in the White House, as well as our national and state capitols.

After I had completed initial investigations into the character of African architecture and its influence on the architecture of the American plantation system, I felt that I had a basic grasp of the way traditional African societies and the dynamics of slavery had shaped the American land use system. My two-part essay was published in two bicentennial issues of *Landscape* under the title "The Big House and the Slave Quarter." The essays, which represented a breakthrough in historical interpretation, were well received, but no one knew what to do with them. Preliminary results of my investigations were quickly taken up by architectural historians eager to fill the gap in historical information. To my disappointment, they did not note the effect of slavery and the threat of white violence on the capacity of contemporary African Americans to exercise agency in shaping their environment.[6]

I sent a copy of my essays to Lewis Mumford, and he replied that he thought I was onto something. However, he stressed that he didn't know much about African American history. "In this," he wrote, "I am your student."

Teaching, Research, and Professional Practice

W HEN WE RETURNED FROM Africa in 1970, the civil rights movement seemed to have evaporated. I had become increasingly disturbed by the great difficulty African Americans face in trying to shape their communities to meet basic human needs. My hope of turning the field of architecture into a tool of transformation was starting to wane.

Not wanting to live in New York City, Jean shared a rented house in Milford, Pennsylvania, where she set up a dark room and processed the black and white photographs from our trip. I took my old job at the Architects Renewal Committee in Harlem (ARCH). People there were interested in the photographs and drawings from our travels in Africa. I worked at ARCH three days a week and spent the other four days with Jean.

When ARCH's executive director, Art Symes, resigned that spring, I applied for the position. When I learned that a friend of mine who had lots of community organizing experience but no architectural training would be competing with me for the job, I was upset. I felt that the ARCH board should hire based on experience and training, and I didn't want to be competing for the job with someone, let alone my friend, who didn't have both. I got into our small old car, intending to take a long ride to let off steam, and ended up in Chicago. In retrospect, my choice of Chicago as a destination made sense. Throughout my architectural training at Columbia University, I had heard hundreds of times about the importance of the Chicago School and its architects, such as Louis Sullivan, Henry Richardson, and Frank Lloyd Wright. I could take advantage of the opportunity to see some of the buildings they had designed.

I phoned Jean to tell her where I was and that I was not coming back to New York. She agreed to meet me later in Colorado, where I wanted to visit some communes and American Indian communities that I had been hearing about. She needed to move out of her rented room in Milford and pack, sell, or give away stuff in our New York apartment. My mother had been staying in the apartment while we were traveling and would remain there, so we could leave most of the furniture. The hardest thing for Jean was moving my large and very heavy collection of books to her mother's house for safekeeping.

While exploring the Southwest with Jean, I quickly realized that the substance of African architecture has a lot more in common with American Indians, sharecroppers, and hippies than it does with the urban centers of the emerging black bourgeoisie in the North. We drove to several remote communes; at least two were using geodesic dome designs for their residences. At one commune, residents had chopped roofs off abandoned cars in junkyards to use as dome sections. We also visited the pueblos and sites of ancient peoples. At one of the pueblos, I had a long conversation with an elder about traditional building techniques and social organization. As he had no prior exposure to other indigenous building traditions, Jean's prints of African dwellings especially intrigued him.

Driving into a Havasupai town near the Grand Canyon, small children made us stop the car, shouting with delight, "What tribe are you? What tribe are you?"

Moving to Berkeley

After a month or so in the Southwest, Jean and I decided to head further west to California. At first, we checked out Los Angeles, but then decided that Berkeley might be a better fit for us—I was considering pursuing a PhD in architecture and had a great respect for the programs at the University of California at Berkeley (UC Berkeley). We arrived in Berkeley in mid-1971.

I was particularly drawn to the work of Christopher Alexander and his colleagues at the Center for Environmental Structure in Berkeley. They were laying the basis for an entirely new approach to architecture, building, and planning and establishing a reputation internationally as thought leaders in the field of design. Alexander proposed a process in which the designer develops a clear statement of problems and needs and builds up solutions incrementally. The problem statements can be used repeatedly and, over time, enrich the vocabulary of what he called a pattern language.

"The difference between a good building and a bad building, between a good town and a bad town," Alexander (1979, 25) wrote, "is an objective matter. It is the difference between health and sickness, wholeness and dividedness, self-maintenance and self-destruction." As models, he pointed to buildings from other times and places—the ideal being a structure that was beautiful one hundred years ago and would continue to be beautiful one hundred years into the future.

Alexander produced a monograph titled *A Pattern Language Which Generates Multi-Service Centers*. The multiservice center—a new building type that had emerged in the late sixties—involved collaboration among many public agencies to bring an array of services to low-income communities in a single building. African American architect Max Bond, a professor and friend from my days at Columbia School of Architecture, built a prototype multiservice center in the Bronx using Alexander's design guidelines; Alexander's pattern language came to be used by public agencies across the United States. I was interested in this building type and intrigued by the idea that the pattern language would help laypeople access solutions to problems they encountered when designing their houses and communities.

Christopher Alexander's methods seemed to offer promising applications for buildings that would meet the needs of inner-city residents, so when I arrived in Berkeley, I called him and introduced myself. He invited me to lunch at the Center for Environmental Structure, a rambling house in the Berkeley hills, to meet and talk with him and his staff. Jean and I showed him our photographs and drawings of African village buildings and told him stories about our trip. He ended up selecting two of our photographs from West Africa to include in his next book, coauthored with several colleagues, *A Pattern Language: Towns, Buildings, and Construction.*

Soon after that, I met Dick Peters, chair of the UC Berkeley architecture department, and Ken Simmons, one of two African Americans on the department's approximately seventy-person faculty. Ken had been a classmate of Max Bond at Harvard. After I told Ken that I was thinking of pursuing an advanced degree at UC Berkeley, he called Max, who had been the only African American faculty member in the architecture department at Columbia, to get a reference for me. Evidently, Max gave me a favorable recommendation since I was soon offered a teaching position.

Having arrived unannounced only days before, the offer surprised me. The whole situation felt surreal at first, but the existing faculty, including Chris Alexander, warmly welcomed me.

I imagined that I would follow a traditional path in architecture: a few years of teaching followed by a career in professional practice.

Teaching at the UC Berkeley College of Environmental Design

From 1972 through 1979, I worked as an assistant professor of architecture at UC Berkeley's College of Environmental Design. I taught studios and seminars on how social, psychological, and environmental factors shape the design of buildings. I also supervised a community design studio where undergraduate and graduate students provided technical assistance to neighborhood groups who were involved in planning projects. Despite my passion for architecture and planning, I was disappointed by the extent to which African Americans and other communities of color were isolated from the processes of planning and design. My goal was to use the studio to build a body of knowledge and planning practice to support just, racially inclusive, resilient communities. I hoped to address and help reverse the legacy of racism in the physical, economic, political, and institutional planning and design of communities.

I suppose the UC Berkeley College of Environmental Design had been eager to hire a person of color since it seriously lacked in diversity. Out of seventy faculty members, only two were African American and only two were women. There were more African Americans among the students, and most took my courses.

While I was teaching at the university, I was concerned with several critical issues, the main among them being:

- How could we get more African Americans and Latinos into the university as students of architecture and planning?
- What were the areas of innovation where there was the greatest possibility for people of color to gain access to professional roles?
- How best could I introduce new course material that would make the field more relevant to people-of-color communities?

Although my experience during the 1960s on the East Coast had been focused on African American communities, I believed that my focus on the unmet needs and unresolved social issues of all poor communities, consisting primarily of people of color, could provide transformative insights and opportunities for the society as a whole. Of course, this was beyond the purview of standard architectural consideration.

Thinking that the building traditions we had observed in West Africa might provide some inspiration for designing housing for the poor, I inquired of a librarian at the university about borrowing slides of buildings in traditional African villages. Shocked by my request, the librarian informed me that the library did not collect images of the homes of ordinary people, but only those of important buildings.

During the time I taught at Berkeley, the field became less concerned with social issues. At the same time, I began to move away from conventional architectural work and toward a greater focus on civic engagement and planning for inclusion, justice, and community resilience.

Influential urban-planning theoreticians of the time, even those dealing with social issues, reflected the field's refusal to confront race head-on. In 1987, John Friedman, a professor of architecture and planning at the University of California at Los Angeles, wrote *Planning in the Public Domain: From Knowledge to Action.* He continued to write prolifically about planning and the processes of urbanization, identifying three bottom-up traditions—Marxist, anarchist, and utopian thinking—but failing to consider the abolitionist and civil rights movements, which, to my mind, contributed to the discipline of planning in important ways. In 1983, Manuel Castells, a professor of sociology and city and regional planning at UC Berkeley, wrote *The City and the Grassroots*, which included a case study of Chicago, focusing on the work of legendary labor organizer Saul Alinsky. However, Castells failed to take into account other changemakers the city had produced, including Elijah Muhammad, Harold Washington, and Jesse Jackson. In 1973, David Harvey wrote *Social Justice and the City*, wherein he argued that capitalism annihilates space to ensure its own reproduction by using disinvestment to cause the decline and abandonment of inner cities, lowering property values, and making acquisition of land for future investment by speculators more affordable. I had witnessed this upsetting process during my childhood in Philadelphia. Unfortunately, Harvey shared the widespread tendency of academicians to overlook the contributions, needs, and agency of African Americans and other people of color. This provided me with yet more evidence of how racial narratives are ignored or hidden.

Tracking Innovations in Architecture and Planning

Feeling fortunate to work with some of the most creative and innovative people in architecture and planning, many of whom were on the UC Berkeley College of Environmental Design faculty, I set out to bridge some of the gaps I observed in the field.

I had the honor of working with Roz Lindheim, a dedicated pioneer of patient-centered health care, in designing community-based primary-care health facilities. Ray Lifchez was another inspiring innovator on the faculty who used psychological methods to develop helpful narratives about design problems or challenges. Ray and I both view architecture as a social art and insist on engaging users in participatory planning processes. He coined the terms "public interest design" and "architecture for the public good," and did a lot of important work designing spaces to support independent living for physically disabled people (Lifchez 1987; Lifchez and Winslow 1979). I also worked with fellow professor Sim Van der Ryn, who had done a number of projects with and for farm workers (Van der Ryn 2005); I admired the social consciousness of his work.

With Sim, I helped create the Natural Energy Pavilion during the 1972–1973 school year. It was a model of off-grid, energy-conserving technologies and constructed on campus near the College of Environmental Design. The pavilion was built from salvaged lumber and included a prototype solar collector, windmill, rainwater reservoir, and composting toilet, among other features. I was looking for ways to use environmental design techniques and strategies for connecting to the overlooked African American tradition of self-reliance. I had been inspired by the model of Booker T. Washington and the do-it-yourself (DIY) legacy of the Tuskegee Institute.[1]

Working on the Natural Energy Pavilion was a tremendous experience for me. Unfortunately, we had to dismantle the exhibit prematurely when students and faculty entering the music department complained about the smell from the composting toilet.

Family Matters

Settling down in Berkeley, Jean and I bought a lot with two small houses; it was cheaper than renting. Our Carleton Street block was mostly African American with a few Japanese families. We were excited about the idea of creating an African-inspired multigenerational compound on our new property and planned to bring my mother to live with us. I built a deck shared by the two houses.

In March of 1972, shortly after moving, we lost my brother Lewie to suicide. After we buried Lewie, I arranged for Mother to come live with us in Berkeley. She had been living by herself in our old apartment near Columbia. Jean and I moved into the back house that was unfinished, and Mother had the bedroom in the more finished front house where we shared the kitchen and living room. It was wonderful to have her sharing our home; she played the role of foster mother to many of our friends who paid frequent visits to the house to talk with her.

Although we had not previously wanted to have children, we had second thoughts after Lewie's death, which had shaken each of us to the core. Our son, Khalil, was born at home in May of 1973. We prepared for the momentous event by attending birth preparation classes and, eventually, a few births, both at home and in the hospital. The journey in West Africa had given Jean confidence that birth was normal and could happen without the hospital. I felt super prepared. The DIY spirit was in the air in Berkeley. We stuck with a home-birth plan with the assistance of Carole, a wonderful self-trained lay midwife. It wasn't easy, but our son was born in our unfinished back house. Mother was beset with worry beforehand but delighted to welcome her only grandson into the world—Khalil Sekaye Lewie David Doak-Anthony. Mother was Khalil's major caretaker as a baby and toddler[2] while Jean tried to reintegrate to a work life.

A few years later, Mother developed lung cancer and had a surgery that we later felt may have shortened her life. She died peacefully at home in July of 1976. I wanted a ceremony to honor her life that would be true to who we were. We had an outdoor gathering at home, including friends as pallbearers, a minister, and a jazz combo, before transporting Mother's body to be buried in Philadelphia. I was grateful for the years we shared before her death and for the way she was appreciated and honored by our community of friends.

A cabinetmaker friend, Priscilla, with help from two of my colleagues, built Mother a beautiful coffin inlaid with rosewood. Two other friends, Maria and Mildred, created lining and pillows using a group of wedding dresses owned by Mildred's mother, local hero Ma Howard, who had devoted years of her life in the 1950s and 1960s—even mortgaging her house—to mount a successful campaign to keep the tracks of the new light rail Bay Area Rapid Transit (BART) system underground through Berkeley.

Jean and I lived separately after I returned from Philadelphia. Our bond had become somewhat tenuous due to my preoccupation with my struggles at the university. I was committed to bringing racial diversity to the College of Environmental Design, to figuring out how to use architecture and urban planning to further social justice, and to gaining tenure. Jean was not interested in being a faculty wife, and I often felt unsupported by her when I came home wanting to rant and complain about the culture of white privilege at the university. She was ready to live independently.

The realization that it takes a village to raise a child encouraged women, and some men, of our circle to share childcare to a far greater extent than their mothers had. I am ashamed to admit that I felt resentful that Jean's attention was so focused on our child—that I was no longer the main object of her attention. Jean was the stronger parent in raising and caring for Khalil. I was focused on developing my career and my public persona, and I wanted to avoid a pattern I had observed in my father. As Lewie and I were growing up, our dad was very present and spent an enormous amount of time with us—most likely compensating for the absence of parents in his own childhood. Before he married my mother, he had begun to develop a dynamic public presence through his work with co-operatives, and he had a lot of potential as a community leader. I appreciated the effort that he put into raising us, but it troubled me that he gave up his public life and leadership role. I decided that I was not going to let that happen to me. I felt that if I didn't push forward and try to make my mark, I would be one of the many thousands before me who had many gifts, but didn't develop them. It seemed vitally important to try to make a mark, even a small one.

Jean and I remained friends and co-parents of Khalil despite our separation. We are family. We still have a bond. I am filled with admiration and gratitude for all that Jean has done to care for and guide Khalil and to help me deal with myriad challenges through the years, including getting the care I've needed as I lost my eyesight.

Khalil has been a guitar player since the age of thirteen. Music is a field I cannot help him with. I had hoped he would take a path African Americans did not usually follow and go into a field like ocean science. In his teen years and later, Khalil received mentorship and encouragement from adult musicians who recognized his talent and his passion for innovation with the guitar. Khalil is father of a son, has married, and has a stepdaughter. I find myself amazed to be a grandfather. My life experiences have taught me that raising children is best as a community endeavor. Bringing up the youth must involve more than just the nuclear family. Now, more than ever, we need to find ways to help our communities rise to the occasion.

Hosting James Baldwin for a Month

In 1974, James Baldwin was invited to participate in a month-long program at UC Berkeley. The organizers, wanting to find a low-profile place for him to stay, sought me out, and we made the arrangements. What a fascinating month it was!

Baldwin was small, wiry, and intense—charismatic and brilliant. Having him around was a delight. He had a unique perspective and filled the house with interesting people and conversations. Folks would come over as early as ten in the morning, and the last ones would leave around two at night. A veritable Who's Who in African American politics and culture came by to visit, including Angela Davis and newly elected African American Berkeley mayor Gus Newport. Huey Newton came with a driver/bodyguard who stayed in his car the whole time and wouldn't come in even when invited.

When we walked through town, people would often recognize Jimmy and strike up a conversation. He was gracious with these interactions and did not seem perturbed when his schedule was thrown off by one or more unanticipated conversations.

Attempting to Introduce New Course Material

In the late 1970s, I shared a popular perception, based on a belief in progress, that with emancipation, life had gradually improved for African Americans: the Civil War had been won. The industrial and commercial society of the North had been on the right side of the struggle against slavery.

I wrote a two-part article, "The Big House and the Slave Quarter," which was published in the Spring and Autumn issues of *Landscape* in 1976. Part one was subtitled "Prelude to New World Architecture," and part two was subtitled "African Contributions to the New World." In documenting the built environment that surrounded slavery, I thought that I had solved the most important mystery about the relationship between African American people and the New World environment. I believed that I had nearly completed the foundation for understanding the spatial experience of African Americans that had been missing in my formal education and that I needed as a professional architect and urban planner. Within the context of a consensus about racial progress, which was easily shared with my colleagues, I planned to write a brief essay on a few items that had been overlooked in the history of building in modern America that would bring the environmental story of African Americans into the present.

As I surveyed historical accounts, however, I learned that the post-Civil War history of American racism against African Americans was much more complex than I had anticipated. What I came to know of this history didn't add up to a well-packaged and comprehensive story of progress for me. Defining racism in terms of slavery and overtly visible "whites only" signs had prevented me from acknowledging less visible forms of racism that were pervasive even in the North.

As I learned more about the aftermath of the Civil War and Reconstruction, I realized how important it was to understand the unique relationships between African Americans and the built environment. Before the end of slavery, enslaved people had a wide variety of living arrangements according to where their labor was being used. With emancipation, old patterns shifted and new arrangements had to be made; this included highly functional black towns.[3] Through all the challenging new experiences they faced, freed African Americans learned to make do. The ability to adapt to changing conditions had helped them survive slavery. After emancipation, they formed new patterns of resilience.

By the end of the nineteenth century, blacks had lost access to political space as policies had been put into place to systematically dismantle their civil rights. New sharecropping arrangements gradually institutionalized the occupational isolation of blacks in the rural South. Schools, urban neighborhoods, transportation, and other public facilities became racially segregated by local ordinances known as Black Codes and, later, by Jim Crow laws. Lynchings and other vicious attacks by white mobs came to define the Southern landscape. African American families and individuals lived under a reign of terror.

Gradually, it became clear to me that conditions for black people from Reconstruction through the end of the nineteenth century had been made with expectations of near-linear progress, but racial realities appeared to be moving backwards. While the conventional liberal perspective attributes the regressive racial policies to the unfortunate backwardness of the South, it seemed apparent to me, however, that Northern industrial society had been complicit in the betrayal of African American people. As the North rebuilt the nation in its own image, its top-down approach abandoned commitment to the full participation of African Americans in society, which had been mandated by the Thirteenth, Fourteenth, and Fifteenth Amendments to the US Constitution.

My idea of how I would further my academic career and get tenure at the university was to publish another article on the black experience from the Civil War to the end of the nineteenth century. My working title was "The Landscape of Freedom." At first, I thought it would be easy to do, but when I started to really work at it, I became disheartened and depressed. A similar situation had occurred in the late 1970s when I had started to develop an essay on the Tuskegee Institute—Booker T. Washington's lifelong project—and its design and construction by Robert Robinson Taylor, the first African American graduate of the Massachusetts Institute of Technology. When I visited the site for research, it seemed not so well cared for, and I was disheartened and upset that such an important milestone in African American history had fared so poorly.

It took me years to figure out the problem—that after emancipation, in many ways, things got worse for black people. It was too painful for me to contemplate the downward spiral from the hopeful, creative efforts that characterized the early days of Reconstruction to the hateful violence of white mob attacks and the gradual degeneration into the kind of inner-city black ghetto in which I grew up.

As I explored the history, I learned that thousands of African American freedmen had been arrested under unjust, arbitrarily applied laws and transformed into convicts. They were leased to entrepreneurs, and their labor was used for rebuilding and industrializing the war-ravaged South. It was the same old story—just as African slaves had labored to build the infrastructure of Northern cities and other enslaved Africans had cleared forested land for plantations and then labored to build and operate them, black Southerners would labor again for white profit.

I wanted to share my growing awareness with my students and colleagues at the university, but only a few black students were interested.

Finally, I said to myself: "I'm out of here. I can't face this." I couldn't provide a good enough explanation to get tenure. At a certain point, I was trying to make it into an optimistic story, but it didn't work. So, I left my teaching job at the university and opened my own office.

Professional Practice

In my professional practice, I looked for places in city development that held opportunities and prospects of yielding to citizen demands. The main promising areas were with projects that had been locked up in controversy and conflict, deindustrialization and plant closures, and divestments of massive land holdings by railroad companies.

One of my first projects was working with Chris Alexander on a redevelopment plan for North Omaha. I was really enjoying the challenges of the project as well as working with Chris, but we had a disagreement about his decision to design and build some new Jewish settlements in Palestine. I didn't want to be associated with that and felt ethically obliged to distance myself from the project.

At this time, I started to figure out what to do in Berkeley. I collaborated with black urban planner Virgus Streets on some consulting for the City of Berkeley. They had a block grant, and most of the money was going to assist black property owners who had previously been overlooked. Eventually, they had a stream of revenue, and there was a movement in Berkeley to look at tenants' rights. We developed a set of policy recommendations for a more balanced program that would also benefit renters. The success of our recommendations led to our getting a consulting assignment on what to do about the West Berkeley Redevelopment Project, which dealt with an area around ten or twelve blocks that had been a subject of controversy for over fifteen years.

The original plan was to make a Silicon Valley of sorts in West Berkeley—tear down all the old houses and build a new place for high-tech businesses. The Republican mayor who had been advocating that plan lost the next election to Democrat Warren Widener, the first African American to hold that office. In the next election, the more progressive candidates from Berkeley Citizens Action gained a majority in the city council, and African American firebrand Gus Newport was elected mayor. The new administration hired Virgus and me to help resolve land use conflicts in West Berkeley.

The West Berkeley Redevelopment Project

Virgus and I were guided by the new and increasingly popular idea of mixed-use development, which offers much in the way of meeting everyone's needs. We developed a plan that was quite successful because it had a little something in it for everybody, including sixty-two units of Section 8 housing and a shared equity home ownership program. The progressives on the city council wanted to create limited equity co-ops to maintain some control of the assets and preserve affordability. The conservatives on the council preferred to allow market forces to work without restraint. At that time, the idea of selling a city-owned, run-down house for one dollar was quite popular, but the result of that approach was that the people who renovated the properties stayed in them for only a short time—as soon as market values rose, the renovators sold the home for a price that moderate-income residents could not afford. We came up with a new strategy—equity sharing—in which the city financed the portion of the down payment and mortgage that the prospective homeowner was unable to afford. This solved the problem of long-term affordability. When the property was sold, the city and the homeowner shared the profits in the same proportions as in the original purchase agreement. This method[4] was well received by all nine members of the city council.

Early on, I saw the wisdom of developing plans that would be unanimously approved. If you only had five votes and you missed a meeting, your opponents might vote to block or reject your plan. Planning projects tended to go through several administrations, so to get something done, we would need a super majority. We were always ready to engage in more communication and try a little harder so our plans would get nine votes.

Many people involved in the West Berkeley Redevelopment Project were passionate about historic preservation. They demanded that the oldest block in the city on Fourth Street and Delaware be rebuilt from the ground up based on photographs from an earlier time. Various other sites and renovated buildings in the area were made available as live/work units.

Several blocks onward were set aside for small-scale commercial use and became a very popular destination for shopping and dining. The site attracted innovative retail businesses that catered to designers and other creative tenants. The design of parking and sidewalks promoted a flow of foot traffic that evoked earlier days and benefitted the merchants. Denny Abrams, who had worked for Christopher Alexander, did a great job as the architect on the commercial development. This was an early example of how abandoned areas of cities can be rebuilt, and I sought to use the solutions in later projects.

Deindustrialization and Plant Closure Conversions

After working on West Berkeley redevelopment, I got involved in the conversion of industrial plant closures. Many businesses had moved their operations overseas, where labor was less costly, or out to the suburbs, where land and buildings were cheaper. The Colgate-Palmolive plant in Berkeley had closed, and we got involved in trying to figure out new uses for it. Three colleagues and I formed a nonprofit development firm and presented a plan to Reuben Mark, the vice president of Colgate, that would have him donate the plant to us in exchange for a tax write-off. After jumping through hoops to get the financing to prove we had enough resources to develop the site, Reuben Mark accepted a counteroffer from a purveyor of second-hand goods who offered him cash in hand with the stipulation that his investment would be returned if he couldn't find a way of making the plant profitable. During the year or so that he occupied the plant, he removed all the valuable plumbing and electrical fixtures. When he demanded the return of his investment, Colgate complied, not realizing that the building had been gutted and was no longer functional.

We got involved in the conversion of the General Motors (GM) automobile plant in South Gate in Southern California. GM had decided to close the plant and move all production to the Midwest. We proposed that they use the facility to produce parts for the two plants that were still operating in the area. GM decided against it. The building stood vacant for many years until it was torn down to build a high school, which was a bit strange since it's in the middle of an industrial area.

Collaborating with Architect Randall Fleming

I had never gotten my license as an architect because I had never found an architect with whom I felt comfortable apprenticing. Even though I had plenty of experience, skill, and connections, I needed to team up with a licensed architect in order to practice. I enjoyed working with Randall Fleming. When I first met him, he complained that he was tired of designing kitchen remodels. He seemed to enjoy the projects we took on. In one project, we worked with neighborhood residents in Oakland's San Antonio district to convert a decommissioned firehouse into a community center. Another big project was the redesign and renovation of twenty-two units of single-resident occupancy housing in downtown Oakland.

In 1983, we did a site feasibility study for the Oakland Ensemble Theater. The city wanted to take control of the space that the troupe had been using. When the troupe members complained that the city didn't understand them and their needs, we advised them to write a play about it and perform it before the city council. It seemed like a whimsical tactic, but it worked, and they ended up being given a great new location.

Randall and I decided to submit a proposal in a competition for Oakland's Central District Development Plan, a process that is undertaken every decade or two. I had gotten many great ideas about designing downtowns from *A Theory of Good City Form*, then the most recent work of eminent urban planner Kevin Lynch (1981), who resided in New England. I contacted him and requested that he partner with us on the proposal and was delighted when he agreed. Our proposal was well received, and we came in second in the competition. The winner, we were told, had previously been promised the job.

Receiving that recognition was good for our reputation and helped us get the commission to work on the Berkeley Waterfront Plan.[5]

Finding Meaning in Work

I often wondered why, after so many generations, African Americans were still marginalized. What were their unmet needs? I asked myself how a physical environment could be developed that met the needs of African American communities while improving the quality of life for everyone. The goal of urban planning and design is to apply intuitive, experiential, and scientific knowledge to the solution of problems. I believed that urban design could help communities achieve social justice objectives and help solve the problems we face in our neighborhoods, cities, and regions. Rather than work in an office visualizing and designing individual buildings, I wanted to use my skills as an architect and planner to foster inclusion, justice, and resilience in our most vulnerable communities.

My professional practice in Berkeley helped me further develop my understanding of the processes of planning, designing, and building cities. I hoped that it would also provide opportunities to address issues of justice and equity. Communities marginalized by the impacts of racism often face health and safety risks such as flood, earthquake, and exposure to toxic waste. Planning for resiliency in the most disadvantaged communities can help residents recover rapidly from such extreme natural or human-caused events.

CHAPTER 8

Crisis and Turning Point

I N THE MIDDLE OF THE 1980S, I experienced a crisis of identity in my personal and professional life. I was feeling uncertain about my role as an architect and as a member of the African American community. I needed to come to terms with crucial changes that had occurred since I embarked on my career in the 1960s. First of all, the natural environment—on local, regional, and global levels— was rapidly deteriorating, and it was unclear what should or could be done to reverse the destructive trend. Second, the nature of the city itself was changing. Gentrification and related dynamics were beginning to revitalize the economies of inner cities while draining the life out of the older suburbs.

Planning the Berkeley Waterfront Redesign

My crisis came to a head while I was working on a plan to develop the waterfront for the City of Berkeley. On the north side of the Berkeley Marina now lies César Chávez Park, a ninety-acre park on former landfill that is a well-loved spot for walking, picnicking, and kite flying. Looking west across the San Francisco Bay from its grassy slopes, one beholds magnificent panoramic views of the San Francisco skyline, the Golden Gate[1] Bridge, and the Marin Headlands. The value of this view, however, has not always been recognized and appreciated. Beginning in the mid-nineteenth century when the gold rush brought hordes of people to the San Francisco Bay Area, the dumping of construction debris, sewage, and all sorts of discards into the shallow edges of the bay became common practice. These landfills served a two-fold purpose: convenient waste disposal sites and the creation of valuable new land on the bay's edge, commonly referred to as bayfill. When the bay was deepened starting in the early nineteenth century to enable larger ships to enter and navigate its harbors, the dredged material was also deposited at the bay's shallow edges.[2]

When I moved to Berkeley in the earlier 1970s, I heard from friends who had grown up in the area that the Berkeley waterfront had been used as a landfill for a hundred years. In 1957, the City of Berkeley declared the site an official dump and constructed dikes to contain municipal waste.[3] They charged residents a fee to deposit their old refrigerators, furniture, leftover building materials, cans, bottles, newspapers, and other refuse on the western side of the railroad tracks.

Most of the land on the eastern shore of the San Francisco Bay, much of it bayfill, was owned by the Atchison, Topeka and Santa Fe Railway, commonly abbreviated as Santa Fe. Controversy arose over proposals by Santa Fe Realty, the company that handled the railroad's properties, to develop this land. Railroads and their holding companies owned huge tracts of land in every major city in California, and many were trying to come up with real estate development plans for the sites.

In the early 1980s, Santa Fe Realty advocated for office and retail development in Berkeley's waterfront that would amount to a new downtown, asserting that this was the best use for the land because it would result in the highest monetary value. If the city decided to keep the land as open space, Santa Fe threatened to sue, protesting that by doing so, the city would be denying the company the land's full potential value.

The architectural firm I formed with Randall Fleming—Anthony, Fleming and Associates—was relatively new at the time, but we had a good track record with the City of Berkeley based on work mentioned in Chapter 7: Teaching, Research, and Professional Practice. We partnered with ROMA, a well-established waterfront planning firm in San Francisco, and landed the contract to develop a plan for Berkeley's waterfront. In 1984, we developed a report on alternatives and initial evaluation criteria. In 1985, we conducted a series of public workshops. The first workshop focused on the topic of economic development and employment; the second on housing; the third on conservation, recreation, and open space; the fourth on urban design; and the fifth on transportation.

The process of developing these plans made me more aware than ever of the shifting environmental and racial priorities in Berkeley. These perspectives caused me to face profound questions about the direction of my life's work. A large percentage of Berkeley residents had begun to appreciate the San Francisco Bay as a community asset, which represented a shift from attitudes in an earlier period when the railroad (and, later, Interstate 80) separated the bay from the city and the waterfront was used as a landfill.

The Berkeley Waterfront planning process reflected growing understanding of the role of Berkeley in the context of the larger metropolitan region. Many locations east of the waterfront were losing vitality and ideally suited for intensive commercial development. Department stores and retail establishments lay vacant in downtown Berkeley, so the last thing Berkeley needed was a new downtown on the waterfront to compete with its struggling city center.

Another perspective was that Berkeley possessed a unique treasure in the waterfront location: a magnificent view of the Golden Gate Bridge. This was particularly evident to those relatively affluent—and typically white—people who lived in the hills above the flatlands. They argued that the site, running along the bay, would be excellent for completion of a grand shoreline park that would connect Berkeley with the other cities that face the waterfront to the north and south along the east side of the bay.[4]

The racial issue had become increasingly important. Santa Fe, for its part, was gaining public support for its commercial development proposal by promising lots of new jobs for unemployed residents who were predominantly African Americans. Santa Fe had hired a prominent black planning firm to develop and defend their proposal, but advocates for environmental preservation challenged their projections. "You can't eat open space," said a well-dressed man, one of the few African American people to participate in the public hearing. "I support the Santa Fe plan to build a new downtown on this site. Santa Fe has promised us twelve thousand new jobs."

The almost entirely white audience of over three hundred people grew uncomfortable when the African American man spoke in favor of the waterfront development; the white majority in attendance were adamantly opposed to building on the waterfront. Members of the Sierra Club and supporters of the Save the Bay movement were pushing for the property to be developed as a park.

"Our young people need jobs!" he continued. As he spoke, I reflected that the whole idea of citizen participation in urban planning had grown out of the African American civil rights insurgency in the 1960s. By the late 1980s, the innovation of citizen engagement had moved into the mainstream. The overwhelmingly white crowd was not aware that a large part of their power to participate in decision-making processes like this had been fought for and won by black people. Many had no respect and appreciation for the issues faced by black communities. "Go back to South Berkeley," someone muttered.

I, and most black residents at the time, lived in South Berkeley, and I was struck by the irony that I, despite being the chief professional architect of the whole waterfront redevelopment planning process, had been included in such an unguardedly racist dismissal. On hearing this remark, questions that had been bothering me at a deep level for some time began to surface: To what extent had the black community of the fifties and sixties gained a meaningful and ongoing place at the table of public life? Were the quality-of-life advancements that we had won at great cost now threatening to evaporate in the shifting social landscape of America? I thought of my South Berkeley neighbors, who often told me about a time, not so long before, when blacks could not even sit down at a soda fountain in downtown Berkeley, much less apply for jobs there. Now, Berkeley had a black mayor, a black city manager, and four black members of the nine-person city council. Nonetheless, even though around 20 percent of the population was black, less than a handful had shown up to comment on the plan for the waterfront. Something was very wrong.

At the end of the meeting, the people had spoken. The City of Berkeley, after a few more meetings, would decide to create a shoreline park at the Berkeley waterfront, which would create a few jobs for low-income people. To address the problems of unemployment, the City would later commit to a plan that would save some four thousand jobs in the adjacent industrial area. I was reasonably satisfied with the outcome, but was deeply troubled by the lack of black engagement in the planning process.

On one hand, the City of Berkeley had been good to me. They had hired me to work on one of their most important projects, which was leading me toward private professional success. On the other hand, I had a terrible sinking sensation. I could feel myself being drawn further and further from my deepest life aspiration—to use my knowledge of city-building processes as a vehicle for advancing the well-being of the African American community.

I was passionate about getting a critical mass of African Americans involved in the process of making decisions about the development of our communities. I was clear about the direction I wanted to take, but unsure of how to get there. It was becoming starkly evident to me that I needed a deeper footing for my life's work than could be provided by the civil rights movement.

Fragmentation of the African American Community

I had realized for some time that the idea of racial solidarity that animated the civil rights movement of the 1950s and 1960s was no longer applicable in the 1980s. The black community, previously concentrated in inner cities, had begun to disperse. With that dispersal, the coherent structures for civic engagement and rights-building processes that had been developed during the civil rights movement were unraveling. I was seeing the emergence of a new condition that journalist and political analyst Eugene Robinson (2010, 4) would point to a decade and a half later in *Disintegration: The Splintering of Black America*:

> There was a time when there were agreed-upon "black leaders," when there was a clear "black agenda," when we

could talk confidently about "the state of black America"—
but not anymore.

Beginning in the late 1960s, major American cities began elect-
ing black mayors. That political consensus rose through the early
1970s, but gradually faded away. Black people remaining in the
inner cities, whom Robinson identifies as the "abandoned," did not
possess the solidarity and political strength—qualities developed
during the civil rights era—that enabled other African Americans
to use the political system to gain rights. Upper- and middle-class
blacks had marched away with many of the rewards of the civil
rights struggles. Those who remained in the inner city were left
behind, both politically and economically. Caught in a new cycle
of poverty and diminishing opportunity, they were often shuttled
into the prison pipeline.

The movement of middle-class blacks out of inner-city ghettos fragmented and weakened the African American community,
which had once found strength in physical proximity. Ironically,
middle-class black flight from the inner cities was driven by the
victories of the civil rights movement—greater opportunities for
education and better-paying jobs for African Americans. Increasing
numbers of African Americans were better integrated into the larger
society, but that integration was accompanied by a loss of cohesion
and political power within the black community as a whole.

I observed another dynamic, every bit as disheartening, at play.
Blacks were moving to the suburbs to escape the violence, crime,
and lack of good schools that plagued the inner cities. They painfully discovered, however, that all suburbs are not equal and that the
American dream they sought no longer existed in many of the places
to which they moved. The image of the safe, prosperous suburb that
was established during the fifties had faded. The older suburban
residents were aging, and the newer suburban dwellers were more
ethnically and economically diverse. The sense of the suburbs as a
place of privilege was fading fast.

In many ways, the division between the cities and the suburbs
had reinstated the politics of segregation. In doing so, a new politics
began to emerge by the 1980s where the wealthier suburbs were

establishing a base of political power that completely bypassed the cities within their regions.

White flight from the suburbs reached a peak in the late 1980s just as African Americans and other people of color began migrating there from the inner cities. For example, between 1980 and 2010, Oakland, the larger city adjacent to Berkeley on the south, lost 30 percent of its black population[5] as those who could do so moved to the suburbs in search of the American dream. Meanwhile, others of lesser means were forced out of the city by gentrification and the rising rents it generated.

Ultimately, the civil rights laws that were designed to protect African Americans created protections and opportunities for economic advancement and political engagement for other populations as well. The black power movement—itself based on community cohesion—had set off a political chain reaction in which diverse identity groups organized to claim rights, including indigenous peoples, Chicanos/Chicanas, Asian Pacific Islanders, gays and lesbians, women, and environmentalists. As important and positive as these movements were and are, they failed to create or sustain a sense of belonging and solidarity among the diverse members of the larger community—either urban or suburban.

A Crisis in My Career

In the days following that first public workshop on the Berkeley Waterfront Plan in 1985, I kept reflecting on the social and environmental significance of all the changes I was witnessing. My mind was troubled, and I sensed myself urgently searching for something I could not yet name. All I knew for sure was that we were in a new situation—old approaches were not going to work anymore. Even the intersections between different kinds of discrimination were shifting. For example, when Martin Luther King Jr. went to Chicago in 1966 to help integrate the suburbs, the residents threw bricks and bottles at him. The Polish immigrants who had settled there felt threatened by African Americans moving into their neighborhoods. By the 1990s, that neighborhood had become largely Latino. I had to reckon with the inescapable truth that social conditions are dynamic. Old assumptions—no matter how valid they were at the time—cannot serve as a basis for thinking about new, and often more intractable, problems.

From 1985 to 1987, I consulted with the City and County of San Francisco on the development of Mission Bay and produced a series of reports. The area being developed was big enough for ten thousand new housing units, four million square feet of office space for low-wage workers, and a lot of community facilities. I was in on the beginning of that planning process and tried unsuccessfully to get the African American people in San Francisco's Hunter's Point neighborhood interested and involved in the planning process.

Although my career was advancing at a brisk pace, the work was increasingly troubling in that it did not include African Americans and other people of color in the processes of planning and design. Gradually, it began to dawn on me that I could either be successful as a conventional architect and planner or I could try to build a social movement that addressed the challenges faced by the African American community. It was becoming increasingly clear that I could not do both.

My Moment of Truth

At the end of a long week of work, I had settled in for a pleasant evening at home, reflecting on my career as an architect, an urbanist, and an advocate for social and racial justice. I had been a faculty member at the University of California at Berkeley, one of the most prestigious universities in the nation. Now, I was an independent professional with a good reputation, living in a modest house in an upscale neighborhood.

In my living room at sunset, my walls lined with books and my easy chair facing the fireplace, I poured myself a glass of sherry, reached for a book, and settled into the easy chair. The slim volume I had picked was *An Essay on Man*, a long poem written in the eighteenth century by Alexander Pope. The poem articulated a hierarchical concept Pope called the Great Chain of Being, in which bugs and grass were at the bottom, angels were at the top, and humanity was in between.

In a contemplative mood, I reflected on where I, as an African American, might fit. To my astonishment, I placed myself just below white people. At that point, I was forty-five years old and had been actively engaged in the struggle for racial justice for twenty-five years. I was proud to consider my work as a part of the long struggle for racial justice.

Sitting there with my glass of sherry and the book open in my lap, there were no slave traders holding my arms and legs in chains, no plantation owners restricting my movements and activities, no patrolling vigilantes with hound dogs to keep me in my place, no Ku Klux Klan burning crosses on my front lawn, no admissions officers telling me I was unqualified, and no policemen eyeing me suspiciously as an intruder in the neighborhood. I was by myself in my own living room where no one could have influenced my decision, yet I had still placed myself just below white people in my own Chain of Being. What on earth could that mean?

Over the years, I had pondered and worried about how unfair America had been to black people—how many of our young people filled the prisons, how many of our children were being raised without fathers, and how the schools and universities were refusing or failing to educate African American people. Having to think about my place in the universe on top of all that was a burden too heavy to bear.

Ordinarily, I would not have been speculating on such matters. At this point in my life, however, I urgently needed to piece together my experiences in a more holistic way.

Places for Peace

My mentor and friend, landscape architect Karl Linn, had moved to the San Francisco Bay Area in 1985 after taking an early retirement from his professorship at New Jersey Institute of Technology to work full time in the anti-nuclear movement.[6] Karl stayed with me during this period as I was agonizing over whether to close my architecture and planning office.

Karl invited me to join him in collecting and editing papers on the theme of places for peace, which we assembled into a paperback book and presented in October at the 1988 World Congress of the International Federation of Landscape Architects in Boston, Massachusetts.[7] The book, *Places for Peace*, is international in scope and presents case studies, themes, rituals, and ceremonies aimed at lessening the nuclear threat, decreasing dependency on the war economy, and redirecting military spending toward domestic programs.[8]

Working with Karl gave me a respite from my preoccupation with contradictions in my career and allowed me to pursue my thoughts about the environment, cities, suburbs, and race in a larger context. I was inspired by the way that some of the projects in the book addressed social justice issues, as well as environmental ones. We documented the work of citizen diplomats committed to using their roles as architects and planners as a vehicle for reducing international tension. Some engaged in international collaborations on the construction of peace parks for improved cross-cultural understanding and east-west cooperation, including a park built by American volunteers in Tashkent, the capital of the Soviet Republic of Uzbekistan, dedicated to friendship between the two countries. Karl introduced me to many inspiring ideas and projects, such as the Chipko "tree hugger" movement in India and Vandana Shiva's efforts to protect the forests there.[9]

PART TWO

Finding a New Story

CHAPTER 9

A New Beginning

A MONG THE MANY GIFTS of working on *Places for Peace* with Karl was my introduction to the writings of Catholic monk, scholar, and eco-philosopher Thomas Berry. During my days of self-searching, Karl handed me a photocopy of Berry's essay, "The New Story," suggesting that I might find it relevant. The essay, which became part of Berry's first book, *The Dream of the Earth*, published in 1988, was a real turning point for me. Berry points out that humanity is in trouble today because we do not have an adequate story of who we are. This gave me a context in which to think about a larger story.

Berry (1988, 124–32) describes humanity as divided between two dominant stories. On one side are those who believe in the power of science and industry to guide us to a safer and more abundant future; and on the other side are those who center their lives on the religious experience of redemption. The problem, according to Berry, is that scientific materialism has caused us to lose touch with spiritual, ethical, and aesthetic dimensions of life and has led to mass extinctions and an increasingly toxic industrial environment. The adherents of redemption by a divine savior typically have little interest in or connection with the physical world and its environmental and social problems, focusing instead on a heavenly hereafter.

Berry (Ibid., 115, 119) argues that we need a new, unifying story—a creation story that embraces the empirical observations of modern science about the origins of life on this planet, including the genesis of our own species. Ironically, both scientific reductionism and the promise of salvation in the afterlife encourage human beings to be manipulators and consumers of the natural world. Neither of these systems gives humans a basis for belonging. Earlier humans were much more directly connected to plants and animals and mountains and rivers than today's industrial way of life allows. Berry (Ibid., 181-93) asserts that a new creation story could help restore our sense of belonging to the natural world and allow us to reimagine the relationship between European immigrants and indigenous peoples.

In his writings about Earth and the universe, I searched for clues on how to think about race and city planning. *The Dream of the Earth* was like a bible to me; I read and reread it. While Berry's insight into our current predicament electrified me, I was disappointed that in "The Historical Role of the American Indian," he made no mention of other people of color. I wished that he shared my conviction that African Americans also needed a new story—a story that would take us beyond the dignity-sapping narrative of slavery and colonialism and empower us to take leadership roles in responding to our global ecological crisis.

I started to recognize a shift in my thinking about the primary needs of African Americans. In the past, I had focused on increasing opportunities for employment and finding a place in the industrial system. Influenced by the new story that Berry articulated, I placed Earth in a much more central position and started envisioning a new set of opportunities that put restoration and justice at the heart of personal and social transformation.

Connecting with the Environmental Movement

Working on *Places for Peace* had given me a new starting point—a respite from the contradictions I had been facing as I attempted to use my architectural and planning skills to benefit African Americans. I entered a space in which I could think beyond a purely local context and develop a more global perspective. Suddenly, a new awareness of myself, my purpose, and my role in society emerged. I became dramatically aware of the need to tell the story of African Americans and other people of color and to support the development of multiracial leadership for the environmental movement.

After *Places for Peace* was printed and distributed at the conference in Boston, Karl refocused on his earlier work of greening inner cities. He made a one-year commitment to volunteer at Earth Island Institute (EII) in San Francisco, where he began to engage in dialogue with its founder, environmental activist David Brower. Karl aimed to convince David that inner cities and their residents are part of the environment and need protection and advocacy as much as wilderness and the creatures that inhabit it. David invited Karl to present his work on neighborhood commons at an annual meeting of the Sierra Club and proposed that Karl write a chapter on urban barnraising in an EII publication. He also supported Karl in mining his extensive slide collection to create a set of two videotapes chronicling his work in building neighborhood commons in low-income communities.[1] I was pleased to see Karl's work getting the attention it deserved and happy to support the video by being filmed interviewing him about his work.

The story of my growing involvement with EII picks up again in Chapter 13: Forging an Alliance between Environmentalists and Social Justice Activists.

Inspired by the Universe Story

In 1992, Thomas Berry and astrophysicist and cosmologist Brian Swimme coauthored and published *The Universe Story: From the Primordial Flaring Forth to the Ecozoic Era—A Celebration of the Unfolding of the Cosmos.* Rushing to get the book as soon as it came out, I immersed myself in the grand tale of our cosmic origins and billions of years of history. Berry and Swimme relate the story of the cosmos, the story of Earth, the story of humanity, and the story of the future. At last, I was encountering a context in which the answers to many of my questions began to gel.

The story begins with the big bang, which Berry and colleagues refer to as the primordial Flaring Forth, an unimaginably creative moment. From an infinitesimal pinpoint, there exploded what eventually became something on the order of two hundred billion galaxies, each containing as many as a hundred billion or more stars. Humanity as a species, and each of us individually, has come to exist thanks to this creative explosion. We have been formed in the same process of universe development that made the stars and galaxies. Something amazing happened in one of those ancient stars—after growing and becoming increasingly dense, it finally collapsed under its own gravity, exploding and spewing out countless new stars and solar systems, including our Sun.

Earth was born from the demise of this exploding star, which Berry and Swimme called Tiamat.[2] The elements and molecules that make up our world and our physical bodies—oxygen, carbon, hydrogen, nitrogen, calcium, and all the rest—were contained in the gases and dust that burst forth from this supernova.

As the surface of newly born Earth began to solidify, it was bombarded by rocky asteroids, icy comets, and enormous meteorites, which formed deep craters and generated steam. The steam gradually condensed into water and filled the craters and indentations. Within these protected pools, elements from exploded stars combined. Then, after perhaps a few hundred million years, a startling development took place. Complex hydrocarbons were synthesizing and re-synthesizing in water warmed and infused by the molten lava below Earth's crust. Stimulated by lightning from thunderstorms, the natural processes of organic chemistry finally hit on the key that opened the door to life: the first living cell(s) appeared.

The startling development of photosynthesis came early in the history of life—the ability of cells to convert sunlight to chemical energy and use it to do work, like growing a tree hundreds of feet into the air. As life spread throughout the planet, cells filled the depths of the oceans and then lifted off and became part of the atmosphere. Earth demonstrated its power to adapt by altering the composition of its atmosphere to keep itself cool as the Sun grew hotter. A living planet—a complex, self-organizing system—arose with the capacity to maintain the delicate conditions of life.

Life continued its inventions—the ability to move and ingest and digest other living beings—and achieved multicellularity. Over 3.5 billion years, generations of Earth's living beings have invented mouths, teeth, shells, bones, fins, eyes, gills, and organs that can sense and interpret touch, sound, smell, heat, electric fields, magnetic fields, and a host of other environmental conditions. As creatures found their way out of the sea and onto land, their progeny developed lungs, legs, feet, fur, and even wings and feathers for flying. The living systems of this planet have brought forth an uncountable variety of ingenious adaptations to changing conditions.

How does our species, Homo sapiens, fit into the history of life on this planet? According to Swimme and Berry (1992, 143),

> When shape-shifting matter suddenly appeared in human form, a great surprise took place. For a new faculty of understanding was making its appearance, a mode of consciousness characterized by its sense of wonder and celebration as well as by its ability to refashion and use parts of its exterior environment as instruments in achieving its own ends. The story of the human is the story of the emergence and development of this self-awareness and its role within the universe drama.

As I immersed myself in this story, I felt a growing sense of my place in the universe and on Earth. I felt empowered by the discovery that the universe story was large enough to include my unique role, function, status, and relationships, and the parts of my life and work that are important and meaningful to me. I was pleased to realize that I am an end product of billions of years of life in the universe. I began to ask myself how this knowledge of my full ancestry shed light on my life and daily choices.

This new way of thinking began to have a positive impact on my life. One day while in a heated discussion at a gathering of environmentalists, I found myself saying, "I don't have to put up with this. I'm the end product of fourteen billion years of evolution." Everyone stopped and took notice. I was amazed at how good that affirmation made me feel. I discovered that I had a place. Nobody could throw me out.

Telling the Story of African Americans

In her 1992 book *Trauma and Recovery: The Aftermath of Violence—from Domestic Abuse to Political Terror*, Judith Herman observes that victims of captivity or abuse gradually lose touch with their larger environment and begin to increasingly focus their attention on the perpetrators of their abuse. As a therapeutic approach, Herman (1992) recommends that people with post-traumatic stress syndrome find a safe place to tell the story of their abuse. They need to tell their story over and over again until it loses its charge.

Although Herman's 1992 study focuses primarily on prisoners of war and battered women, many of the themes she develops could well apply to African Americans whose ancestors were captured and sold into slavery beginning five hundred years ago and who continue to experience racist attitudes and treatment from society and institutions. In the trauma of slavery, our African ancestors were uprooted from their village communities and cosmological context and placed in a hostile, oppressive, and demeaning environment. After emancipation, abuse and trauma continued, including the Black Codes, Jim Crow laws, housing and job discrimination, racial profiling, and police violence.

As a result, many African Americans—myself included—retain an excessive preoccupation with what white people think and do instead of focusing on overcoming the many very real obstacles to our own self-realization and fulfillment. In an elegant analysis, Joy DeGruy (2005) describes this as "post traumatic slave syndrome" in her book by that name, subtitled *America's Legacy of Enduring Injury and Healing*. How can we undo the damage caused by the ruptures and cruel treatment our ancestors were forced to endure? How can we connect to our present environment when the American civilization that brought Africans to this continent as slaves has never truly faced its white supremacy, the harm it has inflicted, or the obvious injustices on which it continues to rely? America seems unable to avoid retraumatizing those whose ancestors it once enslaved.

Recent African American history is littered with examples of individual and collective betrayal: the dramatic withdrawal of assistance and protection for those freed from slavery when federal support for Reconstruction evaporated; the establishment of seg-regation via discriminatory Jim Crow laws throughout the South; the denial of federal assistance to black farmers; the denial of loans for purchasing homes to black veterans of World War II; the refusal of home-improvement loans to inner-city residents like my fam-ily, which resulted in the deterioration of our neighborhoods; and the allowance of racially restrictive covenants in real estate deeds. White flight resegregated the United States during the 1960s and 1970s; and when African Americans migrated to suburban places, the suburban prosperity they anticipated had evaporated.[3] It re-minded me of how duped and distressed I felt upon learning as an adult that William Penn, who had been one of my childhood heroes, had owned slaves and that his father's enormous wealth had grown out of his participation in the trans-Atlantic slave trade.

What are we to do with the wounds of such betrayals? The di-verse people of European ancestry who surround us black Americans today are not the slave traders who captured our ancestors centuries ago, and our present ecological context is quite different from the environment that our ancestors knew. We have much to learn about how to achieve reconciliation around the intertwined histories of exploitation of both our labor and our shared environment. How do we move from there to effective common action? A crucial first step is to expose and deconstruct the harmful illusion of whiteness.

In June of 1993, I was invited to a conference on ecopsychology, an emerging field that studies the relationship between human beings and the natural world through ecological and psychological princi-ples. There, I met many well-known psychologists. Theodore Roszak invited me to contribute to his forthcoming book, *Ecopsychology: Restoring the Earth, Healing the Mind.* I am not a psychologist, but I was told that Roszak's interview with me, included in the chapter "Ecopsychology and the Deconstruction of Whiteness," turned out to be the most widely read part of the book. In it, I argue that we cannot make any progress in our damaged relationship with nature without taking the whole notion of race apart at the seams.

The monolithic human identity that has been built around the mythology of pure whiteness is destructive. We must find a way to build a multicultural self that is in harmony with our ecological self. We need to embrace human diversity in our dealings with one another and reject the notion that white people are the mainstream and everybody else is "other." An ecopsychology that has no place for people of color and that doesn't deliberately set out to correct the distortions of racism is an oxymoron (Anthony 1995, 277).

We often assume race to be something clear cut and solid; we take it to represent real divisions among peoples of the world when, in all actuality, it is an equivocal ideological concept that has very little biological basis. This separation within the human community is deeply reflected in the separation between people and nature. Nature is also defined as "other" in the same way that people outside the dominant group are "other" (Ibid., 270).

I came to realize that the story of the cosmos can have a transformative effect on the most marginalized populations. For example, when a friend of mine recounted the universe story to an inmate serving a life sentence in San Quentin State Prison, the prisoner remarked, "That changes everything."

"Know from whence you came," wrote James Baldwin (1962) in the famous letter to his fifteen-year-old nephew, "and there is no limit to where you can go." As an African American in the United States thinking about my origins, I am fascinated by the ancient geographic connection between North America and Africa during the formation and breakup of the supercontinent known as Pangaea hundreds of millions of years ago. The formation of Pangaea included the collision between the continents of North America and Africa that produced the Appalachian Mountains. Later, the continents moved apart, forming the Atlantic Ocean. In my mind, the story of African Americans begins many millions of years ago, when Africa and America were one land, and continues for millions of years as they became two geographically distinct places separated by a great ocean. This information is an essential element of African Americans' place in the story of Earth.

The more I read and reflected on the universe story, the more confident I became that the story of Earth's formation and our place in its long evolution can give African Americans and other people of color a sense of identity and belonging. Moreover, the story can serve as a corrective to the extremes of hubris and shame that have enabled our oppressors to weaken and disempower us for centuries.

My generation contributed to and benefited from the breakthroughs of the 1960s. We have come into maturity and are now poised to offer important leadership and support in achieving the quantum leap in human social and ecological relationships that Thomas Berry envisioned. Such leadership, built upon an empowering understanding of the past and an inclusive vision of the future, requires a larger narrative framework in which struggles for human justice are linked with the stories of Earth and cosmos.

Despite some racial slights and dismissals that I experienced as I shared my insights over the years, I have never lost confidence that a comprehensive narrative of the African and African American environmental experience fits well within the story of the universe. As I reflect on writings by Berry and colleagues, I keep thinking of ways that essential elements of the African American experience could enrich the universe story. Although parts of Berry's and Swimme's (1992) accounts might be contested from an African American perspective, I nonetheless feel confident that dialogue and discussion will lead toward a greater understanding of the African American experience while strengthening the ecocentric thesis at the heart of the universe story. I am excited by the prospect of opening new vistas for learning and action by African Americans in the twenty-first century—learning and action that strengthen the possibility of survival for all humanity.

My intention is to contribute to a common story that harnesses the power of the universe story and includes people of non-European descent. Adopting the story of the universe as a framework for thinking about issues of racial oppression can give us a larger perspective in which to conceptualize environmental issues. If we think only in terms of the moment in which we're struggling, i.e., the rapidly changing post-industrial world, we can feel discouraged. We obviously don't have enough time to reconstruct our entire social and economic system. However, placing ourselves within the context of the universe story gives us more time and more space in which to shape our story and our strategy.

Acting on my new thinking about African Americans, the experience of belonging, and environmentalism, I wrote an essay entitled "Why African Americans Should Be Environmentalists,"[4] which appeared in *Call to Action: Handbook for Ecology, Peace and Justice* assembled by David Brower's assistant Brad Erickson (Anthony 1990a). The book consists of short essays by an international roster of activists, including a preface by Jesse Jackson that begins with Antonio Gramsci's famous "An old world is dying, and a new world is struggling to be born" quote and ends with Jesse asserting that environmental justice is a human right. I considered my essay to be the first installment of a new story about and for African Americans and their allies.

Returning to the work of Berry and his colleagues and pondering their vision sharpened my awareness of the three stories that have engaged my attention most vividly and consistently throughout my life—the stories of the Earth, the city, and the struggle for racial justice. This book arises from my commitment to interweave these stories and offer that as an addition to the fabric of the universe story, responding to the invitation at the end of Swimme and Berry's (1992, 5) introduction:

> Our aim is to awaken those sensitivities to the great story
> that enable a rich participation in the ongoing adventure.
> We offer this brief narrative in the hope that others will fill
> in what is missing, correct what is improperly presented,
> and deepen our understanding of the ongoing story.

This chapter and the chapters that follow are my best effort to respond to that invitation.

CHAPTER 10

Deep Time, Slavery, and the Making of the Modern Economic System

S HORTLY AFTER BARACK OBAMA was elected president of the United States, a Kenyan engineer offered to give me a ride home from a gathering. On the way, I struck up a conversation about the recent election. "It must make you feel pretty good to have a president of the United States with ancestors that come from your part of Africa," I said.

"All the presidents of the United States have ancestors that come from my part of Africa," he replied.

I knew what he meant—most scientists agree that our species emerged and evolved in the Great Rift Valley in East Africa, which runs through Kenya north to south. But I was struck by how conscious he was of that fact. He was fully and immediately aware of his lineage. Not all Kenyans or other Africans that I have met share that awareness. I raised the point about the African origins of humanity with an Ethiopian waitress at a local restaurant.

"Really?" she said, "I had no idea."

Africa was the last continent to be explored by Europeans, the last to be colonized, and the last to win its independence from Europe. Considering that humanity's journey began in Africa, its position in human history needs to be lifted up and placed more centrally in our shared understanding of who we are as human beings.

Human History Begins in Africa

By writing about human origins, I want to reach beyond the story I learned about my heritage that doesn't begin until the seventeenth century CE when Africans found themselves captured, enslaved, and transported to distant lands. For many years, I have been searching the work of paleontologists and archeologists for access to knowledge of our African ancestors. One of my challenges was to orient myself and move beyond the myth of Africa as the "Dark Continent," a viewpoint promulgated by nineteenth-century Europeans, who categorized the land as "unexplored" and its people as "primitive," "exotic," and "uncivilized"—unequivocally and irredeemably other. This viewpoint led to the conclusion that any contribution Africa might make to world culture is unimportant when compared with the high achievements of Europe and that, at best, Africans represent an earlier stage in human evolution.[1]

Today, however, there is general agreement among scientists that the human species emerged through an evolutionary process that began in Africa. Most scientists believe that between five to seven million years ago, a shift in the tectonic plates created a huge rift valley stretching from Ethiopia to South Africa that blocked the rain coming in from the Indian Ocean.[2] As the rift valley dried up and plants began to die, our tree-dwelling hominid ancestors came down from the trees in search of food and learned to walk across the landscape on two feet, arguably leading to the emergence of human intelligence in East Africa. The two accounts of human evolution that I find most convincing are *The Journey of Man: A Genetic Odyssey* by Spencer Wells (2002) and *The Real Eve: Modern Man's Journey Out of Africa* by Stephen Oppenheimer (2003).[3]

Although ongoing archeological discoveries will continue to require revisions in theories, most scientists believe that modern humans developed in Africa as a separate branch of hominins starting about two hundred thousand years ago, or possibly earlier,[4] when they began to fashion tools for hunting and their brains grew larger. Many species of hominins had developed earlier, including our ancestors and their cousins who were hunter-gatherers for millennia. Eventually, Homo sapiens (also known as anatomically modern humans) became the last hominin species to survive. Thus, the human journey began in Africa.

Evidence shows that our forebears improved their tools, developed language, arts, and agriculture, and built cities throughout Africa. At some point between fifty and eighty-three thousand years ago,[5] a small group of hunter-gatherers genetically similar to the San people (also known as Bushmen or Basarwa) crossed the Red Sea, which had shrunk to a width of about ten miles, into the Arabian Peninsula and continued eastward along the coast. It is likely that they left Africa and chose to travel along the coast to avoid the effects of glaciation or drought in the inland environment.

Extensive genetic research and mapping suggest that modern nonAfricans sprang from this exodus out of Africa. Both Spencer Wells and Stephen Oppenheimer explain the routes and branches that these people took although they give different starting dates. According to Oppenheimer (2003), ancient humans left Africa around 83,000 BP[6] and moved southward into India and Australia (70,000 BP), northward into central and eastern Asia (60,000 BP) and then west into Europe (50,000 BP), and northeast across the Bering land bridge into North America (22,000 BP) and then down into South America (12,500 BP).[7] Wells (2002, 108) has the process starting later—around 50,000 years ago.

The journey out of Africa resulted in humans inhabiting all major continents and adapting their skin color and other traits to the different climatic conditions in which they settled. This peopling of the continents is quite amazing, but I feel that much greater respect should be given to the peoples of Africa—not only those who migrated to other continents in the deep past and those who were captured and sold into slavery (the African diaspora) but also those who continue to reside in the first home of human beings.[8] Tragically, the most recent phase of massive forced movement out of Africa, starting early in the sixteenth century, was accompanied by the extraction of Africa's wealth, enriching transcontinental business interests while impoverishing the continent's people.

The essential point is that, contrary to what schoolchildren were taught for many generations, Homo erectus did not originate in the Middle East ten to twelve thousand years ago, but instead originated on the African continent 1.8 million years ago—and the history of all modern humans began in Africa around two hundred thousand years ago. In its version of the human story, the narrow lens of Western civilization has excluded or marginalized Africans and descendants of the African diaspora. We have inherited a tendency to tell the human story as if it began in Greece, but the real journey of *everyone*'s ancestors—not just those whose ancestors were captives of the slave trade—began much, much earlier in Africa. In a sense, all Americans, descendants of slaves and slave owners alike, are African American.

We need to lift up the first two hundred thousand years of modern human experience and validate its importance, moving it out of the shadowy edges where it has been marginalized and into a central place in human history. We also need to recognize and celebrate our more ancient ancestors.[9] The fact that we all descended from common ancestors several million years old throws questions into bold relief: How did the bonds of solidarity become broken, and what can be done to repair them?

Ancient and Medieval African Cultures

The second chapter title of Clive Ponting's *A Green History of the World*, "99 Percent of Human History," refers to the amount of time our species spent as hunter-gatherers. Ponting (1991, 52–55) reflects on the changes that accompany the transition to agriculture, arguing that because of this transition, we tend to value that which looks like us and discount or downplay the unfamiliar. We also tend to see the migrations out of Africa as main story and the people who remained on the continent as less deserving of our attention. Similarly, we tend to focus on signs that our ancestors had begun tilling the soil to grow crops and domesticating animals for various uses as the beginnings of civilization.

Recently, such perspectives have come under critical review. Ponting and many others point to the ecological damage farming practices have caused and suggest that we need to reexamine and revise our concepts of development when it comes to designing and maintaining sustainable human settlements. Whether and when particular peoples developed agriculture was often related more to environmental conditions than to any evolutionary instinct. Why go through the trouble of farming when nature provides all that you need?[10]

For several millennia, between around 7,500 and 4,500 years ago, the enormous Sahara Desert became a fertile land with rivers and lakes teeming with fish, forested hillsides, and grassland plains with wild game (Davidson 1966, 10). During that time, people moved through the green Sahara to and from the north, south, and west, sharing their cultures and technologies and developing elementary forms of farming. These people left remarkable paintings on stone depicting human activities, cattle, and wild animals.[11] As the climate became warmer and drier, most of the inhabitants dispersed to the north, east, and south. Some of them must have settled in the increasingly habitable and extremely fertile Nile River Valley, whose swamps and marshes were drying and forming solid earth. Others developed nomadic cultures, leading camel caravans through the desert (Ibid., 14–18).

I first encountered this sort of climate-informed historical anthropology when reading Basil Davidson. It was through Davidson and other historians and anthropologists, as well as my own travels through West Africa with Jean, that I developed a strong sense of the ancient roots of African culture.

When researching humanity's African roots, I, like Davidson in *Lost Cities of Africa*, limited my focus to Africa south of the Sahara. I didn't want to get caught up in the academic and general controversy surrounding Egypt and its origins. No one could deny that Egypt was the most advanced educational center in the ancient world, and for a long time, it was standard practice for youth from the Mediterranean territories and the Near East who aspired for knowledge to travel to Egypt and study with masters there (James 1954, 7, 15, 18, 45, 48, 53, 58). However, racial prejudice embedded in Eurocentric thinking led scholars of the so-called Enlightenment to insist that Egypt's highly advanced civilization had to have been European rather than African.

If people believe that Africans are uncivilized creatures with no history prior to their contacts with Europeans, it is easier to justify enslaving and colonizing them. Davidson (1966, xxii–xxiii) provides an eloquent critique of this devious manipulation of public opinion in his preface to *Africa in History*.

In many of his books, Davidson presents a broad outline of Africa's grand and complex history, which was hidden or ignored for centuries and is still being discovered and debated today. Whenever possible, he quotes or summarizes ancient reports or letters written, for the most part, by those with direct experience of the events and circumstances they recount. Voices from the past help to bring history to life and offer insight helpful in constructing the future. By ignoring such histories while simultaneously ignoring specific communities in planning our future cities, we lose out on a tremendous amount of wisdom.

Great civilizations in African history—the Kingdom of Kush with its wealthy capital city of Meroë in present-day Sudan, the Land of Punt between the Middle Nile and the Red Sea,[12] and the Kingdom of Aksum with its center located within present-day Ethiopia and Eritrea—participated in extensive trading networks that linked Africa's interior to Asia and Europe via the Indian Ocean and the Mediterranean Sea. For some time, Aksum was the chief supplier of African goods to the Roman Empire, and its kings traced their lineage to King Solomon and the Queen of Sheba (Davidson 1966, 43–44). In the fourth century CE, the ruler of Aksum, Ezana of Axum, became a Christian and made Christianity the official religion of the kingdom (Ibid., 216–18). In the twelfth century CE, King Lalibela of the Zagwe Dynasty in present-day northern Ethiopia directed his artisans to carve eleven churches out of sub-surface, soft volcanic rock—today, the Lalilbela churches are places of pilgrimage and included in the United Nations Educational, Scientific and Cultural Organization (UNESCO) World Heritage List.[13]

When Muslim legal scholar Abu Abdalla Ibn Battuta passed through Cairo in 1326, he must have heard tales of the lavish pilgrimage to Mecca two years earlier by Mansa Musa, the emperor of Mali, who had crossed the Sahara with a retinue of thousands and a hundred camels loaded with unworked gold (Dunn 1986, 290–92). Later, Ibn Battuta traveled along the east coast of Africa and, in one of his famous travel narratives,[14] described the wealthy, multicultural trading centers of Mogadishu, Mombasa, Kilwa, and cities throughout Mozambique as some of the most beautiful places he had ever seen (Hamdun 1995, 16–25; Dunn 1986, 123–28). When the first Europeans—the Portuguese—arrived in East Africa in the late 1400s, they found busy and prosperous port cities enjoying trade goods with trading partners from as far away as Persia and India (Davidson 1970, 176–81). Many cities in East Africa had also been trading with China for centuries, but China had shut down their maritime industries only a few decades before the Portuguese arrived (Ibid., 181–91, 195–97).[15]

Further south lay the impressive stone-work structures known as the Great Zimbabwe, which were constructed between 1050 and 1450 CE—around the same time as the cathedrals in Europe. It was the capital of a Bantu-related civilization that later became the center of the Mutapa Empire and, after that, the Changamire Dynasty (Davidson 1970, 145–47, 262–64).

In West Africa, mastery of iron-working and access to gold helped Ghana become the first trading state in the region around 500 CE. Later, the Mandinka kingdoms of Mali thrived and even held in submission for a half century the powerful Songhai Empire with its great capital city of Gao. In the autumn of 1351, Abu Abdalla Ibn Battuta set out from the capital city of Fez in northern Morocco to visit the Mali Empire, formerly ruled by Mansa Musa, whose extravagant pilgrimage from Africa's west coast to Mecca twenty-seven years earlier had become world news. Ibn Battuta crossed the Atlas Mountains and the Great Desert, joining a caravan that followed one of the trans-Saharan trade routes. He reached the palaces of the new ruler, Mansa Suleiman, Musa's older brother, and spent months exploring the middle-Niger River territories, the same area that Jean and I visited in 1970 (Hamdun 1995, 29–75; Dunn 1986, 290–305). One of the high points—for Ibn Battuta and for us—was visiting the Djinguereber Mosque in Timbuktu, one of the world's capitals for higher learning in the fourteenth and fifteenth centuries and home to one of the world's largest libraries.[16]

A year after we left Africa, an archeologist couple, Roderick and Susan McIntosh, and their colleagues started excavating a series of *tells* (ancient mounds containing remains of successive settlements) near the town of Djenné, Mali. These tells mark the site of the ancient city of Djenné-Djenno. In 2005, I came across Roderick's recently published book, *Ancient Middle Niger: Urbanism and the Self-Organizing Landscape*, and was excited to learn what their excavations had revealed:

> No kings, apparently no armies, no palaces nor citadels—for the longest time we were frustrated in our attempts to imagine the social glue holding together these vast popula-tions. . . . Each [tell] frustratingly resides as a city within a larger urban cluster. (McIntosh 2005, xii)

For many years, archeologists and anthropologists determined whether the inhabitants were "civilized" based on the presence of castles, fortresses, and weapons at sites being unearthed and stud-ied. At Djenné-Djenno, the McIntoshes and their colleagues found signs of coppersmithing and goldsmithing, trade goods from areas outside the region, and ironwork with tools and ornaments, but found no weapons and no evidence of state power (McIntosh 2005, xii).[17] It is an example of heterarchical (in contrast to hierarchical) urbanism. Djenné-Djenno offers an alternative view of the human past and, perhaps, a hopeful model for the future.

Deconstructing Europe's Rise to Dominance

In geographical terms, the peoples of northern and western Europe —Spanish, Portuguese, Dutch, and English—were poorly situated to take part in the burgeoning trade routes that connected Mediterra-nean Europe, Africa, and the Middle East to China and India. They had not yet discovered that they were closer than other seafaring nations to a resource-rich continent across the Atlantic Ocean to the west. All they knew was that they wanted in on the lucrative trade routes to the east. With trade routes through the Middle East controlled by the Ottoman Empire, Europeans were motivated to begin exploring the South Atlantic while West Africans were busy improving their very serviceable overland routes to Mecca and other points eastward (Brown 2007, 190).[18]

Self-serving mythologies aside, the peoples of northwestern Europe in the fifteenth century could make no claim to more advanced culture or greater scientific and technological knowledge than any other people. Meanwhile, between 1000 and 1500 CE, "Chinese, Indian, and Islamic cultures played leading roles [in the exchange of technology, inventions, and socio-religious ideas] while Europe played catch-up from its location as a backwater" (Brown 2007, 186).

In addition to the advanced cultures in Africa, the Middle East, and China, there were highly civilized societies in the Americas. In *1491: New Revelations of the Americas before Columbus*, Charles C. Mann (2006, 396) documents what he calls the "great antiquity, size, and sophistication of [New World] Indian societies." For example, when Cortés invaded the Aztec Empire in 1519, Moctezuma's capital city of Tenochtitlan, on the site now occupied by Mexico City, was larger and more opulent than any European city (Ibid., 141).

Geography scholar James Blaut (2000, 2) expresses what has now become the majority view among scholars: "I believe that the rise of Europe—that is, the surging of Europe past other civilizations in wealth and power. . . resulted not from any unique, pre-existing internal qualities, but from Europe's location on the globe." On the eve of the European expansion in 1500, the people of northwestern Europe, whom we now think of as representing dominant global societies, were lagging in comparison with the African urban centers of that era. By contrast, many enslaved Africans, ancestors of contemporary African Americans, came from cities and villages with traditions that were well established long before the arrival of Portuguese explorers. Europe, Blaut (Ibid.) explains,

> acquired incalculable riches from the Americas after 1492. This led to the rise to political power of the merchant capitalist class and its allies, and in many other ways led, directly and indirectly, to the awakening of Europeans to the rest of the world and the transformation of Europe's society and economy. Here was an entire hemisphere, North and South America, six times the size of Europe itself, almost

emptied of its population by the importation of Old World diseases during the sixteenth century.

The Columbian Exchange and the Global Economy

Columbus sailed across the Atlantic in 1492 in search of a westward route to Chinese and Indian trading centers, but instead touched ground in the Caribbean, specifically the Bahamas, Cuba, and Hispaniola (island home of present-day Haiti and the Dominican Republic).[19] This was the birth of the so-called Atlantic Community. As is well known, the conquest, enslavement, and genocide of the indigenous Americans began at that moment.

In 1972, historian Alfred W. Crosby published *The Columbian Exchange: Biological and Cultural Consequences of 1492*. The term "Columbian Exchange" refers to the widespread exchange of animals, plants, culture, human populations, communicable diseases, technology, and ideas between the American and Afro-Eurasian hemispheres following Columbus's voyage. The exchange continued with colonization and trade by Europeans in the Americas and the exponential growth of the slave trade in Africa and the Americas.

We are usually taught to think of the Industrial Revolution of the late eighteenth and nineteenth centuries as the decisive turning point toward modernity. While its technological innovations did indeed revolutionize the world, the Industrial Revolution rested upon the economic foundation of the capture, imprisonment, and enslavement of at least twelve million people who were transported from Africa across the Atlantic and used as an energy source to build and operate plantations. In *The Empire of Necessity: Slavery, Freedom, and Deception in the New World*, history professor and journalist Greg Grandin (2014, 28) succinctly explains the role of slaves in the new economy:

> Enslaved peoples were at one and the same time investments (purchased and then rented out as laborers), credit (used to secure loans), property, commodities, and capital, making them an odd mix of abstract and concrete value.

The consistent pattern in this prelude to industrialization is that enslaved people were treated above all as property to be used at their owner's will, like farm animals.

Simultaneously, agricultural land was treated as though it were a kind of mine from which one could simply extract raw materials. In general, the plantations destroyed rich and complex New World ecosystems, such as rainforests and wetlands, installing in their place monocultures—especially sugarcane, rice, tobacco, and cotton, and later, indigo, coffee, and chocolate (Merchant 2002, 41–42, 46, 53).

The story of the combination of slave labor and environmental plunder (accompanied by the displacement and genocide of native peoples) is usually told as though it begins after Columbus sailed across the Atlantic in 1492, but it begins, more accurately, with the so-called Age of Discovery—a loosely defined period from the fifteenth to eighteenth centuries marked by extensive overseas exploration by Europeans, the rise of European influence and colonialism, and the beginning of globalization. The Age of Discovery, also known as the Age of Exploration, began in 1418 when Prince Henry of Portugal commissioned ships to explore the west coast of Africa. In 1419, the Portuguese discovered the small uninhabited island of Madeira about 280 miles off the coast of Morocco and measuring just thirty-five miles long and fourteen miles wide. The pattern that the Portuguese followed in colonizing the island became the basis for later colonization efforts in the New World and elsewhere.

Madeira's colonization by the Portuguese began within a year after its discovery. *Ilha da Madeira*, or Madeira Island, meaning "wooded island," was brimming with tall, lush trees when the Portuguese arrived, and by 1472, 280 tons of wood was being exported per year, finally peaking at almost 2,500 tons in 1506. After a few colonists landed and attempted to grow food for themselves with mixed success, commercial interests arrived, aggressively clearing all the trees from the coastal plateaus, selling the wood at a high price in Europe, planting sugarcane, and importing slaves to work the fields. The harvested sugarcane was transported to mills where the juice was crushed out and boiled down to sugar in boilers fueled by Madeira's forests. When cultivation with natural rainfall did not yield the level of sugarcane production desired by investors, they ordered slaves to perform the extremely hazardous task of building stone *levadas* (aqueducts) that would carry water down from the mountains to irrigate the fields. Hundreds of slaves died. The dramatic story of how the Portuguese exploited Madeira's natural resources using the enforced labor of enslaved Africans is recounted in *A Forest Journey: The Story of Wood and Civilization* by John Perlin (1989, 249–62).

Within one generation (1472–1506), Madeira became Europe's number one supplier of sugar, but by the end of that generation, sugarcane production on the island began to plummet and soon stopped altogether when the last of the island's available trees had been chopped down. Without wood for the boilers, sugar could no longer be produced at a profit. The investors' solution was to pull up stakes, "discover" another untapped natural resource, take some slaves, and start over again. Excited by the return on capital investment demonstrated on Madeira, Spain instituted sugarcane production on Hispaniola very shortly after Columbus had discovered it. Portugal developed sugar production in Brazil while the English, Dutch, and French also got involved in varying degrees, mostly in the West Indies (Moore 2000, 414, 417–25).[20] The main difference between plantation development in the New World and that on Madeira was the presence of native populations in the Americas that settlers killed, expelled, enslaved, or otherwise subjugated.

Eventually, sugar became the basis of the global economy, and millions of people—including slaves—became addicted to it. Rum, distilled alcohol made from molasses, became a booming global business to the point where it became so highly prized that it functioned as a kind of currency in the New World. Millions also became addicted to tobacco, coffee, and chocolate—plants whose monoculture production wiped out vast swaths of precious New World biodiversity.

Wealth extraction industries in the New World came at a profound cost to the local people and environment. The Spanish Empire became the most powerful economy in the world for more than a century (from the early 1500s to the mid-1600s) thanks in large part to silver mining in New Spain (present-day Mexico). In the process, between 1558 to 1804, the Spanish chopped down 151,000 square miles of forests for charcoal—an area larger than the country of Germany (Studnicki-Gizbert and Schecter 2010, 99). Silver smelting also resulted in the introduction of staggering amounts of highly toxic mercury to the New World environment (Nriagu 1994, 167).

The wholesale plunder of New World ecosystems for profit rapidly and irreversibly changed our planet (Berry 1999, 3). Nonetheless, the fact of this huge ecological transformation has mostly disappeared from public consciousness thanks to the tunnel vision of Eurocentrism and US-centrism in the dominant culture's conception and conveyance of history.

Every bit as important, but just as effectively consigned to the hazy fringes of historical narrative, is the fact that the wealth that underlay the technological explosion of the past 250 years was generated through the enslavement of millions of Africans and African Americans, the wholesale plundering of mineral and botanical resources in the Americas, and the genocide of millions of indigenous Americans. We cannot even begin to understand the convergence between the so-called achievements of Western civilization and the impending ecological collapse we are now inheriting without bringing the legacy of racial exploitation into the open.

From 1500 to 1800, five-sixths of all trans-Atlantic voyagers were enslaved Africans. During this three-hundred-ear period, between twelve and fifteen million Africans arrived in the Americas as slaves while millions more perished along the journey, commonly known as the Middle Passage (Games 2008, 52). It was surely the largest human migration of all time. Even though they were forced to come in what were essentially portable prisons under the most miserable conditions imaginable, Africans were making a westward migration that completed a circling of the globe that had begun with the eastward migration out of Africa some fifty to eighty millennia earlier.

I believe that, traumatic though it was, the period in which millions of Africans were rudely transformed into African Americans—in the span of approximately four centuries—was also a major turning point in the history of humanity on earth. Millions were captured, torn from their homes, transported across the Atlantic Ocean, and sold. Required to labor for their "owners," they produced vast wealth that supported lifestyles of leisure and refinement for the slave masters and financed the development of the Industrial Revolution. With its enormous scale and intercontinental scope, the Atlantic slave trade was an early manifestation of globalization.[21]

Cities Shaped by the Atlantic Slave Trade

To understand the contemporary challenges of race in American cities and the relationship between African Americans and urbanization, we must examine the role of the trans-Atlantic slave trade in the development of maritime cities. Contemporary forms of urban inequality in the United States can be traced to unresolved issues and injustices lingering from the slave trade era.

The labor of African slaves laid the groundwork for the transformation of the global economy.[22] Between 1500 and 1800, around forty or fifty maritime cities and towns emerged on four continents and in the Caribbean—their growth fueled by profit from the slave trade. Records show, for the first time, that the deforestation that accompanied the development of the silver and gold mines and sugar plantations of this period, as well as ship building and construction of urban centers, brought about irreversible climate change (Grove 1995, 1). Writing in the early sixteenth century, Cristobal Colon noted that "since the removal of forests that once covered those islands [Madeira, Canary, and Azore Islands], they do not have so much mist and rain as before" (Moore 2000, 425).[23]

At the time of the American Revolution, New York City had a larger population of slaves than any other city in North America except Charleston, South Carolina. New York City and Charleston were not the only maritime cities in the seventeenth and eighteenth centuries whose increasing prosperity was based upon profits from the slave trade and plantation agriculture. In the sixteenth and seventeenth centuries, close to fifty settlements in the British Isles, France, Spain, West Africa, the Caribbean, and South and North America were built as a direct consequence of the slave trade.

Numerous cities, particularly port towns, grew and thrived on the wealth generated by the slave trade. Liverpool, a shipbuilding town in England, prospered to such an extent during this period[24] that most of its streets are named after prominent slave traders.[25] Other cities whose growth was financed by the slave trade include Amsterdam and Rotterdam in the Netherlands; Bristol, Manchester, and London in England; Nantes in France; Lisbon in Portugal; Seville in Spain; Gorée and Dakar in Senegal; Elmina in Ghana; Lagos in Nigeria; Port Au Prince, Santo Domingo, Nassau, Kingston, and Havana in the Caribbean; Bahia in Curaçao; Rio de Janeiro, Porto de Santos, Porto de Paranaguá, and São Sebastião in Brazil; Montevideo in Uruguay; Buenos Aires in Argentina; and New Orleans, Charleston, Baltimore, Philadelphia, and Providence in North America.[26]

My interest in the mercantile cities of the Atlantic Basin originated from my trip with Jean to Africa in 1970 when I began to realize that these cities owed their growth and prosperity to the slave trade. After my "The Big House and the Slave Quarter" essays were published in *Landscape* magazine in 1976, I tried to decide whether to follow up with an essay about the Civil War and Reconstruction or with another about slavery in the development of the cities of the Atlantic Basin. I put both projects on the backburner for many years. My interest in the mercantile cities of the Atlantic was restimulated when I lived in New York City while working at the Ford Foundation during the first decade of the twenty-first century. On my return from a visit to India, I made a quick side trip to Liverpool, England, to visit the International Slavery Museum, which had opened in August of 2007. A first of its kind, the museum looks at historical and contemporary slavery and explores human rights issues. The vision for the museum, set out by its founding director, Dr. David Fleming, in the brochure I picked up, particularly moved me:

The transatlantic slave trade was the greatest forced migration in history. And yet the story of the mass enslavement of Africans by Europeans is one of resilience and survival against all the odds, and is a testament to the unquenchable nature of the human spirit. . . .

. . . Our aim is to address ignorance and misunderstanding by looking at the deep and permanent impact of slavery and the slave trade on Africa, South America, the United States, the Caribbean and Western Europe. Thus we will increase our understanding of the world around us. (International Slavery Museum 2017)

The mercantile cities on the Atlantic rim can be seen as both a tragedy and a triumph of globalization. The tragedy is the wanton desecration of people and nature by a small group of humans who appropriated planetary resources and the wealth and labor of human populations to satisfy their greed and desire for self-aggrandizement. This dubious accomplishment transformed living environments into industrial units of production whose benefits and burdens accrue to all of us. For indigenous cultures destroyed by mercantilism, for populations left behind by the rank opportunism of European expansion, and for descendants of captured and exploited Africans, it is essential to retell the story of the slave trade and the rise of wealthy maritime cities.

Slavery and the Modern Economic System

Slavery was at the heart of a trans-Atlantic triangular trade pattern. Merchant ships sailed from Europe to Africa exchanging manufactured goods—guns and gunpowder, rum, glass beads, metals, and textiles for ornamentation (Tibbles 2000, 1)—for black people at a profit and then transporting their human cargo across the ocean and selling the enslaved Africans to colonists, merchants, and planters in North America, the Caribbean, or South America for another round of profit.[27] Finally, the ships transported goods grown and harvested by African slaves—sugar, rice, tobacco, and cotton—back to Europe for a third round of profit. At the core of city building in places like Liverpool was a plainly expressed and unambiguous desire to take advantage of this very profitable system. The huge accumulations of capital generated by this process funded maritime enterprises, factories, and the development of port cities, as well as the lifestyles of the elite.

People had been captured and sold in Africa (and in many other places) since ancient times (Davis 2006, 27–47), but the trans-Atlantic slave trade marked the beginning of a different relationship between people and planet Earth as a whole, particularly with its oceans. Before Europeans mastered the arts of shipbuilding and seafaring, the Atlantic Ocean had been a barrier. Subsequently, it became a connector, and England's proximity to it was a big advantage in the new game of transporting people and goods from one continent to the other.

Raw materials from the New World built wealth in Europe and the colonies. Meanwhile, in the American South, descendants of African people worked the land—in some places, as many as twelve generations—without receiving the benefit of their labor. Slaving under the hot sun, they cleared forests, drained swamps, unloaded ships, built roads, and planted and harvested cash crops that made their masters wealthy.

In *The Half Has Never Been Told*, Edward Baptist (2014) draws on slave narratives, plantation records, and other primary sources to create a poignant narrative demonstrating how US entrepreneurs used slavery to create a cotton empire and build a modern industrial capitalist economy. The labor of African slaves was used not only for plantation agriculture but also to build infrastructure in emerging urban centers, like New York City:

> Slaves constructed Fort Amsterdam and its successors along the Battery. They built the wall from which Wall Street gets its name. They built the roads, the docks, and most of the important buildings of the early city—the first city hall, the first Dutch and English churches, Fraunces Tavern, the city prison and the city hospital. (New-York Historical Society 2016)[28]

In 1991, construction workers in Lower Manhattan discovered a seventeenth-century burial ground for both free and enslaved Africans during an excavation for building a federal office building. After years of scientific, archeological, and historical research, the General Services Administration partnered with the National Parks Service to dedicate, create, and open the African Burial Ground

National Monument and visitor center in 2007.[29] I was fortunate to be living in Manhattan at the time and closely followed the reports and reflections in the media. I wondered about the relationship between the Lower Manhattan of the seventeenth and eighteenth centuries and the Lower Manhattan of the twenty-first century—an integral center of the global economy. I asked myself what the significance of this rediscovery might be for contemporary urban planning and development. My first thought was that people would become more conscious of the impact and significance of historical underpinnings like the kidnapping and exploitation of African people. Such awareness can lead to a deeper understanding and greater capacity for resolving problems we face today.

In the eighteenth and nineteenth centuries, entrepreneurs in the North capitalized on the expanding production and trade of cotton and sugar in the South to make New York City the leading port and global financial center. It is no surprise that African Americans—enslaved and free—provided the bulk of the labor that built not only the New York infrastructure but also the White House, the US Capitol, and other early government buildings.[30] In order to assume any kind of moral authority in today's world, Americans need to understand and acknowledge their enormous debt to black people, as well as to the indigenous people from whom they took the land. It has become increasingly apparent that Americans owe enslaved Africans and their descendants deep appreciation and an enormous debt of gratitude. No amount of reparations could repay the debt incurred.

Recognition of the price paid in human life and liberty for economic advancement—and the costs of resources extracted as nature's systems were exploited—must inform and guide us as we work to transform our cities and regions. We must forge a new path illuminated by justice, respect for the dignity of each and every human being, and determination to maintain and restore the web of life as the foundation for health and sustainability.

CHAPTER 11

The Landscape
of Freedom

THE 1893 WORLD'S COLUMBIAN Exposition in Chicago, also known as the Chicago World's Fair, was an immense attraction that commemorated the four-hundred-year anniversary of Columbus's arrival in the New World and celebrated the achievements of many nations while emphasizing America's progress and accomplishments. However, when Frederick Douglass, Ida B. Wells, and other black leaders approached the fair organizers and offered to create an exhibit that celebrated African Americans and their achievements since emancipation, they were advised to inquire whether any of the state selection committees would be interested. With no black representation on any of the committees and no white committee members willing to grant them entry, African Americans found themselves completely shut out (Foner 2005, 215). Not to be defeated, Wells used her journalistic and organizing skills to produce[1] an eighty-one-page pamphlet titled *The Reason Why the Colored American Is Not in the World's Columbian Exposition.*

Wells (1893, 1) wrote the preface for the pamphlet, immediately challenging the racism of the Chicago World's Fair:

> That which would best illustrate her [America's] moral grandeur has been ignored. The exhibit of the progress made by a race in 25 years of freedom as against 250 years of slavery,

would have been the greatest tribute to the greatness and progressiveness of American institutions which could have been shown the world.[2]

Since Frederick Douglass had once been Haiti's consul general, he was asked to represent Haiti at the fair. Wells and Douglass used the opportunity to distribute the pamphlet at a table in front of the Haiti exhibit.[3]

In my architectural training, the Chicago World's Fair had been spoken of as a high point in the evolution of American architecture. The attentive planning of the layout of the fair was a prelude to the discipline of city planning. The massive neoclassical buildings designed by prominent architects of the day housed the exhibits. Except for Louis Sullivan's Transportation Building, the buildings were not particularly innovative, but they certainly demonstrated Chicago's recovery from the devastating fire of 1871. The enormous Ferris wheel was an extravagant device intended to rival the Eiffel Tower at the World's Fair in Paris in 1889. The backstory of African American exclusion and protest at the event was particularly relevant to me and my understanding of black people's contributions to the field of architecture. Despite the absence of an exhibit to celebrate it, the experience of African Americans after emancipation tells a rich story—one that I have come to call the Landscape of Freedom.

Abolition

The abolitionist movement started on the slave ships. Many of the sailors charged with boarding captive Africans onto ships were not completely in agreement with the idea and practice of slavery. Some of them had been coerced or tricked into service, and others had been trapped by limited opportunities for employment. Some sailors were quite sympathetic to the slaves despite being in positions of dominance over them. When English abolitionist Thomas Clarkson, for example, undertook the collection of first-person accounts of atrocities on the slave ships, his best informants were the sailors. He printed their accounts and distributed the tracts widely to inspire public outrage and advance the cause of abolition (Rediker 2007, 321–31).

Boycotts organized by English women—the main purchasers of food for their families—of slave-grown sugar from the Caribbean islands during the 1790s made significant impact (Davis 2006, 232–49). In 1833, the British Parliament received over five thousand anti-slavery petitions with 2.5 million signers, including one unwieldy half-mile-long petition sewn and pasted together (Ibid., 237).

In the United States, the main actors in the struggle for abolition were former slaves. Their dignified and articulate testimonies awakened the conscience of many whites and dispelled ignorant assumptions that blacks were inferior. Stories of the brutal and demeaning life conditions they had endured under slavery were very effective in awakening listeners to the evils of the practice. Their white allies were also crucial in the struggle.

Naturally, African American people, both enslaved and free, supported the abolition of slavery although it was rarely safe to express such an opinion. Benjamin Banneker, the famous black surveyor, scientist, and farmer who helped design the layout of the nation's capital, corresponded with Thomas Jefferson about the almanacs Banneker produced. In his letters, he criticized Jefferson for having slaves and urged the ending of slavery, which he compared to the enslavement of the American colonies by the British crown. Abolitionist groups first published Banneker's letters in a pamphlet and, later, included them in the 1793 edition of the almanac (Cerami 2002, 168–74, 193–94). Banneker's writings laid a foundation for later abolitionist leaders, including Frederick Douglass, an escaped slave, who became a leading spokesperson for the movement.

The abolitionist movement in the United States started to gain momentum in the early 1800s after the new nation was established. In the late 1830s, Frederick Douglass discovered William Lloyd Garrison, a white man passionately devoted to immediate abolition who was publishing a periodical called *The Liberator*. Later, they were joined by Sojourner Truth, another escaped slave who was also active in the women's movement. Harriet Tubman, another powerful abolition activist, returned to the South nineteen times to lead groups along the Underground Railroad—she led a total of three hundred individuals to freedom (Bradford 1886, 6). These courageous and inspiring individuals and others like them traveled around the country lecturing about the evils of slavery.

In the fifty years after the American Revolution, every Northern state had outlawed slavery. It had once seemed likely that it would disappear in the South as well, but the invention of the cotton gin in 1793 led to a massive increase in cotton production, making slavery indispensable to both the South and the North, a process documented extensively in *Empire of Cotton: A Global History*, Sven Beckert's (2014) prize-winning account of the origins of modern capitalism. The national economy depended on cotton, which, it seemed, could not exist without the labor of enslaved workers. According to historian David Blight (2013),

> slaves were the single largest financial asset in the entire American economy, worth more than all manufacturing, all railroad, steamship lines, and other transportation systems, put together. The only thing in the American economy worth more as simply a financial asset was the land itself [that had been prepared for agricultural use by the enslaved of earlier generations when they cleared forests and drained swamps].

Historian Edward Baptist (2014, 352) completes the picture, explaining that

> The 3.2 million people enslaved in the United States had a market value of $1.3 billion in 1850—one-fifth of the nation's wealth and almost equal to the entire gross national product.[4]

To lose the essential resource of slave labor was unthinkable to most whites, but an increasing number of people began to see the enslavement of human beings as a violation of God's law. Those moved by this deep moral conviction, however, naively hoped that slavery could end by the power of love and the spirit of repentance.

The set of laws known as the Compromise of 1850 ended the trading but not the owning of slaves in Washington, DC. It described borders and stipulated whether slavery would be allowed or restricted in some newly admitted states. It also amended the Fugitive Slave Act of 1793 to stipulate that any citizen, in either the North or South, could be required to help catch a suspected runaway. The law imposed large fines and prison sentences for aiding fugitives and made it easy for unscrupulous men to kidnap free blacks on mere suspicion (or, more accurately, suggestion) and sell them into slavery—as the free-born Solomon Northup experienced when he was kidnapped in New York and sold in 1841 to a Louisiana plantation, where remained as a slave until his release twelve years later.[5] Popular reaction to the injustice of the law strengthened the abolitionist movement.

Another big boost to the abolitionist cause came from Harriet Beecher Stowe, a white wife, mother, and part-time writer, who wrote *Uncle Tom's Cabin: Life Among the Lowly*. The anti-slavery novel was serialized in the *National Era*, an abolitionist periodical, in 1851 and published as a book in 1852, appealing to a wide audience and drawing sympathizers to the abolitionist movement. It was later adapted to the stage and translated into over sixty languages.

Emancipation

Freedom from enslavement had long been dreamed of and prayed for. On January 1, 1863, near midnight, word went out that Abraham Lincoln had signed the Emancipation Proclamation. Almost three years later, in December of 1865, the Thirteenth Amendment was added to the US Constitution, banning slavery in all the states.

Toward the end of the Civil War, Congress established the Bureau of Refugees, Freedmen, and Abandoned Lands, commonly called the Freedmen's Bureau. As the first federal social service agency in the country, it assisted the transition of four million black people from slavery to freedom in the aftermath of the Civil War and helped manage the lands abandoned by plantation owners. The bureau also established over 4,300 schools in the South (Schneider and Schneider 2000, 364).

In the wake of emancipation, the American Missionary Association[6] began working with the Freedmen's Bureau and the Union Army to establish schools and institutions of higher learning. The 117 historically black colleges and universities in the United States, most notably Tuskegee Institute (now Tuskegee University) and Howard, Atlanta, and Fisk Universities, are some of what remain today of the bureau's efforts. During the post–Civil War period, African Americans celebrated their emancipation by constructing hundreds of new churches, schools, and towns across the United States.

In Charleston, South Carolina, during the final year of the Civil War, the Confederates had converted the city's Washington Race Course and Jockey Club into an outdoor prison where Union captives were kept in horrible conditions. By the time the war ended, at least 257 prisoners had died of disease and been hastily thrown into a mass grave behind the grandstand. After the Confederate army evacuated the city, black workmen went to the site and gave the Union dead a proper burial. They also built a high fence around the cemetery, whitewashed it, and inscribed on an archway over an entrance the words "Martyrs of the Race Course."

On May 1, 1865, in cooperation with white missionaries and teachers, a grand parade was staged on the racetrack to honor the Union dead: three thousand black schoolchildren came first, carrying armloads of roses and singing "John Brown's Body," the Union marching song; several hundred black women followed with baskets of flowers, wreaths, and crosses; and then came black men marching in cadence followed by contingents of Union infantrymen. Within the cemetery enclosure, a choir of black children sang "We'll Rally Around the Flag," "The Star-Spangled Banner," and spirituals before Bible readings by a series of black ministers. After the ceremony, the crowd moved to the infield to picnic, listen to speeches, and watch soldiers drill (Blight 2011).[7] Undoubtedly, my ancestor William Jervay was among their number and a proud participant in the day's events.

The Hope of Reconstruction

In *Reconstruction: America's Unfinished Revolution 1863–1877,* historian Eric Foner (1988, 95–96) conveys the exuberant and hope-filled spirit of the freed people:

The rise of the independent black church provides only the most striking example of the thriving institutional structure blacks created in the aftermath of emancipation. A host of fraternal, benevolent, and mutual-aid societies also sprang into existence. Even before the Civil War, free blacks had formed fraternal organizations, and secret societies of various kinds had existed among the slaves. In early Reconstruction, blacks created literally thousands of such organizations; a partial list includes burial societies, debating clubs, Masonic lodges, fire companies, drama societies, trade associations, temperance clubs, and equal rights leagues. . . . Although their activities generally took place away from white observation, they appeared in public in the processions and celebrations that seemed ubiquitous, especially in Southern cities, during Reconstruction. . . . [T]hese voluntary associations embodied a spirit of collective self-improvement. . . . [T]he spirit of mutual self-help extended outward from the societies to embrace destitute nonmembers. In 1865 and 1866, blacks in Nashville, Jackson, New Orleans, and Atlanta, as well as in many rural areas, raised money to establish orphanages, soup kitchens, employment agencies, and poor relief funds. In some areas, such as a poverty-stricken corner of West Virginia, black organizations contributed money to aid suffering poor whites. . . . Perhaps the most striking illustration of the freedmen's quest for self-improvement was their seemingly unquenchable thirst for education. . . . Access to education for themselves and their children was, for blacks, central to the meaning of freedom.

For a brief period after emancipation, up until 1877,[8] life improved for most black people. For the first time in US history, African

Americans, the majority of whom had been enslaved, could own their own bodies. They could make decisions about where to live and how to spend their time. They could form families and build community institutions. They could choose when, where, and for whom to work. The Thirteenth, Fourteenth, and Fifteenth Amendments to the Constitution were passed, and African American men had the right to vote. For the first time, African Americans were elected to state legislatures in the South. My ancestor William Jervay was among these. Born a slave on a South Carolina plantation, he fled as a teenager to join the Union army. After the war, he started and operated a small store in Charleston and after five years, had saved enough money to buy a 257-acre farm. He served in South Carolina's constitutional convention and then in the state house (1868–71) and senate (1872–76) (Egerton 2014, 54).[9]

New Methods of Forced Labor

Meanwhile, shortly after the war ended, on Good Friday, April 14, 1865, President Abraham Lincoln was shot and died the next day. His vice president, Andrew Johnson, was a Southerner. Although not from the slaveholding class, he opposed abolition and colluded with disgruntled Southerners to keep the status of African Americans as close to slavery as possible.[10] The former slaveholding states quickly passed laws, known as the Black Codes, severely restricting the freedom of the emancipated people and ensuring their availability as cheap labor. Many states required black adults to sign yearly labor contracts and black youth to be apprenticed as unpaid laborers until adulthood; noncompliance carried the risk of arrest for vagrancy and enforced servitude to pay off the fines and court costs to which were added the costs of board, clothing, and medical care, which seemed never to be paid off.

Practices like debt peonage[11] and convict leasing became prevalent. Many black people were apprehended on fabricated or flimsy charges and quickly convicted and sentenced. When fines and charges were levied and the prisoners became debtors, a white man would usually appear and insist on paying their fines, which made them indebted to him. He could then hire them out as unpaid workers to planters, mine operators, road and railroad contractors, and lumber and turpentine harvesters where they were subject to beatings, shackles, insufficient food and clothing, and unsafe living and working conditions. Many died as a result.[12]

Journalist Douglas Blackmon researched the forced-labor practices that helped extend slavery long after the Civil War and shared his findings in 2008 in *Slavery by Another Name: The Re-Enslavement of Black Americans from the Civil War to World War II*. In 2012, he collaborated with director Sam Pollard on a companion documentary film of the same name for PBS. In a short video on the making of the documentary, Blackmon takes descendants of siblings of Green Cottenham, the previously unknown but emblematic character on whom he focused in the book, to a small graveyard where Scipio, their ancestor who was brought from Africa, is likely buried. In a voice-over, Blackmon marvels at the

> forgiveness that African Americans have shown—the willingness to forgive and move on. . . . All this represents, in many ways, such terrible things. It would be legitimate for them to be angry at this, and yet there's none of that. There's just an honest willingness to try to understand their own story. (Pollard, Allan, and Blackmon 2012)

Understanding my own story and understanding our collective story has been an important part of my life's work and is an important part of what I'm trying to do in this book. I appreciate Blackmon's perspective, which celebrates our compassion and resilience and highlights the heroic nature of our story.

Blackmon (2008) chronicles unsuccessful federal attempts to outlaw and end the worst abuses. Following the abolition of slavery, most workers were treated more cruelly than they were during slavery since they no longer represented a valuable investment and could be easily replaced. The Radical Republicans, a faction of politicians within the Republican Party who held a majority in the US Congress after the 1866 elections, declared the Black Codes illegal, but did not have sufficient authority and federal support to curb the profitable practice of convict leasing.

The Black Agrarian Movement

After emancipation, black people worked to create sustainable, land-based lifestyles. They wanted the freedom and dignity of having land of their own. Up until the end of the nineteenth century, many African Americans, both enslaved and free, were inspired by the democratic ideals expressed by Thomas Jefferson even though he owned black slaves and profited from their labor. There was a general feeling that a way to create a future for the black community was to get control of land and engage in subsistence farming to meet the needs of local communities.

There were several movements that involved cooperative relationships with whites who were also engaged in agriculture. Practicing the craft of farming was a central theme in African American culture throughout the nineteenth century and into the twentieth. There were many who were attached to the agrarian way of life, and there were several institutions that sprang up all around the country that included agricultural programs in their curriculum. In fact, the land-grant colleges were established around the idea of serving the local community through sharing research grounded in local needs (particularly agriculture), a major theme in the historically black colleges.

Tuskegee Institute, one of the most notable black colleges, was built on the idea of teaching people to work the land and develop a range of other skills necessary for survival and self-reliance. Its founder and chief exponent, Booker T. Washington, became a passionate advocate of scientific agriculture and industrial education. In fact, it was Washington I had in mind when developing the Natural Energy Pavilion at UC Berkeley with its off-the-grid, self-reliant architecture and engineering.

Another prominent figure on the Tuskegee faculty was George Washington Carver, who performed remarkable experiments and discovered scores of new uses for familiar plants. Care for the land

and farm animals was central to the environmental experience of African Americans.

Not surprisingly, African Americans encountered obstacles to land ownership—for them, it was never a level playing field. For example, when President Lincoln signed the Homestead Act in 1862 in the middle of the Civil War, land that had been confiscated from the Native Americans was given to white settlers who were willing to develop it—African Americans were not eligible. Big land grants, meanwhile, went to the railroads. After the Civil War, most of the abandoned plantation lands acquired by the Freedmen's Bureau were returned to former slaveholders. The black people who had been working these lands—in many cases, for several generations— were reduced to sharecropping or eviction. Despite such difficulties, historian Kimberly Smith (2007, 72) states that "by 2010, southern blacks had acquired about 15 million acres of land, and nearly 17 percent of southern farm owners were black."

By the mid-1880s, African Americans had established many local chapters of the Colored Farmers' National Alliance and other agrarian and labor organizations. Within a few years, thousands of black and white chapters of the Farmers' Alliance had formed. In 1891, a broad network of farmers, many of whom had formed economic cooperatives, established the People's Party and called for a national subsidy program, reform of the credit system, and enforcement mechanisms to regulate railroads.

African American Struggle for Economic Rights

The upsurge of political activity by African Americans quickly became a threat to Southern Democrats who saw it as a second Reconstruction. Threatening and exclusionary tactics, including physical attacks, ballot manipulation, discriminatory laws, and poll taxes, were frequently utilized by Southern Democrats to discourage and prevent African Americans from voting. Lynchings, along with attacks and assassinations of political leaders who supported the rights of the freed people, increased during the late nineteenth century. By 1896, the Democratic Party had succeeded in suppressing the black vote in the South, and the violence, racist propaganda, and intimidation against blacks continued on an even broader scale. Booker T. Washington, who became a spokesman for African Americans, especially after the death of Frederick Douglass, preached a gospel of economic self-reliance and accommodation to white demands for disenfranchisement and segregation.[13] W. E. B. Du Bois (1903) devoted the third chapter of *The Souls of Black Folk* to a sympathetic but critical examination of Washington's expressed ideas, which Du Bois felt underlay the trend toward political disenfranchisement, civil inequalities, and withdrawal of access to higher education for capable and aspiring black youth.

Many, if not most, white Southerners felt it was their patriotic duty to "redeem" the South, which meant protecting or restoring white supremacy. Accomplishing that mission required ruthless willingness to use violence and terror, as well as dishonest dealings with the freed people and their allies. In his 2014 article titled "The Case for Reparations," Ta-Nehisi Coates recounts the story of Clyde Ross. When Clyde, born in 1923, was a child,

> Mississippi authorities claimed his father owed $3,000 in back taxes. The elder Ross could not read. He did not have a lawyer. He did not know anyone at the local courthouse. He could not expect the police to be impartial. Effectively, the Ross family had no way to contest the claim and no protection under the law. The authorities seized the land. They seized the [family's] buggy. They took the cows, hogs, and mules. And so for the upkeep of separate but equal, the entire Ross family was reduced to sharecropping.
>
> This was hardly unusual. In 2001, the Associated Press published a three-part investigation into the theft of black-owned land stretching back to the antebellum period. The series documented some 406 victims and twenty-four thousand acres of land valued at tens of millions of dollars. The land was taken through means ranging from legal chicanery to terrorism. (Coates 2014)

If the promise of Reconstruction was the full participation of black people in American society, its failure betrayed them. For the most part, land was returned to or remained in the hands of the Southern aristocracy; the system of sharecropping replaced slavery.

The conventional environmental narrative ignores the African American experience. Such a narrative also tends to ignore the diversity of European experiences with the land they left behind—the exploitation and mistreatment of the Irish, Jewish, and Italian people, for example.

After the Civil War, a New South emerged with the formerly rebelling states functioning like colonies—a source of raw materials and cheap labor—to the industrial North. What changed on the plantations? Ex-slaves scattered across the landscape, building cabins throughout the fields (approximately thirty to forty acres per house site). Fields became smaller and crop patterns became diverse as each black family now worked a separate plot of land. Roads and trails were constructed to provide access to the scattered settlements. Freed blacks constructed churches, schools, and even whole towns and utopian communal experiments.[14]

In her *Washington Post* article on black towns, journalist De-Neen Brown (2015a) describes Zora Neale Hurston's hometown of Eatonville, Florida, along with twenty-one others. Hurston had revisited Eatonville in the early 1930s to collect stories and information for her upcoming folklore collection, *Mules and Men*, and paints a delightful picture of the town: "Eatonville, the city of five lakes, three croquet courts, three hundred brown skins, three hundred good swimmers, plenty guavas, two schools and no jail house" (Ibid.).[15] It sounds quite heavenly, but despite the hopeful spirit and the promise of black communal growth in those years, the towns and communities the emancipated people established were largely doomed in the face of unrelenting efforts to restore white supremacy.

Generally, to the extent possible, blacks were confined to rural areas or, if allowed in the cities, to certain occupations and neighborhoods. All this and much more is covered in C. Vann Woodward's (1955) *The Strange Career of Jim Crow*, a classic analysis of the state of affairs in the South. Descriptive text on the back cover of my second revised edition explains that since the book was quoted so often to counter arguments for segregation, Martin Luther King Jr. called it "the historical bible of the civil rights movement."

The dark undercurrent in the story of post–Civil War America is white mob violence. Growing numbers of books document the horrors black Americans endured—murders, beatings, and lynchings, along with arson and theft of black homes, neighborhoods, and towns. In *The Wars of Reconstruction: The Brief, Violent History of America's Most Progressive Era*, history professor and prolific writer Douglas Egerton tells the stories of hundreds of black activists and officeholders who stood firm against whites determined to "redeem" the culture of white supremacy. Egerton (2014) details the long chain of assassinations; house, church, and school burnings; voter intimidation and attacks; and other acts of white violence aimed at dismantling Reconstruction and ushering in Jim Crow. At the same time, he chronicles acts of resistance and self-defense by newly empowered black leaders.[16]

In *Buried in the Bitter Waters: The Hidden History of Racial Cleansing in America*, journalist Elliot Jaspin (2008), curious about why there were so many all-white towns in the United States, unearths stories and reports of white mobs during the first part of the twentieth century that drove blacks from their homes and towns—the book focuses on twelve such incidents.[17] Historian and journalist Scott Ellsworth's (1982) *Death in a Promised Land: The Tulsa Race Riot of 1921* chronicles a dramatic series of events that left a thriving black business district in shambles.

The Great Migration

In her bestselling book *The Warmth of Other Suns: The Epic Story of America's Great Migration*, Pulitzer Prize–winning journalist Isabel Wilkerson (2010, 39) explains what blacks who left the South were fleeing from:

> Across the South, someone was hanged or burned alive every four days from 1889 to 1929, according to the 1933 book *The Tragedy of Lynching*, for such alleged crimes as "stealing hogs, horse-stealing, poisoning mules, jumping labor contract, suspected of killing cattle, boastful remarks" or

"trying to act like a white person." Sixty-six were killed after being accused of "insult to a white person." One was killed for stealing seventy-five cents.

Between World War I and the 1970s, approximately six million black Southerners moved to the cities of the North to escape the indignities of Jim Crow policies and the constant threat of retaliation for minor, and often imaginary, offenses with various degrees of punishment, including death by lynching (Ibid., 9). The migration was the nation's largest and longest protest against racial injustice. Wilkerson (Ibid., 178–79) selected three individuals from among the many she interviewed and presented their stories in some detail; each represented a different decade, point of departure, and destination.

> The Great Migration ran along three main tributaries and emptied into reservoirs all over the North and West. One stream . . . carried people from the coastal states of Florida, Georgia, the Carolinas, and Virginia up the eastern seaboard to Washington [DC], Philadelphia, New York, Boston, and their satellites. A second current . . . traced the central spine of the continent, paralleling the Father of Waters, from Mississippi, Alabama, Tennessee, and Arkansas to the industrial cities of Cleveland, Detroit, Chicago, Milwaukee, Pittsburgh. A third and later stream carried people . . . from Louisiana and Texas to the entire West Coast, with some black southerners traveling farther than many modern-day immigrants. . . . They traveled deep into far-flung regions of their own country and in some cases clear across the continent. Thus the Great Migration had more in common with the vast movements of refugees from famine, war, and genocide in other parts of the world, where oppressed people, whether fleeing twenty-first-century Darfur or nineteenth-century Ireland, go great distances, journey across rivers, deserts, and oceans or as far as it takes to reach safety with the hope that life will be better wherever they land.

The drama of this massive migration is poignantly rendered in the paintings of Jacob Lawrence.[18] A powerful image impressed me deeply: an African American mother entrusting the care of her son to a black Pullman porter as she sends the boy north by train in hope of greater safety and opportunity for him. I must have seen that image in a play or story or the work of another artist because I was unable to find it in the two books of Lawrence's paintings that I was able to examine.

CHAPTER 12

The City at
a Crossroads

B Y THE END OF World War II, when I was a young child living with my family in Philadelphia's Black Bottom neighborhood, the majority of the black population in the United States lived in urban areas. In moving to the city, blacks had to consider what would be an appropriate relationship to their new urban environments. While newcomers were bemused when whites moved away as soon as a single black family moved into their neighborhood, they were in fact witnessing another version of Jim Crow, or "James Crow" as those who had made the journey in California had called it (Wilkerson 2010, 211). Some white urban residents were willing to tolerate blacks as a marginalized population in the cities as long as they remained in ghettos. The implied message was that if blacks want to live in "white" cities, they should get used to the idea that the American mainstream is white—by definition, inheritance, and privilege.

The invisibility of blacks in mainstream popular and scholarly narrative about cities seems to suggest that blacks were not present in North American cities prior to, say, 1950 or that they were present but insignificant and played no important roles. This perspective underestimates the agency of black people and the influence of racist housing policies. It also reinforces the perception of black communities as contained by and subordinate to so-called white people rather than as actors in their own right.

The Racialization of Space

The dynamics of white supremacy have been clearly reflected in the built environment across generations. On the slave ships, space was rigidly divided with whites free up on the decks and blacks chained down below. The design of housing on the plantation reflected the same racial hierarchy. With the Civil War and emancipation, the pattern shifted temporarily as the new status of the freed people required new living arrangements. Emancipated blacks eagerly built their own churches where they could sit where they liked and listen to a black minister. Their next priority was schools to educate themselves and their children. They gathered in black conventions to educate and organize themselves politically, and they worked lands that had been abandoned by Confederate planters fleeing Union troops. In *Rehearsal for Reconstruction: The Port Royal Experiment*, female historian Willie Lee Rose[1] (1964) gave a moving account of the challenges, triumphs, and eventual failure of early Reconstruction efforts in the South Carolina Sea Islands, which were captured by Union troops in the first year of the Civil War.

The defeated Confederates in the South would not tolerate the flowering of independence in their former slaves and set about reducing blacks to a condition as close to slavery as they could manage. In order to reestablish white supremacy, they created a culture of racial segregation reinforced by violence and intimidation. A strict definition of race was used to dictate who could live where within the cities and between cities and outlying areas. Drawing on the same spatial tactics that informed the organizations of slave ships and plantations, they shaped the social and occupational stratification of society—prohibiting anyone defined as Negro from equal access to the ownership of property, the benefits of scientific knowledge, and the comforts and rituals of daily life. Whites created rules about who could live where and used them as tools of domination and racial subordination. Naturally, blacks resisted such arrangements. The stories of these dynamics and their implications for planning have been largely invisible, both in public awareness and in the training and practice of environmental and urban development professionals.

As David Sibley (1995) explains in *Geographies of Exclusion: Society and Difference in the West*, white space is, first of all, a space of exclusion. The color symbolism of white and black is used to mark pure and defiled territory. Laura Pulido (2006, 23) writes about differential racialization in *Black, Brown, Yellow and Left: Radical Activism in Los Angeles*, describing how in "different places and times and at various scales, particular groups may be subordinate, dominant, or in some intermediate position." In the racialization process, population groups are assigned different degrees of access to and governance of physical territory on the basis of their racial or ethnic identity. The meanings embodied in these racialized spaces are clearly conveyed by the differences between the spaces assigned to the subordinate and the dominant groups.

The philosophy of "separate but equal" masked the reality of discriminatory Jim Crow laws and practices in both urban and rural spaces throughout the American South. White supremacists made it known that housing and neighborhoods, schools, public marketplaces, restaurants, hotels, and churches were for whites only.[2] The limited accommodations that were open to blacks were routinely substandard. For example, the textbooks given to black schoolchildren were ones thrown away by the white schools due to defacement or wear and tear (Wilkerson 2010, 84). For black people in the South, interacting with white people was often demeaning and dangerous. Limited opportunities for education and employment and the dangerous consequences of speaking one's mind drove the Great Migration from the South to the cities of the North and West.

The rate of black migration increased during World War II. Whites, particularly those who had arrived in the cities earlier than blacks, pushed back in response to the influx of African Americans, using violence to express their resistance. They formed chapters of the Ku Klux Klan (KKK) and neighborhood associations based on race. Ethnic whites, such as those from southern, central, and eastern Europe who had previously seen themselves as low on the social hierarchy, had an opportunity to rise by abandoning their ethnic identity and becoming white. In general, the white populations began to see race as black and white.

Racial ideologies were coded into the real estate industry with the development of restrictions and policies that steered black people to black neighborhoods and kept them away from white ones. Under President Franklin D. Roosevelt, Congress created the Home Owners' Loan Corporation in 1933 and the Federal Housing Administration (FHA) in 1934 to make home ownership more affordable—insuring mortgages in order to lower interest rates and the size of down payments. The FHA rated neighborhoods according to their stability and reliability for loan repayment. Neighborhoods where black people lived were rated D, colored in red, and usually considered ineligible for FHA backing (Coates 2014). Philadelphia's Black Bottom neighborhood, unsurprisingly, was colored red and rated D on Home Owners' Loan Corporation maps from 1937, two years before I was born there.[3] This practice, known as redlining, excluded black people from most legitimate means of obtaining a mortgage and from loans for property improvements and repairs. The widespread practice of mortgage discrimination continued from the 1930s to the 1960s—a period corresponding to the greatest influx of black migrants from the South.

Many black families, eager and often desperate to purchase a home, resorted to buying from contract sellers. These real estate entrepreneurs would scare white sellers into selling at a low price and then sell the house at more than twice what they paid to an African American family on a contract that demanded a much higher than normal down payment and monthly installments. The first time the buyer missed a payment, ownership would revert to the seller, who would evict the buyer, retain all the payments as profit, and go on to sell the property to another desperate black family. As Coates (2014) observed, "Contract sellers became rich. North Lawndale became a ghetto."

Suburban Sprawl and Inner-City Abandonment

After World War II, a new version of white space emerged based on the movement of white families to the newly built suburbs. African Americans had poured into the cities to take on jobs in the factories that had multiplied for the creation of wartime materials. Now, the factories were being converted for production of consumer goods, including automobiles, which made suburbanization possible. A series of public policies supported the construction of suburbs, white access to them, and restriction of African Americans. The National Interstate and Defense Highways Act in 1956 created the infrastructure that supported suburban development. The chosen routes of the freeways often went through vibrant black neighborhoods, dislocating thousands of African American businesses and neighborhood centers and destroying millions of homes. Another support for suburbanization was the FHA-guaranteed loan, which was largely unavailable to blacks. The US government spent huge amounts of money creating the suburbs and the highways that connected them and subsidizing the white people moving into them.

The Servicemen's Readjustment Act of 1944, also known as the GI Bill, provided college tuition and home loan benefits to veterans, but did not extend equally to returning black soldiers. Poor whites who served in the army and received these benefits when they came out were able to enter the middle class for the first time.

In the 1950s and early 1960s, I witnessed the damaging effects of urban renewal on African Americans who were displaced from the run-down, historic neighborhoods where they had settled. Later, I learned that the settlements of other ethnic minorities, particularly Catholic Irish, Italian, and Polish, had been intentionally destabilized by Protestant ruling elites who considered them politically threatening and had used African Americans to break up Catholic ethnic communities. Blacks, desperate for larger, cleaner housing, were assisted in purchasing homes in white ethnic neighborhoods. Once they moved in, property values fell; and the residents fled in fear to the suburbs where their ethnic identities gradually faded and they became "white."

Some of these ethnic European communities were determined to remain the majority in their neighborhoods, and they responded to black newcomers with violence. Leaders like Martin Luther King Jr. were not exempt from this violence. In 1966, King was hit on the head with a rock and fell to his knees shortly after arriving to lead a protest march in Marquette Park, a primarily Lithuanian community outside Chicago. E. Michael Jones (2004, 505) describes the event, which included thirty injuries and the torching of fifteen cars belonging to the marchers. Isabel Wilkerson describes the same incident (Wilkerson 2010, 388–89) and other instances of violent white reaction to blacks moving into previously all-white neighborhoods, or trying to (Ibid., 320, 372, 375).

Cities were being abandoned by the white population, and the loss of jobs, population, and tax base accompanied that abandonment. Upon losing tax income from the upper and middle classes, cities deteriorated further, exacerbating white flight. At the same time, home loan and insurance policies favored the suburbs heavily, making it almost impossible for the new city dwellers to improve or protect their buildings. Real estate policies were, at times, openly racist, denying title transfers, coverage, or loans to whole blocks if a Jewish, Catholic, Asian, or black family were to move in (Gotham 2002).

My family bought a three-story, ten-bedroom house in 1945 in a mostly white neighborhood. We were on the frontier of racial change in Philadelphia. The block soon became 100 percent black. When all the white people had moved to the suburbs, the neighborhood began to deteriorate. Once separated into ghettoes, discriminatory practices in banking compounded the depreciation of whole neighborhoods.

Although antidiscrimination laws have been put in place since, the effect of generations of lost wealth accumulation continues to take its toll. In *Black Wealth / White Wealth*, Melvin Oliver and Thomas Shapiro (1995) point out that the difference in wealth from home ownership between white and black Americans is even greater than the wage gap between the two groups.

The ugly side story is that devalued real estate makes for attractive long-term investments that benefit investors and developers but not renters. When physical improvements finally begin to reach the neighborhood, long-time residents are displaced by rising rents. We have seen this process of gentrification take hold in countless inner cities over recent decades.

With suburbanization, the majority of European Americans in the United States gradually came to think of themselves as a uniform population—whites—presumed to be naturally superior to non-European Americans. This sense of superiority provides the basis for the system of white supremacy, which is still used to justify dominating, marginalizing, and exploiting non-whites. The reality is that African Americans and other people of color are at the heart of the human community in the United States and elsewhere. We must reject any vision of community that consciously or unconsciously—intentionally or unintentionally—overlooks, minimizes, marginalizes, or otherwise devalues the experience and contribution of people of color in the United States. Such a vision is racially biased, if not racist.

The consequences of this abandonment of inner-city neighborhoods by whites moving to the suburbs are well documented in many studies. In *When America Became Suburban*, Columbia University planning professor Robert Beauregard (2006) finally identified a phenomenon I had been observing for decades in my personal, academic, and professional lives: "parasitic urbanization," a process whereby new growth saps the life out of existing structures. It was clear to me much earlier that the suburbs were sucking resources and opportunities out of the inner city.

Study after study reinforced my belief that persistent poverty among blacks in the United States is due to the high degree of deliberate segregation they experience in American cities. The racial policies, urban renewal strategies, and housing and transportation initiatives of federal, state, and local governments, along with private interventions during and following World War II, devastated and impoverished once-thriving urban neighborhoods.[4] This was the canvas against which the civil rights and black power movements in the North came into being. The upshot of the racial apartheid was that by 1966 and 1967, civil disorders had broken out in cities across America.

The Kerner Commission Report

Civil unrest was rampant in American cities during the late 1960s when I was completing my architecture studies at Columbia University. Several short-lived uprisings occurred in Harlem; Rochester,

New York; Elizabeth, New Jersey; Chicago; and Philadelphia during 1964, but a six-day insurrection in August of 1965 in Watts, an impoverished, black neighborhood in South Central Los Angeles, caught the nation's attention. It was followed by outbreaks in Chicago, Cleveland, Omaha, Tampa, and Buffalo, culminating in a two-week uprising in the summer of 1967, first in Newark and then in Detroit. The intensity of these insurgencies moved President Lyndon Johnson to action.

President Johnson appointed an eleven-man National Advisory Commission on Civil Disorders to investigate the cause of the civil unrest. He requested Otto Kerner Jr., the former governor of Illinois, to head it. The Kerner Commission, as the commission became known, published a report that became available in paperback all over the country in 1968. The commission concluded that the nation was moving toward two societies: one black and one white—separate and unequal. The white part was suburban and thriving while the black part, in the inner city, was in decline. Unless conditions were remedied, the commission warned, the country faced a system of apartheid in its major cities.

> To pursue our present course will involve the continuing polarization of the American community and, ultimately, the destruction of basic democratic values. The alternative is not blind repression or capitulation to lawlessness. It is the realization of common opportunities for all within a single society. . . . What white Americans have never fully understood—but what the Negro can never forget—is that white society is deeply implicated in the ghetto. White institutions created it, white institutions maintain it, and white society condones it. (National Advisory Commission on Civil Disorders 1968, 1)

The Kerner Commission report identified unjust policies that isolated African Americans and prevented their educational and economic advancement. It called for legislation and policy reforms to promote racial integration and enrich the ghetto—making resources available for jobs, job training, improved public schools, and decent housing.

We believe that the only possible choice for America is. . . a policy which combines ghetto enrichment with programs designed to encourage integration of substantial numbers of Negroes into the society outside the ghetto. . . . The primary goal must be a single society, in which every citizen will be free to live and work according to his capabilities and desires, not his color. (Ibid., 19–20)

Unfortunately, none of the Kerner Commission's recommendations were implemented—neither on the national nor the local level.[5] Not surprisingly, when Martin Luther King Jr. was assassinated in April of 1968, insurrections broke out in many cities, including the student takeover of the president's office at Columbia when I was an architecture student there. The fact that the recommendations had not been taken up lingered and festered within me. Many white people thought the "Negro problem" had been eliminated by civil rights legislation, but that was neither my view nor one widely shared among black people.

It was clear that something had to change. The Kerner Commission's diagnosis of corrosive inequities and its warning of worsening conditions in the inner cities and increasing racial conflict was continuing to be played out. America had become suburban and white. These suburbanites had their own view of what the world was like, which was quite different from the reality I and other black people faced daily.

A Demographic Shift

Congress passed the Immigration and Nationality Act of 1965, a companion to the Civil Rights Act of 1964, to eliminate racial discrimination in immigration. Previously, 70 percent of all immigrant slots were allotted to natives of just three countries—the United Kingdom, Ireland, and Germany—and went mostly unused while there were long waiting lists for the small number of visas available to those born in Italy, Greece, Poland, Portugal, and elsewhere in eastern and southern Europe. The new legislation opened the doors for immigration of people from Asia, Latin America, and Africa, ushering in a major shift in the demographics of the American population. American life had always been multicultural, starting with the indigenous cultures and the Mexican inhabitants of the lands that became the American Southwest. Then came the waves of immigrants from various parts of Europe, and the smaller waves of Chinese, Japanese, Filipino, and Mexican immigrants.

After the legislation in 1965, the ongoing war between capitalism and communism on the world stage resulted in an influx of refugees from Asia and Central America. Africans came, fleeing civil wars. The US Census Bureau (2015) estimates that by 2044, the majority of the US population will be people of color. It is increasingly obvious that we need new strategies for promoting justice in a multiracial society. We are shifting from a black-versus-white framework to a much more complex pattern, coming into more direct relationships with people from all over the world as shifting migration trends make racial diversity a fact in American cities. We are becoming a multiracial nation and need new awareness and a new story that reflects this new reality.

As I pointed out in Chapter 10: Deep Time, Slavery, and the Making of the Modern Economic System, the racialization of space had its origin in European reliance on forced labor and, later, on support for colonial expansion. The parts of the environment that were controlled and named by Europeans became white space. A negative meaning was assigned to unfamiliar, unconquered areas; for example, Africa was often referred to as the dark continent. Our understanding of the relationship between the human community and the natural world has been distorted and fragmented by racism. Such distortions disempower us and cloud our understanding of the roots of our current social and ecological crises. In order to work together for change, we need a truthful history of the genesis of the unjust power relations that now hold sway in the system of white supremacy.

The Sustainability Revolution

Alongside the growing pressure for racial justice, the environmental movement was coming into its own with rising awareness and more frequent discussions about sustainability. The movement got a jump-start in early 1969 when a Union Oil offshore pumping station had a blowout near Santa Barbara, California. A successful attempt to cap the hole triggered the buildup of pressure that caused breaks in a fault on the ocean floor, releasing oil and gas from deep below. Over two hundred thousand gallons of crude oil poured forth and was spread by wind and waves into an eight-hundred-square-mile slick. Incoming tides pushed the thick tar to nearby beaches, polluting thirty-five miles of prized coastal real estate.[6] Much worse accidents have happened before and since, but this one garnered a huge amount of public attention and stimulated legislative attempts to increase environmental protection.

The first Earth Day was held that spring. Wisconsin senator Gaylord Nelson had initiated the event after touring the damaged shoreline and getting the idea of holding a nationwide teach-in—a technique derived from the Freedom School movement of the South —about protecting the environment.[7] Some people consider Earth Day in April of 1970 as the start of the environmental movement, but consciousness about the need for environmental protection and restoration had been prepared by Rachel Carson's 1962 book *Silent Spring*, which raised public awareness and concern about the poisoning of land and life forms by the byproducts of the industrial age. Carson's research showed how the use of pesticides harms many living species, including human beings, and how the chemical industry and its regulators turned a blind eye to these effects in pursuit of profit. Although the 1969 moon landing was driven by a nationalist competition between the United States and the Soviet Union, images broadcast into many American living rooms of our blue-green planet floating in space engendered a new awareness of Earth as the shared home of all human beings. Earth Day in 1970 was the largest demonstration that had happened on environmental issues, marking the consciousness of millions of people taking on the responsibility of caring for planet Earth as their home.

Jean and I were in Africa that April. We returned with a large collection of photographs and drawings about traditional African architecture. By fall of 1971, I was teaching in the architecture department at UC Berkeley, collaborating with Sim Van der Ryn on demonstrations of appropriate technology and teaching the first courses offered at the university on energy conservation. I was seeking new ways to integrate my consciousness as an African American with this emerging global identity. I was eager to share my observations of community participation in natural building with my students and colleagues, but there was no context for it. There were hardly any students or faculty of color. As this global consciousness of the need for sustainability was taking shape, I was in search of the roots of my identity. I carried a lingering awareness of unfinished business from the civil rights movement and began thinking of ways to incorporate those concerns into the new paradigm.

In 1972, Donella Meadows, Dennis Meadows, Jørgen Randers, and William W. Behrens III released a groundbreaking report, *The Limits to Growth: A Report for the Club of Rome's Project on the Predicament of Mankind*. This historic document detailed the disastrous consequences of unchecked economic and population growth on a planet with finite resources. The oil embargo of 1973 made Americans across the country painfully aware of the level of our dependence on fossil fuels and how central such natural resources had become to our lives and the economy.

The collapse of the Soviet Union, beginning in 1985, produced a softening and gradual dissolution of the American consciousness that had seen planet Earth as a battleground for the opposing ideologies of communism and free market capitalism—opening up space for the consciousness of global solidarity. In 1987, another groundbreaking report, *Our Common Future*, was released by the World Commission on Environment and Development, commonly known as the Brundtland Commission after Gro Brundtland, the popular Norwegian politician who chaired the commission and went on to serve as Norway's first woman prime minister and, later, to direct the World Health Organization. The report defined sustainable development as development that meets the needs of the present without compromising the ability of future generations to meet their own needs. The report gave priority not only to the structure of the natural support system that is the living fabric of Earth, but also included the needs of the world's poor in its definition of sustainability.

Many futurists felt that this upsurge of interest in sustainability would generate a new vision for all people on the planet and a reason to set aside our differences and collaborate toward a common goal. Between World War II and the fall of the Soviet Union, US public policy began to open up to the need for more viable life support systems. By 1988, guided by the essays in Thomas Berry's *Dream of the Earth*, I felt that I needed to shift along with the universal forces at work in the world. I was ready to make a change.

A New Vision for the City

I had been empowered by seeing myself in the context of the new story about sustainability proposed by Thomas Berry (1988) in *Dream of the Earth*. I felt it could provide a space for all human groups to work together, transforming our cities, our regions, and our relationships to one another and the planet we share. I imagined African Americans and other people of color playing leadership roles in this great work of planning and redeveloping our metropolitan regions based on ecological balance and social equity.

Our cities are embedded in and dependent on Earth's living systems—bioregions, ecosystems, watersheds, climate, and atmosphere. Many ecological writers heralded this shift in our relationship with the planet—from seeing it as an endless trove of resources to be exploited and manipulated to experiencing it as our companion on a journey through time. I was inspired by the idea that our cities could be redesigned from this new perspective.

For me, Detroit is the poster child for a new vision of the city with opportunities for healing people of color while repairing the damage humans have caused to the planet and to fellow humans. The city saw huge growth from fossil-fuel-based industries, then increasing ethnic diversity from the influx of people of color seeking employment opportunities, and then white flight and suburban sprawl, resulting in an impoverished urban core and an increase in greenhouse gases from automobile exhaust. This was more or less the pattern in many of our big cities that now need to shift toward an emphasis on environmental and social justice.

In 1910, Detroit was 99 percent white, a population almost exclusively of European immigrants. As the auto industry grew and more jobs were created, African Americans began arriving in the city. During World War II, Detroit was one of the cities dubbed the "arsenal of democracy," and weapons manufacturing boomed. African Americans and Latinos came to the city in increasing numbers to work in the war industry, and, subsequently, in the auto industry that mushroomed after the war ended. After 1950, however, the population of Detroit dropped steeply as the white population fled to suburban enclaves. From 1950 to 1989, the population had dropped by almost half. This flight of the white elite left a hollowed-out tax base, and an impoverished urban core with over ninety thousand vacant lots.[8]

Detroit is a paragon of the industrial revolution, and, for Detroit, that revolution has come to an end. The growth spurred by fossil fuels has created fragmented regions with an unsustainable relationship to planetary resources and growing inequalities in wealth, health, and opportunity.

As we begin to rebuild our cities and regions, we will not be able to make shared decisions about how to protect our common future unless we unweave the legacy of racial apartheid. We must lift up the accounts of non-European people in humanity's journey to the present moment. We must reconstruct and recount the migrations of people across the planet, forced and voluntary, including the capture and enslavement of our ancestors. Racism has disempowered us and clouds our understanding of the roots of our current social and ecological crises. In order to work together for change, we need a truthful history of the genesis of the unjust power relations that now hold sway in the system of white supremacy.

Residents in people-of-color communities know through first-hand experience the ecological costs of our current unsustainable patterns of life. People of color need to be at the table, and to exercise leadership, as we make decisions about moving toward an ecologically responsible society. We cannot afford to continue squandering the assets that people of color can contribute to the challenge of transforming our society.

CHAPTER 13

Forging an Alliance between Environmentalists and Social Justice Activists

I N 1988, George H. W. Bush won the U S presidential election; he had run on the promise of being the "environmental president." After his election, he met in Washington, DC, with a group of environmental organizations known as the Big Ten, which produced a book called *Blueprint for the Environment: A Plan for Federal Action and Advice to President Bush from America's Environmental Community*. The book, written by environmentalist and historical preservationist T. Allan Comp (1989), lists detailed steps for 575 recommended actions for the federal executive departments—the Department of State, the Department of Justice, the Department of Education, and so on. Glaringly absent are the Department of Housing and Urban Development and the Department of Labor. These omissions are very revealing. It seems clear to me that the environmental movement gained much of its acceptance from the establishment by saying, "We're not connected with that whole mess in the cities. We're not going to bother with that." The separation of the environmental movement from urban issues left a big hole full of problems just under the surface.

Joining Earth Island Institute

The same year the Big Ten made their recommendations, Karl Linn introduced me to David Brower, founder of Earth Island Institute

(EII). After we interacted a few times, David invited me to join the EII board. I was skeptical about the value of getting involved with a bunch of environmentalists whom I was certain had little understanding of how racism causes social and environmental injustice and even less interest in finding out. I understood that the issues people were complaining about—global warming, chopping down trees, or squandering resources—could not be addressed without considering the predicaments and needs of workers and inner-city residents.

I was, however, impressed by the work of one of the projects EII supported: the Environmental Project on Central America (EPOCA), which was one of the inspiring case studies in *Places for Peace*. EPOCA was promoting environmental protection in Nicaragua and facilitating the formation of cooperatives by agricultural workers and small farmers. In June of 1989, when David Brower and revolutionary Nicaraguan leader Daniel Ortega[1] co-hosted the Fourth Biennial Congress on the Fate and Hope of the Earth in Managua, I said to myself, "Maybe these white people are not so hopeless."

I have often been asked to participate on the boards of nonprofits. Sometimes, these invitations are motivated by a genuine impulse of wanting to do the right thing, to create programs that respond to the needs of communities of color within the context of the organization's mission. Other times, it's simply tokenism—the organization has no intention of modifying its practices in any way, but, if challenged, can say, "Look, we have a person of color on our board."

I think the invitation to join the EII board was motivated by the pressure they were under to respond to demands for more diversity. The environmental movement had come under heavy criticism regarding the absence of people of color in membership, staffing, and leadership.

The EII board was composed primarily of European-American men. The few women who joined the board were uncomfortable with that. Some board members hoped that my participation would bring in greater sensitivity to issues of diversity and social justice. I realized, however, that the principal people there thought that my joining showed a new maturity in people of color "who finally *get* our issues." The notion that, somehow, people of color would be bringing something that white people had to "get" was largely missing. In other words, they didn't realize that my joining would bring them new challenges.

In some ways, it was one-sided. I knew this would be the case long before I joined the board. I had to decide whether or not I was going to try to learn how to fit into their organization even if I was not given the respect I thought I deserved. I saw potential in EII's ability to communicate that ecological issues had to be addressed and so I decided that it was worthwhile to ally with them.

When I finally accepted David's invitation to join the board, I had one important demand: I would be willing to join, I told him, if the board could create a project that would focus on the urban issues that the environmental movement had been avoiding. He agreed that EII would sponsor the new organization that Karl Linn and I had been envisioning. We called it the Urban Habitat Program.

I was the only person of color on the EII board. The advisory board, however, had two women of color, Vandana Shiva and Winona La Duke, who were personal friends of David and greatly respected and appreciated his work. Like them, I was happy to be allied with someone who was in favor of reversing the ecological destruction of the planet.

As I mentioned in Chapter 8: Crisis and Turning Point, Karl Linn was very interested in reforestation and grassroots environmental protection. He had been telling me about the Chipko movement in India, where women were resisting the destruction of their forests by embracing trees threatened with logging, and I was amazed when I realized Vandana had been a part of that. I was impressed by her clear and powerful passion and presence, as well as by the courage of the Chipko women who were putting their lives on the line in the face of approaching chainsaws. The determination of these women to protect the trees made me think about Harriet Tubman and the escaping slaves as they made their way toward freedom. It also made me question the sincerity of Western environmentalist claims about having a relationship with the natural world. The Chipko women clearly had it, but did we?[2] Further, I wondered where the men were.

A great benefit I received from my years at EII was learning a lot about global environmental issues and movements. I was now committed to dealing with environmental issues in concert with bringing about social justice. My article, "Why African Americans Should Be Environmentalists," had signaled the need for an alliance between African Americans and progressive white environmentalists. I quickly realized that the alliance we envisioned would have to be multiracial. It would also need to address issues of gender and class and be intergenerational.

Positioning People of Color in the Environmental Movement

Although the black power movement was a powerful force during the 1960s, many people had negative reactions to what they perceived as our separatism. Most African Americans were receptive to the idea of black power—eager to feel more empowered and to know more about our roots. Many, however, had some reservation because of their strong connection to Martin Luther King's vision of racial integration. Similarly among whites, although many appreciated the power of Malcolm X's message, quite a few of them consciously or unconsciously began to experience a sense of loss, feeling that there was no longer a place for them in the black liberation movement.

Several movements sprang up and attracted whites who had identified with the civil rights movement, including the anti-nuclear, women's, gay and lesbian, and environmental movements. Feeling excluded by the separatism of black power, other communities of color were inspired by the possibilities of discovering their roots and demanded opportunities to express their own power. The result was a proliferation of social movements that had many different bases. Each of these social movements was built upon a sense of sovereignty that implicitly excluded those who did not belong.

The African American community was not large enough or strong enough to bring about the changes needed to achieve social equity. We needed to combine the inspiring and important lessons learned in the 1960s with the work of building more unity and accountability among the various identity groups.

The black community in the 1980s had considerable diversity, as it does today. There were middle-class blacks who had the option of moving wherever they liked. There were the stars of sports, entertainment, and politics who had lifestyles beyond our wildest dreams. People of multiracial identity and recent immigrants from Africa and the Caribbean were two other significant groups.[3] At the same time, there was a large and growing number of young people of color being targeted for the criminal justice system by schools designed to fail them.

Fragmentation could be seen occurring throughout the whole society. The vision of blissful suburban lifestyles composed of prosperous white nuclear families was being shattered by youth rebelling against the superficiality and duplicity of their parents' culture and by longing for personal and social liberation. Separatism, which I had found new and exciting in the 1960s, no longer compelled me. The only way I could foresee a unified African American culture was through building a unified culture for everyone, grounding ourselves in empathy and deep caring about one another's issues and concerns.

I was still trying to get clear on what the new story could be for black people when suddenly my mind shifted and I realized it's not just black people who need a new story. All people need it. This was beyond anything I previously thought possible. "Gee," I thought, "Adam must've felt like this." I was looking back through time and felt only a brief moment away from when the first hominids, our common ancestors, came down from the trees six million years ago. I was carrying millions of years of human experience within myself. I was amazed to be there, right at the beginning, experiencing myself as somebody who had a front row seat to the origins of humanity and of our planet. My new challenge was to construct an origin story that included us all.

Creating the Urban Habitat Program

We started the Urban Habitat Program (UHP) in 1989 with the mission of building multiracial leadership for sustainable metropolitan communities in the San Francisco Bay Area. We recognized that the environmental movement had little or no interest in urban communities. We saw an urgent need to develop leaders of color who could address structural inequalities in regional land-use and transportation planning. Our strategy was to combine education, advocacy, research, and coalition building to advance environmental, economic, and social justice.

The way Earth Island Institute (EII) was set up at that time, there were a score of projects that were all relatively autonomous. Once we got approval to start UHP, we had to raise our own money and set our own priorities. The EII board and the organization were pleased, I think, because they were getting something for nothing. We were the second largest fundraiser of the twenty projects within the organization. EII didn't have to come up with any money for our operation; it didn't have to come up with any ideas or initiatives; and it got the benefit of being associated with our program, which was getting lots of national attention.

UHP also benefitted from the partnership. At that time, there weren't many organizations focused on environmental issues in people-of-color communities. As a project of EII, we were able to get more resources than we would have had we set up as an independent organization.

We were very grateful to Jane Rogers, the program officer at the San Francisco Foundation, who gave us our first grant of fifty thousand dollars and continued to support us. Her husband, Michael Fischer, who was the executive director of the Sierra Club at the time and later became a program officer for the Hewlett Foundation, gave us a five-hundred-thousand-dollar grant to continue our program.

In 1990, Karl and I helped Richard Register, founder of the Bay Area-based organization Urban Ecology and author of *Ecocity Berkeley: Building Cities for a Healthy Future*, organize the First International Ecocity Conference in Berkeley. We had been talking with him about why there were virtually no people of color attending his meetings. I explained to him that people of color need to receive personal invitations to get involved in organizations that have historically excluded or do not explicitly include them. They may see a flyer, but likely won't assume they will be welcome without some prior personal contact.

For the conference, I invited psychologist Victor Lewis, attorney and philosopher Shariff Abdullah, and singer and activist Cordell Reagon to join me on a panel about environmental racism. The panel should have been a plenary session since an overflow crowd attended it. At the end, Cordell, who had been a Student Nonviolent Coordinating Committee organizer in the 1960s and was the husband of Bernice Reagon, founder of the black women's a cappella ensemble Sweet Honey in the Rock, broke into song and led the audience in "Where Have All the Flowers Gone?"

All the panelists, except for Abdullah who was based in Portland, Oregon, became founding members of UHP. Additional founding members were Karl Linn; Eleanor Walden, folk singer and longtime progressive educator; Arthur Monroe, art curator; Ellie Goodwin, a young African American woman who, as a receptionist at the Natural Resources Defense Council, took on the challenge of representing that organization on matters of race; and Luke Cole, about whom I will share more later. Our mission was to build multiracial leadership for sustainable communities in the San Francisco Bay Area while the mission of EII was to protect the global biosphere. Starting UHP under the umbrella of EII allowed me to shape a new institution that embodied ideas that had inspired me in the civil rights movement and to bring those ideas into the context of an emerging global vision.

We were inspired by the community design movement and its goals, which were articulated in Paul Davidoff's famous 1965 essay, "Advocacy and Pluralism in Planning." In the essay, Davidoff argues that the established urban planning tradition falsely claims that its work is based on the public interest. He asserts that planning work is actually based on competing private agendas and goals and argues that minorities should have a right to develop their own plans with technical assistance and have their proposals be debated in the public sphere. Communities should be able to make decisions that impact their neighborhoods.

Our concept was to apply the intentions and strategies of the community design movement at the metropolitan level since public interest was being decided there. The concept of working toward regional equity was beginning to emerge at the center of new ideas about balancing the need for environmental protection and restoration with the creation of a healthy economy. Serving on the EII board gave me an opportunity to be in touch with creative thinking about the environment from around the world. We needed to have people who were deeply rooted in their own communities and issues and able to have empathy for the issues of other communities. A multicultural coalition was more likely to be able to have a broad appeal and rise above the narrowly defined politics of cultural identity.

I studied affinity groups and what accounted for their successes or failures. John Friedman's (1979) *A Good Society* was particularly helpful. I followed his guidance on group size—at least five, to ensure survivability when people left, and no more than twelve, to protect against splintering into warring groups. I initiated a structure for ensuring multicultural representation and gender balance: we had twenty representatives—ten men and ten women—from five ethnic groups (African American, Asian American and Pacific Islander, Latino, European American, and Native American). The core group of paid staff would represent at least three ethnic groups, and no ethnicity would have a majority. Every time we hired new staff, we would evaluate who we might be missing. Being vigilant about what we meant by multicultural, we avoided slipping into patterns where our cultural biases would take over.

I learned about various cultural groups and how awareness and attitudes are rooted in human and environmental values. For example, a Chinese American staff member shared her memories of playing in the family bathtub where her mother kept sea creatures. She speculated that those early experiences influenced her decision to become an environmental lawyer specializing in issues of marine biology. Likewise, I remember shopping with a Latino staff member who had a story about each type of produce we walked past since he and his family had labored to pick them. We learned to cast off the various stereotypes we had about each other, appreciate our diversity, and find common ground.

We concluded early on that most of the established environmental issues were also social justice issues. Environmentalists were afraid that if they allowed any reference to economic and social issues, the questions about jobs and economic growth would block action on substantial ecological threats—worries about endangered species could be easily derailed by worries about an endangered economy.

When issues surfaced at EII, people rarely considered the social implications. At UHP, we were not asking people to relax their commitment to protecting the environment or conserving resources. Rather, we were saying, "Integrate an understanding of the social issues into your approach and create a proactive strategy to deal with them."

The mythology of the environmental movement grew out of a distorted understanding of how North America was settled. Legislation to create protected areas to conserve trees, water, and wildlife disregarded the land rights of native people who had cared for the land for millennia and the land rights of Mexican people who had settled on the land long before the masses of European immigrants came west in their covered wagons. Conservationists failed to understand the anger and frustration of the descendants of people who had been defrauded of their lands. An important reason that the land was still in a condition worthy to be saved was that it had been cared for by people who lived there for generations, using it for sustenance rather than for profit. The conservationists were not wrong in wanting to preserve and protect the land, but they were incredibly wrong in their lack of understanding and respect for the people who had a longtime relationship to that land.

The conservation movement grew out of the hunting and fishing recreational interests of the relatively well-off leisure class. They considered being in the outdoors an opportunity to relax and have fun. In the 1960s, however, especially with the publication of marine biologist Rachel Carson's *Silent Spring* in 1962, the conservation movement underwent a big change. Carson's account of how dumping, spraying, and dusting toxic chemicals was poisoning our water, air, and soil generated a change of consciousness and spurred the formation of the modern environmental movement.

During our first decade, UHP faced many challenges. We sought to strengthen relationships with old partners, build collaborations with new allies, and convert enemies into allies. Our first challenge was to broaden the movement without diminishing its power. Running through our work was a single theme: expanding the influence of the environmental justice movement and its activities without diluting its focus.

We initially focused on preventing and mitigating pollution, which was endemic in people-of-color communities. Gradually, we expanded our focus to include food justice since opportunities to purchase healthy fresh food were severely limited in those same neighborhoods. I wanted to challenge the idea that communities must choose between jobs and the environment. I'll never forget how I felt one afternoon when I stood on Third Street in San Francisco arguing with an acquaintance about air quality. He was asserting that the industry that was polluting the air was essential to our economic wellbeing. I was losing the argument until a truck came by spewing toxic exhaust in our direction, overwhelming us both. My opponent was silenced, and I won the argument by default. No one should have to choose between having a job and being able to breathe.

Shortly after starting UHP, I was elected president of the EII board. In this new role, I could help develop thinking and resolve conflicts within the established, mostly white, environmental movement. As board president, I was dealing with many international environmental projects that addressed a full array of concerns about the biological health of the planet. Most of the projects were driven by the traditions of preservation and conservation. The biggest project, for example, was the Marine Mammal Project, which was concerned with the effects of fishing practices on the safety of marine mammals. I tried to support as many projects as I could in my role as spokesperson for the organization, but my particular interest was in the question of human settlement and the interplay between environmental considerations and how we address urban issues. I frequently participated in conferences and public meetings—and, occasionally, in lobbying efforts when it seemed like my voice might help to push legislation through. It was a great learning experience and an opportunity to look at issues more deeply. This was a major new beginning in my life, and seeing all the EII projects through the lens of the universe story filled me with wonder.

Appointment to the Berkeley Planning Commission

As I began working with EII and developing UHP, I continued consulting for the Berkeley Planning Commission. In 1990, I was asked to become a member, and soon after joining the commission, I was elected its chair. In that capacity, I was charged with addressing the conflict between jobs and the environment in the West Berkeley Plan. Fortunately, I had credentials with both environmentalists and labor supporters because of my work with EII and my commitment to economic health in the black community, where unemployment was, and is, a serious problem. I had gained the important skill of resolving conflicts within communities around land use through my work conducting public meetings on controversial planning issues.

I became involved in one such issue—managing negotiations and public hearings on a proposal by Bayer Corporation on how to develop the property formerly owned and operated by the Colgate-Palmolive Company. I was very familiar with that property since I had partnered with four colleagues on an unsuccessful proposal to Colgate to receive a tax write-off by donating the plant to our nonprofit. Bayer had also purchased and taken over operations at the adjacent Miles-Cutter laboratories, which had been conducting extensive drug experiments on animals. These properties were part of the West Berkeley Plan, which covered all of West Berkeley from the city of Emeryville on the south to the city of Albany on the north.

The initial objection to Bayer's proposal was the height of the building—eighty feet in an area zoned for forty-five. Berkeley residents with homes in the hills argued that the building would disturb the skyline and obstruct views of the bay. Next was the threat of additional pollution. The plant required the use of chlorine gas, which would be deadly if it were accidentally released. In the middle of the controversy Bayer offered to develop a biotech academy to train African American youth for jobs in the growing biotech industry. Animal rights activists objected to the idea of youth being trained to think that experimenting on animals was acceptable. The issue was resolved when the Planning Commission suggested that a course in animal ethics be added to the curriculum and Berkeley's Humane Commission have oversight on the treatment of animals in the facility.

In politically conscious Berkeley, a huge controversy arose over the fact that Bayer's parent company, I. G. Farber, had built the Nazi concentration camp at Auschwitz and set up a factory nearby operated by Jewish slave labor. The Berkeley library had three books that documented these horrors, and they were always checked out.

We went through an arduous and lengthy community process. We had solved all the details and conditions of transferring the property to Bayer except for the legacy of I. G. Farber and Auschwitz. At the last meeting, a woman who had been involved in the process from the beginning got up and spoke:

> I'm Jewish. I lost my parents in Auschwitz. I live across the street from this plant, and I'm not planning to move. I'll be looking at it every day for the rest of my life. Nevertheless, I will ask the city council to approve this plan for it is in the best interest of the community.

People stood up and applauded.

Protecting Jobs and the Environment in West Berkeley

Many people had moved to West Berkeley because they liked the idea of residing in a live-work environment. Later, particularly if they were raising children, they became aware of the ways in which the industrial processes around them were a nuisance, or even harmful, and they sought to have industry phased out. How could these issues be reconciled? I led in the development of a plan for a 160-block area in West Berkeley that protected four thousand manufacturing jobs while strengthening environmental legislation to reduce pollution. Those two goals were usually considered incompatible.

We approached labor unions and asked which jobs they wanted to protect. At the first meeting, they specified two thousand jobs. Another two hundred jobs were still at risk. Environmentalists said they would develop legal protections for the two thousand jobs and support zoning regulations to protect fifty of the remaining jobs. We forged agreements block by block, rolling up our sleeves to tackle one problem at a time.

The Environmental Justice Movement

Back in 1984, six years before joining EII and starting UHP, I was living in an upscale neighborhood in North Berkeley when a community organizer named Francis Calpotura knocked on my door requesting a donation to the Center for Third World Organizing, a racial justice organization empowering and training people to fight against toxics in primarily people-of-color neighborhoods.[4] "That's nuts," I thought, "there are more important things to focus on—like failing schools and unemployment." That was my first exposure to the idea of environmental justice.

Gradually, I became aware that inner-city residents feel the brunt of a host of environmental problems, such as air pollution, industrial waste, mercury poisoning in fish, lack of safe drinking water, inadequate public transit, food deserts,[5] insufficient urban green space, lead poisoning, and heat-related stress. Low-income communities of color are especially impacted.

Toxic waste dumps, with hazardous waste from other communities, tend to be located near impoverished communities, which are most often communities of color. You won't find toxic waste dumps near wealthier communities. Or consider water usage: If you live in a wealthy California suburb and have a large lawn, you may consume as much as five hundred gallons of water per day. If you live in the inner city or an older suburb, you may consume around fifty gallons a day. If you are homeless, you're lucky to get five gallons per day.

Environmental justice calls for fairness in the distribution of benefits and burdens resulting from our industrial way of life to all the communities that contribute to society's wellbeing. People of color, working people, and poor people are often more burdened by environmental excesses than wealthier segments of the population while receiving fewer environmental benefits. There is no reality to the view that environmental issues concern only the privileged classes.[6]

Environmentalists have often ignored such social justice dimensions. To address these issues, an environmental justice movement of hundreds of grassroots organizations has emerged in the United States and globally. Many are based in local neighborhoods and single workplaces. Some are in barrios or on Native American reservations.

We need to be concerned not only with the siting of hazardous waste but also with the siting of everything—schools, grocery stores, parks, prisons, universities, and freeways. The siting of toxic facilities is a symptom of a much bigger problem that symbolizes a community's lack of capacity to shape the environment in ways that sustain it and are ecologically sound.

I was reminded of when the civil rights movement protested separate drinking fountains. Although the separate drinking fountains were clearly an egregious affront to our dignity, they were symptomatic of much deeper problems: racism and white supremacy. Toxic waste dumps are not only an egregious affront to the people living nearby and an enormous violation of public health; they are symptomatic of a system in which people without wealth and political connections have little or no power over decisions that affect the spaces in which they live.

The *Race, Poverty, and the Environment* Journal

In March of 1990, I was invited to speak at the annual Public Interest Law Conference hosted by Land Air Water (LAW) in Eugene, Oregon. Unsurprisingly, I was one of only two people of color in attendance. During the rideshare with three others from San Francisco to Eugene, I got to know environmental public interest lawyer, the aforementioned Luke Cole. After the panel, I told him how weird I felt participating in a conference about the environment with a thousand lawyers and only one other person of color. Luke was sympathetic and drew up a flier calling for an impromptu caucus. About thirty people came, and as we went around the room, we learned that people of color were fighting environmental justice battles all across the country. We agreed to collect their stories and publish them. Luke came up with the name *Race, Poverty, and the Environment (RP&E): A Newsletter for Social and Environmental Justice.* Back in the Bay Area, Luke joined the UHP board and partnered with me in publishing *RP&E*, which became an indispensable forum for dialogue and sharing of news and resources.

Coming from a privileged background, Luke was an outstanding model of what a person with privilege can do. One of his ancestors helped found Hartford, Connecticut, in the 1600s. He was educated at Stanford University and, later, Harvard Law School. He used his education and skills to fight for the rights of marginalized communities. In the mid-1990s, he represented residents of Kettleman City, a majority Hispanic community, in California's San Joaquin Valley in their campaign to stop Chemical Waste Management, Inc., the largest waste management company in the country, from building a toxic-waste incinerator there. Kettleman City was already the site of a vast toxic-waste landfill. A state court ruled that the permitting process was flawed and prohibited the company from constructing the incinerator. Luke is recognized as a champion of environmental justice.[7]

I attended Luke's wedding to Nancy Shelby at the Chalone Vineyard in Soledad, California. Many of the affluent and cultured members of the Luke's family were there and so were local farm workers whom I recognized by the clay on their boots. I was moved, seeing this family who had been so well taken care of blazing a trail to make sure that those with fewer opportunities also had a chance. In 2009, Luke died in a car wreck at the age of forty-six. He and Nancy—who survived the accident with injuries—had been vacationing and visiting one of Luke's brothers in Uganda.

Luke and I published the first issue of *RP&E* on Earth Day in 1990. In addition to our statement of purpose, the front page contained an impassioned message from David Brower about building bridges between environmentalists and people affected by environmental racism. Its eighteen pages contained nine additional articles, including an essay by Gar Smith (longtime editor of *Earth Island Journal*) on "Community, Freeways and Environmental Racism," along with resources, job opportunities, and upcoming events. My essay on "Why African Americans Should Be Environmentalists" got a lot of attention. The publication was well received and appreciated.

I photocopied that first issue and carried a box full of newsletters onto the bus. I handed copies to several African American passengers. Soon, they were in a lively debate about environmental issues. After I got off to transfer to another bus, I noticed someone shouting at me. A man had asked the bus driver to wait for him while he ran across the street to get a copy.

The publication started as a newsletter and quickly became a journal. In each issue, we focused on a particular topic that we recognized as one of the hot issues of the time. We wanted to bring in voices from the community responding to the emerging issues. As our theme coalesced, we would identify a guest editor who would then find eight to ten people to write articles for that issue. Not only was *RP&E* helping make visible the ways in which the burdens of degradation fell on people of color, but it was giving people an opportunity and a platform for expressing their ideas. It turned into a learning process for everyone. It was a way of building community around particular issues, and it also contributed to movement building.

We took every environmental topic we could think of and explored the related substantive issues. In the process, we were building communities of people engaged in those issues. We developed a language of environmental justice that not only honored its roots in fighting toxic pollution but also related it to transportation, land use, the greening of our cities, and other environmental issues.

RP&E is still being published today—in print, online, and podcast formats. It is in the process of being reimagined as a joint publication model in which groups share sponsorship and editorial direction. Its primary publisher is Movement Generation, an organization that emerged in 2007 with a focus on justice and ecology and a mission to stimulate and facilitate visioning and dialogue among grassroots leaders from low-income communities and communities of color. Its stated aim is to inspire and engage in "transformative action towards the liberation and restoration of land, labor, and culture" (Movement Generation 2017). It feels similar to the spirit and purpose with which we started UHP.

Reaching Out to People-of-Color Communities

In 1988, I heard about the 1987 report, *Toxic Wastes and Race in the United States*, published by the Commission for Racial Justice (CRJ) of the United Church of Christ. When the report reached us at the newly formed UHP a year later, it was like a bolt of lightning that reminded me of the impact of Rachel Carson's *Silent Spring*. I was searching for ways to bring people-of-color communities into the planning process, and the report provided a new way of researching and organizing around environmental issues. It demonstrated that new development projects had almost never benefited communities of color and, more often than not, would create new burdens instead. No wonder our communities were skeptical of new development schemes and reluctant to participate in processes for planning them. *Toxic Wastes and Race in the United States* provided a way to explain all this to our communities.

The report was so powerful and timely that I decided to go to New York to meet with Charles Lee, the CRJ research director and primary author of the report. We hit it off well, and he invited UHP to be advisors to a conference CRJ was planning—the first National People of Color Leadership Summit in Washington, DC, in October of 1991. It was a major undertaking that only CRJ, led by Ben Chavis, could pull off—it was the only organization with both the resources to bring everyone together and the stability and authority to make it a success.

At the National People of Color Environmental Leadership Summit, UHP led a large delegation of forty-five people from the San Francisco Bay Area and northern California. The majority were Asian Americans, some of whom went on to form the Asian Pacific Environmental Network. The summit was attended by around six hundred people from all over the United States and a few from other countries. I think that the majority were working on anti-toxics issues. There were some groups, particularly Native Americans, concerned with sacred lands and issues related to indigenous people.

Half of the attendees were delegates who could vote on behalf of their communities for resolutions that were adopted while the other half were individual participants and observers.

Anti-toxics campaigns had the strongest representation at the gathering. Realizing that polluting industries are routinely sited in low-income communities of color, community leaders were passionate about environmental justice issues, which had begun to generate many campaigns and organizations. One of the major achievements of the summit was the identification and drafting of the *Principles of Environmental Justice*, which began by affirming the sacredness of Earth, the interdependence of all species, and the right to be free from ecological destruction and then listed seventeen agreed-upon principles. Article 12 affirms the need for "urban and rural ecological policies to clean up and rebuild our cities and rural areas in balance with nature, honoring the cultural integrity of all our communities, and providing fair access for all to the full range of resources," and Article 17 requires that "we, as individuals, make personal and consumer choices to consume as little of Mother Earth's resources and to produce as little waste as possible; and make the conscious decision to challenge and reprioritize our lifestyles to ensure the health of the natural world for present and future generations" (Delegates to the First National People of Color Environmental Leadership Summit 1991). It is a powerful document that serves as the foundation of the environmental justice movement.

We tried to position our work at UHP in a way that would expand the horizons of many of the groups that were there. We introduced the importance of thinking about sustainability and issues of inner-city abandonment, suburban sprawl, and equitable access to transportation. These were appreciated particularly by delegations from metropolitan regions in the Northeast—Philadelphia, New York, Boston, Washington DC, Detroit, and Chicago. Our reception by some of the anti-toxics groups was less enthusiastic, however, as they felt that the purpose of the environmental justice movement was primarily to deal with hazardous waste and saw other issues as less relevant.

At the summit, I took the opportunity to introduce the idea of transportation justice. I criticized transportation investments in the San Francisco Bay Area, which involved disinvesting in buses, on which poor people depend, in favor of light rail, which serves wealthier suburban commuters. Another problem I addressed was the common pattern of heavy investment in highways, which led to inner-city abandonment and suburban sprawl. I suggested that community development corporations could advocate to reverse this trend. I sat on a panel that included Eric Mann of the Labor Community Strategy Center and Barry Commoner, an ecologist, activist, and former presidential candidate. A national movement for transportation justice grew out of the summit, and UHP was part of that process.

The summit included many powerful and eloquent people. An inspiring participant and key organizer of the event was sociology professor Robert D. Bullard. Known by many as the father of the environmental justice movement, he was drawn into environmental justice research in 1979 when his wife, lawyer Linda McKeever Bullard, asked him to collect data for a lawsuit she had filed to oppose the permitting of a landfill in a middle-class, primarily black neighborhood in Houston, Texas, where 85 percent of the residents were homeowners. He soon discovered that 100 percent of city-owned landfills in Houston were in black neighborhoods although blacks made up only 25 percent of the population. That was the beginning of decades of research, advocacy, and activism.

In 1990, Bullard published his first book, *Dumping in Dixie: Race, Class and Environmental Quality*, which chronicles struggles against hazardous dumping in five people-of-color communities—in Louisiana, Alabama, West Virginia, and two in Texas. He has been a leader in the environmental justice movement and has probably written more books about environmental justice than anyone else.[8]

Bullard emphasized the issue of transportation justice early on with a wonderful book that he edited with Glenn Johnson and Angel Torres called *Highway Robbery: Transportation Racism and New Routes to Equity*. He included the work of UHP on the Bayview-Hunters Point light rail project, the Bus Riders Union founded by Eric Mann, and several other transportation projects that had their beginnings at the summit. While *Highway Robbery* focused on US transportation policy as a source of toxic pollution and dislocation, which we agreed with as an important issue since a shockingly high percentage of people of color live near freeways and are exposed to toxic pollution from auto exhaust, we argued that it was equally vital to think about how people get to jobs, markets, hospitals, and schools. Considerations of access are also integral to transportation justice.

I came to the environmental justice movement with twenty-five years of experience as an architect working for racial justice and striving to use the insights, practices, and benefits of architecture, landscape architecture, and urban planning to improve the quality of life for African American and low-income communities. Encountering the emerging environmental justice movement of the late 1980s onward, I found a curious gap. Most practitioners in fields of environmental justice were unfamiliar with the community design movement even though its origins and goals were remarkably similar to their own.

The community design movement used design to address African American issues. It allied with the civil rights movement and engaged in protesting the injustices of large-scale planning projects like urban renewal and the construction of freeways through African American neighborhoods. Environmental justice was centered on toxic pollution and public health. The younger folks leading the movement had only a dim notion of the struggles for urban justice that had occupied our efforts during the 1960s—struggles for equal opportunities in education, jobs, and housing. They were focused on anti-toxics, which was arguably the most important issue that emerged in the environmental movement in the nineties. I was amazed at the depth and effectiveness of the environmental justice movement that emerged in grassroots communities in the late 1980s and early 1990s. Since then, the movement has become a worldwide phenomenon, growing well beyond anti-toxics.

Older folks at the summit who were concerned about unresolved issues from earlier struggles felt marginalized, and the younger generation felt that the older folks were selling out by not prioritizing environmental justice issues. I was in the middle—I could relate to the growing influence and power of anti-toxics activism, but I also had a sharp memory of the unresolved issues from the 1960s, primarily those around social and economic injustice and the struggle against pesticides in rural areas pioneered by farm workers in the sixties and seventies.

UHP played a unique role in the emerging environmental justice movement of the 1990s. Our allies in Washington, DC, succeeded in getting the Clinton administration to adopt Executive Order 12898 to promote environmental justice in all federal agencies. Arnoldo Garcia of the UHP staff was appointed to serve on the National Environmental Justice Advisory Council.

We developed strategies that would encourage investment in inner-city neighborhoods and counter incentives that contribute to urban sprawl. We also promoted counter-gentrification strategies designed to stabilize multicultural and economically diverse urban neighborhoods. Today, UHP, with its office in Oakland, continues to use education, advocacy, research, and coalition-building to advance environmental, economic, and social justice in metropolitan regions, primarily in the San Francisco Bay Area.

In 1991, UHP worked with Leonard Pitt of the Earth Drama Lab to organize an Eco Rap contest. Young people went on "toxic tours" to major sites of pollution in the Bay Area and composed rap poems. Finalists presented their compositions at a major concert at Justin Herman Plaza in San Francisco. The contest was judged by their favorite radio disc jockeys. AK Black won the contest and went on tour to communities throughout the Bay Area.

I enjoyed helping shape the environmental justice movement while building bridges to groups with other issues. It felt like we were creating a movement capable of transforming society as a whole. I came under criticism, however, by Richard Moore, who organized the Southwest Network for Environmental and Economic Justice, a grassroots organization that covered several southwestern states. He had authored a letter criticizing mainstream environmental organizations for their lack of racial diversity. He told me, "What we want is poor people who are on the front lines of environmental struggles. You being president of the Earth Island Institute doesn't match up with that." He was a powerful leader of the Latino population, and he challenged me—in some ways that were good and in other ways that I thought were baseless.

One of the disagreements I had with Moore was that I wanted to be organizing people who are in the same metropolitan region in order to put pressure on the powers that be within that region. He was more interested in a multistate approach, organizing all of the rural populations throughout a multistate area. I felt it was more likely that people living in a metropolitan region and acting collectively within it would have an impact on shaping that region whereas trying to organize people across five or six states might be like whistling in the wind.

Understanding the Metropolitan Region

Metropolitan regions are the form of twenty-first-century urbanism and the building blocks of our global economy. A metropolitan region is made up of the cities, suburbs, rural places, and surrounding wilderness areas linked to a single bioregion.

When my colleagues at UHP and I learned of Myron Orfield's (1997) work with metropolitan regional analysis and planning, we invited him to prepare a report on the San Francisco Bay Area. With maps and charts, Myron showed what we all suspected: that the suburbs were not monolithic. Long before it became evident to many policy makers, the newer suburbs had been moving further and further out at the expense of older inner-ring suburbs.

Myron demonstrated to us that poverty was predictably spreading to the suburbs. When a majority of schoolchildren in a suburban community were eligible for free school lunches, those communities would, in the absence of any contrary trends, begin a downward spiral. In a curious way, Myron's maps provided an entry point for me, enabling me to see beyond the veil of racial segregation to the metropolitan region as a whole. My staff, however, was not yet ready to go there.

Conventional political wisdom has held for a generation that the suburbs are monolithic. According to this view, suburban residents uniformly benefit from growth and have nothing in common with communities of color left behind in the inner city. Furthermore, people assume that collaboration between the inner city and the suburbs is impossible because these communities are too divided by race and class.

Myron's 1998 analysis of the Bay Area region helped us to understand the importance of suburban communities and raised our awareness of the suburban poverty that was becoming increasingly prevalent. In 1998, we published his report called *What If We Shared?*, in which he proposes that all of the cities in a region put 40 percent of their tax money into a common pool and then redistribute it based on need. To determine need, he recommended creating a map of the region and identifying those cities that had a high percentage of students who qualified for free lunches, which he had found to be a reliable indicator of the places where poverty most needed to be addressed. This strategy had worked when he was in the state legislature in Minnesota (Urban Habitat Program 1998). Myron continues to be a very important influence on my thinking.

Transportation Justice

Following the 1956 passage of the National Interstate and Defense Highways Act, our cities and growing suburbs made a radical break from earlier policy that had tied new housing and commercial development to investment in public transit. In the older pattern, new neighborhoods were built around retail stores and trolley lines that connected them to city centers, other growing districts, and the city's edge. Streetcar suburbs, like the West Philadelphia neighborhood where I grew up, were typical of communities developed for the upper, middle, and working classes in cities across the United States.

African Americans arrived in the cities in large numbers just as this uniquely American form of metropolis was breaking up and being replaced by suburban development centered around the automobile and highways. Urban renewal projects funded by the federal government wrecked the older pattern of metropolis as whites who could afford it fled to the suburbs, buying cars and feeding them gasoline.

The challenge of global warming requires that we move away from the nation's love affair with the automobile and support the development of real transportation choices, including public transit, bicycling, and walking. African Americans and other communities of color, having grown up in abandoned cities, are now positioned to play an important role in advocating for transportation justice, an important element in building the new metropolis.

Eric Mann, whom I met at the National People of Color Environmental Leadership Summit, was the head of the Labor Community Strategy Center in Los Angeles. While organizing to keep a General Motors (GM) factory in the neighborhood of Van Nuys open, he discovered that air pollution was killing people. While he was negotiating with GM, he told them that they were responsible for the poor quality of the air in Los Angeles. He documented this in his brilliant 1991 book called *L.A.'s Lethal Air*. For the book's cover, he chose a telling image: a photograph of kids playing basketball in the shadow of a freeway. In the opening pages, he writes about young victims of homicide whose autopsies revealed that a third of their lung capacity had been lost as they grew up breathing the unclean air produced by the siting of freeways and other sources of toxicity.

To combat air pollution, Eric organized the Bus Riders Union. He started organizing people to pass out leaflets on buses in order to motivate bus riders to protest and pressure the transportation agency to design bus routes and schedules that would meet the needs of low-income residents. Then, as now, Los Angeles was putting a lot of money into light rail while neglecting the bus routes, which are the primary way that people of color get around in the city. Eric and the Bus Riders Union had a strong influence on transportation policy and made a big contribution to transportation justice.

One of our projects at UHP was promoting a new route in San Francisco's light rail system to connect downtown with Bayview-Hunters Point. The majority of Bayview-Hunters Point residents were African American, and the area was economically depressed. We managed to have two hundred million dollars for construction of the new line transferred from a Caltrain project connecting San Francisco to Palo Alto and other points in the wealthy peninsula. We argued that before we start connecting people in the suburbs, we need to serve people who are already in the city, connecting them to downtown and jobs.

Military Base Conversions

The threat of war with the Soviet Union evaporated after its collapse in 1991. In its absence, the nation faced the challenge of closing five hundred military bases and re-missioning the national laboratories. These facilities employed large numbers and, thus, were central to the economies of many regions. How could elected officials, who were expected to bring home the bacon, lead their constituencies in reducing their reliance on and investment in the military?

The representative for what was then California's ninth congressional district,[9] Ron Dellums,[10] played a complex role as an opponent of US military expenditures while also serving as chair of the House Armed Services Committee, which oversees the military budget. He was accountable and responsive to the top military and political actors in the country and had to negotiate the military budget with them. Ron was the first one out there suggesting his district as the site to begin military base conversions. He did not hesitate to point out that the military is not a jobs program—killing people should never be a jobs program.

Having been a marine, a peace activist, and the most radical left congressman of the time, Ron Dellums embodied this contradiction and the spirit of this challenge. He was a model of the kind of leadership we wanted to develop when we started UHP. He exemplified the kind of transformational politics that we need now as we face climate change. We must cut back on our use of carbon dioxide and make a big shift in regional and national priorities while simultaneously working to be sure that poor people and people of color don't get short shrift.

I had been working on the conversion of the Colgate-Palmolive plant in Berkeley and a General Motors auto manufacturing plant in South Gate, a suburb of Los Angeles, both of which had been closed, so I had some experience dealing with large-scale closures. I was pleased when Ron put me in charge of the East Bay Conversion and Reinvestment Commission (EBCRC). He brought federal government officials to our commission meetings, including the head of the Environmental Protection Agency, the secretaries of the Departments of Commerce and Defense, and even President Bill Clinton. In 1996, EBCRC produced a report, *Defense Conversion: A Road Map for Communities*, which was essentially a crash course on sustainable development. We laid out a strategy for conversion of the five military bases and one national laboratory in Alameda County. The report describes all of the dimensions of economic opportunity—the creation of jobs, solutions for housing, and more—that these military bases could offer. We used the document to model military base conversions for the rest of the country.

Another important report, "Reintegrating the Flatlands: A Regional Framework for Military Base Conversion in the San Francisco Bay Area,"[11] was produced for UHP by Martha Matsuoka[12] and James O'Connor.[13] They made the case that the flatlands altogether should be considered as an ecological and social unit.

Ron Dellums envisioned an East Bay region-wide commission to figure out what to do with the military bases in his district. I mentioned to his staff that I would be interested in serving on the commission if I were appointed as its head. Dellums agreed. The commission consisted of about forty people, including all the mayors from his congressional district, along with the heads of many agencies and several community groups.

Converting a very strong militaristic infrastructure into something that would be compatible with and supportive of community life and sustainable development was challenging. We needed to be careful to examine our assumptions.

When we took on the project, I hadn't realized there were herons to consider. Birds love these military bases, and we had to figure out a place for them in our plan. Someone came to us with an attractive plan full of hills and natural-looking phenomenon, but another person who had more knowledge about herons described to us how the birds wouldn't actually like that landscape; herons like to make themselves at home on the airstrips because from there, they can see predators approaching from hundreds of feet away. Observing that dialogue made me realize how easy it is to design something that looks like a good home for wildlife, but actually is not.

Soon after, I was appointed to the Presidio Council, a body that would make recommendations and provide oversight for the conversion of the Presidio military base in San Francisco into a national park. We moved the offices of UHP to the Presidio to participate in this process more fully.

When Vice President Gore came to the Presidio to discuss the emerging plan for conversion of the facility, we gave him the 1995 report UHP had prepared: *Sustainability and Justice: A Message to the President's Council on Sustainable Development*. The report argues that public policy on sustainability should incorporate the three Es—environment, economy, and social equity—and gives examples of the ways in which that was happening or could happen. We put forward the idea that the popular understanding of sustainability needed to expand beyond dealing exclusively with issues of the environment and consider social equity.

The Presidio occupies fourteen thousand acres; it was a site with many buildings that could be preserved and converted for community use. Social equity and social justice needed to be at the heart of our planning process. We got the second lease (the first lease went to Mikhail Gorbachev for a house near Crissy Field) and used the building that had previously been the Red Cross headquarters for UHP. From here, we oversaw and participated in the planning for the Thoreau Center. We did not do everything that we thought could be possible, but we did put forth a number of good ideas.

During this time, I was invited to Charleston, South Carolina, to speak about the emerging environmental justice movement. Many people of color—African Americans, Latinos, and others—were there. I took advantage of being in Charleston to find out more about my ancestor, my great-great-uncle William Jervay. My assistant, Sharon Fuller, and I visited a few libraries and museums and eventually found some information about his time serving in the South Carolina legislature. We learned that he had been involved in planning the conversion of Civil War battlefields and the construction of a streetcar-based transportation system throughout Charleston. Sharon looked at me and said, "This is your résumé."

Urban Habitat Leadership Institute

Although the founding mission of UHP was to build multiracial urban environmental leadership for sustainable metropolitan communities in the San Francisco Bay Area, we did not initially have a formal structure for achieving that goal. We simply learned by doing. In 1993, we applied for and received a grant from the Columbia Foundation to create the Urban Habitat Leadership Institute.

Some people objected, arguing that trainees would sell out or use their newfound skills for personal gain instead of community betterment. I sympathized with their point of view, thinking about some of the black men from the civil rights movement who became elected officials. At the same time, I recognized that I could not have accomplished all that I had if I had not pursued leadership positions.

We moved forward, selecting our first cohort of fifteen people representing various community-based organizations and developed a program based on problem solving in the community. *The Leadership Challenge: How to Make Extraordinary Things Happen in Organizations* by James Kouzes and Barry Posner (1987) presented a particularly useful model for project-based learning. It was based on five simple and powerful tools for leaders and advocates of change to follow:

1. Challenge the process: find a way to stand up and say no to business as usual.
2. Develop a new vision: develop new ideas of what the movement or the organization should be doing.
3. Find resources to support the new vision: seek funding from foundations or the private sector.
4. Model the way: become the embodiment of the new vision.
5. Celebrate: learn how to mark successes and achievements by creating a widely shared appreciation.

Every time we faced a challenge or a problem, we did those five things.

Revisiting Academia

Around 1993, I returned to UC Berkeley briefly to teach a class called Race, Poverty, and the Environment. The class met one afternoon each week, and for a couple of hours before the class, I held an open seminar at a popular café near the university. There were a lot more students of color than when I taught there in the 1970s, and I thoroughly enjoyed the discussions that emerged in this more diverse setting. At the end of the first semester, I was honored to deliver a commencement address for the College of Natural Resources and the next spring for the Department of Geography.

In 1995, Harvard University contacted me at UHP and asked if I would consider being a fellow at the Harvard Institute of Politics. The appointment would give me a three-month sabbatical, and Harvard would cover my expenses and offer a small stipend. I would have the run of the campus, sitting in on classes as I wished, and all I would have to do was meet with a group of undergraduate students for conversation once a week; no preparation would be required. Michael Fischer, former executive director of the national Sierra Club, had recently been a fellow, and he had recommended me. I received this invitation during the winter holidays.

As I reflected upon the fellowship, I recalled that Harvard was the first university to grant a doctoral degree to a black student—first to W. E. B. Du Bois in 1895 and then to Carter Woodson in 1912. I had been deeply influenced by the writings of both men during my university days at Columbia, and I felt honored by the invitation.

I enjoyed my sojourn at Harvard. Each year, they run an orientation program for freshmen members of Congress. They also issue a special invitation to six fellows to participate in the program, typically heads of state who had recently lost an election or their representatives who needed time to reflect and transition to a new assignment.

Republicans, who controlled Congress at that time, had put a lot of pressure on Harvard to include more Republican fellows—threatening to move the orientation program to a different institution. So, I was in a group of three Democrats and three Republicans. My relations with the Republicans was strained at first, but became more collegial toward the end.

The time I spent at Harvard was like a vacation for me. All I had to do was to meet students once a week and talk with them about my work and their aspirations.

Leaving Earth Island Institute

The Urban Habitat Program (UHP) remained at Earth Island Institute (EII) for eight years. In 1997, I had a major disagreement with my colleagues and decided to resign. At issue was a controversy over traditional logging rights of local Mexican communities who had been pursuing land-based livelihoods in the Carson National Forest in New Mexico for generations. By this time, I had internalized the most important environmental values, but I had not succeeded in causing my environmentalist colleagues to internalize the imperative of racial justice. They were demonizing the Latino community-based logging enterprise as if it were on a par with transnational corporate logging operations.

I had come to understand the forest as a living ecological system that performs many important services not only for the human community but also for the whole planet, including the production of oxygen, mediation of the temperature, and purification of the water. Hundreds of these functions were being destroyed by the timber companies, which had clear-cut large percentages of the national forests. So, I agreed with my colleagues in the John Muir Project at EII on the urgency of stopping the clear-cutting and embraced the idea of zero-cut (no logging allowed) in principle. However, in the situation in New Mexico, I sided with the locals who insisted that their tradition of selective logging for small-scale commercial use would sustain both the forest and their local economy.

UHP asserted the need to understand that local communities are dependent on the forests for certain things, like firewood. We suggested introducing a category called "inhabited wilderness," which, by this time, had been established in Alaska and other places where indigenous people had longtime relationships with public lands. We thought that this might be a way to keep intact the argument for eliminating timber sales while honoring the practices of rural people who depend upon the forest for subsistence and, after all, know things about caring for the trees that most of us who live in cities do not.

We didn't ask our colleagues at EII to change their basic point about zero-cutting. We did ask them to tell the truth about the history of the land and how exploitation of people of color accompanied environmental destruction. We asked them to tell the truth about violations of people's human and land rights. We also asked them to include people of color in their planning and outreach activities.

I was shocked when EII accused us of being part of the "wise use movement," a corporate-funded campaign that advocates unrestricted access to public land for logging, mining, drilling, motorized recreation, and all commercial enterprise. *Do these white people really own planet Earth? Do they own the sun and sky?"* I asked myself. *"Why do they assume that they are the only ones who have a stake in saving our planet?"* It was clearly time for UHP to leave EII. We made the break without airing our differences publicly, expressing gratitude for our years there.

The controversy over inhabited wilderness illustrates what I see as a fundamental problem with the environmentalist mythology—the idea that, somehow, we can save nature by separating it from human activity. That human activity and the environment can coexist sustainably is evident to me in the history of indigenous peoples and their long relationships with the land. The value of such interactions was acknowledged in the Alaska National Interest Lands Conservation Act in 1980. The legislation included the setting aside of ten national parks, nine of which allow Alaska natives, whites included, customary and traditional subsistence use (Catton 1997). I am convinced that sustainable land use by indigenous people and other land-based communities should be seen as one of our global environmental imperatives.

Forming the Social Equity Caucus

The Bay Area Alliance for Sustainable Communities (BAASC)—originally named the Bay Area Alliance for Sustainable Development—was an attempt to organize and develop a sustainability plan at a regional level as the President's Council on Sustainable Development (PCSD) aimed to do for the nation.

In 1996, I was approached by Richard Clarke, retired chairman and CEO of the Pacific Gas and Electric Company (PG&E), and Michele Perrault, international vice president of the Sierra Club, both of whom were members of PCSD, to help form a regional group. I identified seventy or eighty groups that were strong advocates for social justice and invited them to a meeting. I imagined that they would ensure that social justice considerations would not be overlooked in the work of BAASC and similar groups.

The Bay Vision 2020 Commission had been created in 1989. The goal of its thirty-six members was to seek solutions to problems that cross city and county boundaries, such as traffic congestion, long commutes between home and job, shortages of affordable housing, loss of valued open space, urban sprawl, air pollution, and economic weakness. Advocates for environmental and commercial health were strongly represented, but only three members were advocates of social justice, and these members had no political base. I wanted to create a seat at the table for social justice groups and to create a democratic body capable of representing a consensus of community groups around a set of agreed-upon principles.

The BAASC continued to collaborate with the Bay Area Council, the Sierra Club, and the Association of Bay Area Governments (ABAG). After some initial mistrust, I became great friends with Sunne McPeak, who headed the Bay Area Council, the largest Bay Area trade organization with over two hundred of the biggest businesses in the Bay Area. She is a remarkable person and a sincere supporter of social equity. She explained her position on the Bay Area Council as follows: "This is where the money is; I'm going to be in charge of it."

For most of the first year, we collaborated with other Bay Area groups and worked on creating an agreement, laying out ten principles for sustainability that we would develop and follow as we went forward. It was signed by 60 percent of the counties and cities in the Bay Area.

In 1997, Sunne was very instrumental in putting together our next major effort, the Smart Growth Strategy/Regional Livability Footprint Project, which we undertook collaboratively with ABAG and the Metropolitan Transportation Commission. This project sought to define what kind of development should occur in the Bay Area and where it would best be located. It was an early plan for how the region would grow in a manner compatible with the three Es—environment, economy, and equity.

Sunne and I shared ideas on how to do something about the forty-five neighborhoods throughout the Bay Area where the majority of residents were below the poverty line. We worked together and developed the Community Capital Investment Initiative (CCII), an investment pool targeted to reduce poverty in those forty-five most vulnerable neighborhoods. CCII used new underwriting standards based on the triple bottom line. We raised about 150 million dollars in investment capital to create a family of funds—first, for businesses located in the forty-five poorest neighborhoods; second, for brownfield[14] cleanup; and third, as a Smart Growth Fund for businesses that followed practices of the triple bottom line.[15]

We decided to form the Bay Area Social Equity Caucus, a regional body of seventy-five social justice organizations, to oversee our work at BAASC. We invited Manuel Pastor, founding director of the Center for Justice, Tolerance, and Community at the University of California at Santa Cruz, and Grantland Johnson, the secretary of California's Health and Human Services Agency, to join us in hosting the first meeting of the Bay Area Social Equity Caucus at our offices in the Presidio. Sixty-eight people attended. Using the documentation that we had received from Myron Orfield and a draft compact for a sustainable Bay Area,[16] we presented our case for metropolitan regional equity organizing. The participants listened attentively.

While most people responded favorably, representatives of the Center for Third World Organizing, who were seasoned community organizers, pointed out that we did not have an organized base.

At best, they felt, we would be ineffective. In the worst case, we would be easily co-opted. Given the realities of displacement and disenfranchisement faced by our communities, however, we felt we should proceed despite the risk of failure and lack of unanimity. The Bay Area Social Equity Caucus continued to meet and work with the BAASC for the next couple of years.

Leaving the Urban Habitat Program

Increasingly, I felt I needed to move on to the next stage of my journey and confront the deeper questions of my life. Though there were still things to be done at the Urban Habitat Program (UHP), I had begun to feel restless. I needed to be more systematic about building leadership. I hadn't written my book. I knew a lot about how cities worked, but I hadn't confronted the reality of the suburbs, where, it seemed, the power lay. I was approaching my sixtieth birthday and wasn't sure what would be next. My successes at UHP were due to the fact that I had adopted a new story, but I hadn't really thought through the next steps.

I had been at the helm of UHP for ten years. During my time there, my personal interest gradually shifted to building relationships with business leaders and elected officials, which seemed necessary to achieve the goal of social transformation, but tougher questions remained—most importantly, how to build real power in low-income, grassroots communities. I announced my resignation from UHP and began letting go. We engaged CompassPoint, a consulting organization for nonprofits, to help us search for new leadership. Joe Brooks, an experienced rent control advocate and San Francisco Foundation program officer, became chair of the Urban Habitat Advisory Board and led the search for a new executive director. He has continued providing guidance to the organization ever since.

A New Opportunity for Collaboration

In 2000, the Regional Livability Footprint Project was well underway. ABAG was planning a series of countywide meetings in each of the nine counties that make up the Bay Area metropolitan region, focusing on the question of how the region should grow. Given our limited time and resources, there was no way we at UHP could mobilize our communities in time to take part. As a result, no communities of color could participate in these important meetings.

Around that time, I learned about the work of Dr. Paloma Pavel, whom I had met earlier on several occasions. Paloma had chaired the department of organizational development and social change at the California Institute of Integral Studies. It was the first graduate program in the United States that applied organizational development to social change, going beyond the narrow focus on efficiency and business success. She had also founded a nonprofit: Earth House Center. Paloma has an impressive educational background, including graduate work in public policy and organizational development at the London School of Economics and Political Science and Harvard University. She is a creative, dynamic, and articulate educator dedicated to social justice. She explained that she was experimenting with performance art as a way of linking community engagement to public policy. She invited me to take part in a performance she was planning in a warehouse in West Berkeley.

My role in Paloma's performance art show was a five-minute, spoken word piece on environmental justice that led into a recording of "Strange Fruit," the song popularized by Billie Holiday about the lynching of black men in the South. Although theatrical performance was unfamiliar territory for me, the evening was a success. Paloma and I became friends. I explained to her that I was leaving UHP and told her about the upcoming ABAG countywide meetings and my dismay that people of color would not be part of the dialogue.

Paloma proposed making a documentary film that would feature the concerns and voices of the disadvantaged communities usually left out of the public planning process. I was enthusiastic about the idea. She collaborated with Emmy Award–winning filmmaker Rick Butler in 2001 to document interviews with around fifteen people of color who had worked with the UHP over the past few years. We called it *Voices from the Community: Smart Growth and Social Equity*. The Association of Bay Area Governments agreed to show the short video at the beginning of each of the countywide meetings held in the region's nine counties. It was a big hit and provided a good introduction to a sustainability planning process that would include protections for the region's most vulnerable residents. The communities of color involved in making the film were introduced to the planning process and participated in it by sharing their perspectives.

Next Steps for the Urban Habitat Program

The advisory committee selected Juliet Ellis, who had been my personal assistant, as the new executive director. I felt confident in her ability to lead the organization forward. UHP thrived under Juliet's tenure. She gave the organization strong direction, moving operations from the Presidio to offices in Oakland at Fourteenth Street and Broadway, close to the Twelfth Street BART station, and creating a 501(c)(3) for UHP in order to give the organization greater strength and flexibility. She led the formation of a board of directors and changed the mission statement to emphasize building power in low-income, people-of-color communities. She continued to run the Bay Area Social Equity Caucus and organized and led several state of the region gatherings that focused on social equity.

Under Juliet's watch, the Urban Habitat Leadership Institute evolved into the Boards and Commissions Leadership Institute (BCLI), providing specialized training for the particular commission or board the participant wished to join. These organizations are essentially government-sponsored volunteer agencies, and their success depends upon the knowledge and skill of their members. UHP BCLI graduates serving on boards and commissions, such as planning, community development, transportation, housing, and environment, now number over 150.

She put the organization on a sound financial basis and created such an efficient operating system that she was able to take long maternity leaves during which everything went smoothly. Working as a team with the board was an important element in her success.

UHP played a unique role in the emerging environmental justice movement of the 1990s. Founding it had helped me to develop strategies to counter suburban sprawl and inner-city abandonment.

It also helped to sharpen my awareness of and effective response to conflicting forces in my life that had begun to trouble me during my childhood.

UHP served as a bridge for me from my beginnings in the advocacy planning movements of the 1960s to the forefront of strategizing for regional equity. It was a knowledge generator framing new ideas for metropolitan development, collecting and sharing stories, and creating planning tools for low-income communities and communities of color. UHP is a channel for collaboration and professional development for urban planning professionals and warriors for justice and sustainability from communities of color throughout the United States.

I challenged foundations to incorporate social and environmental justice considerations in their funding strategies. Gradually, I gained a national reputation as a leader in the environmental justice movement. I spearheaded many programs, bringing together local and regional resources for socially equitable and sustainable regional development. However, I continued to be troubled that the mainstream thought leaders in metropolitan planning were all European American men. I was looking for opportunities to bring diverse community voices into the regional equity conversation.

CHAPTER 14

Laying the Groundwork for a National Movement

S URROUNDED BY FREEWAYS, parking lots, and tall buildings, we sometimes think that our cities—and the racial hierarchies therein—have, like the mountains and rivers, been with us a very long time. Nothing could be farther from the truth. In 1800 (not that long ago in the greater scheme of things), only 3 percent of the human population lived in cities (Population Reference Bureau 2016). According to the United Nations (2014), 54 percent of the world's population was living in cities in 2014, and the proportion is expected to increase to 66 percent by 2050.

The rapid pace of urbanization places enormous pressures on water, food, and energy resources and on the global climate. Issues of inequality, public health, poverty, and violence move front and center as millions of people seeking opportunities to survive, and hopefully to thrive, pour into shantytowns that surround the burgeoning cities of developing countries. In the United States and other developed countries, structures of spatial segregation in urban regions isolate poor people from beneficial economic activities and increase inequality.

Movements for social justice linked to sustainability are transforming the ways we think about, plan, design, build, and live in cities and regions. Building the next metropolis presents many opportunities to create ecologically sound, economically viable, equitable, and healthy communities while also undoing the legacy of racism.

Recruited by the Ford Foundation

In early 2001, Angela Blackwell, who had recently founded Policy-Link, a national research and action institute dedicated to advancing economic and social equity, invited me to meet Cynthia "Mil" Duncan. Mil had published *Worlds Apart: Why Poverty Persists in Rural America* in 1999 and had just been named director of the Ford Foundation's Community and Resource Development Unit. She was in the process of building a team responsible for supporting national and international work on community development, youth, and the environment and was looking for a program officer to head the foundation's Metropolitan Sustainable Communities Initiative.

Having left my job as executive director of the Urban Habitat Program, I arranged to have a position as a visiting faculty member at the College of Natural Resources at the University of California at Berkeley. Under my agreement with the university, I would raise the money to pay for my position. My primary goal would be to work on my book.

I listened attentively as Mil described the position she was seeking to fill and the salary and benefits that the Ford Foundation was prepared to offer. To tell the truth, I really wasn't interested in becoming a program officer at the foundation. I had endured a winter at Harvard in 1996, and the idea of returning to the East Coast was not appealing. Besides, I was looking forward to staying in Berkeley and working on my book. At the end of our meeting, however, Mil made me an offer that was too good to refuse.

I must admit that the potential of taking my work at the Urban Habitat Program to a national scale appealed to me. Funders can play an important role in catalyzing social movements not only by providing grant money to support key organizations but also by encouraging new partnerships among organizations that may not have previously worked together or even encountered one another. Plus, I was looking forward to laying eyes on the Ford Foundation building again.

Back to New York

When I was an architecture student at Columbia University in the mid-1960s, I went with fellow students to visit the Ford Foundation's enormous new headquarters shortly before its completion. It is a spectacular twelve-story L-shaped building made of steel, concrete, pink granite, and glass. The building frames two sides of an indoor terraced garden and atrium with glass walls that extend up to the roof and a cantilevered skylight, bringing light into the building and enabling most of its occupants to view the garden and one another. Other offices have a view of the East River. It is one of the most splendid buildings in New York.

Working from this citadel that reflected many of the realities of the global economy did cause me some apprehension. The Ford Foundation, after all, was created by Henry Ford, a key figure in exploding the reach of the automobile industry to a global level. In other words, the wealth from which the Ford Foundation had sprung was built from initiating a global dependence on petroleum. Learning of the role I would play on the forefront of efforts to create a sustainable economy that relied on a new and equitable pattern of development settled my qualms. I reported for work in June of 2001 and was given an office on the seventh floor overlooking the atrium. The view was spectacular!

When I arrived in New York that June, I stayed in an apartment that the foundation keeps on the Upper East Side while I looked for a place of my own. I looked at apartments all over Manhattan and finally decided to move into a building four blocks from the foundation offices so I could walk to work.

Ford Foundation's Change of Direction

The Ford Foundation had been a presence in my life since the middle of the 1950s when I was a teenager. Through my interest in urban planning, I became aware of the foundation's Gray Areas Program, with its overt purpose to find ways to fund areas that had been overlooked in the development of our cities. I learned much later that it was also intended to smooth the way for the expansion of downtowns by means of urban renewal, which demolished housing in African American neighborhoods. The director of the foundation's Division of National Affairs, who had been an aide to Philadelphia's mayor, managed the program. The program started in Philadelphia, where it began to materialize the vision I had encountered when my third-grade class visited the Better Philadelphia Exhibition, and was then expanded to four other cities. The Gray Areas Program took a top-down approach, which was very different from the participatory, community-based revitalization practices I later learned from Karl Linn.

In the United States, the foundation has focused increasingly on the ways that metropolitan fragmentation and sprawl exacerbate patterns of residential segregation and concentrated poverty. After observing how development, growth, and wealth were being generated in suburban enclaves while inner cities stagnated, the Ford Foundation started investing in what were called community development corporations (CDCs).[1] The foundation funded these individual development organizations in cities across the country, beginning in the 1960s when Robert Kennedy started the Bedford Stuyvesant Restoration Corporation, which then became a national model.[2] CDCs like Bedford-Stuyvesant were an instrument for people from predominately African American neighborhoods to undertake housing and economic development as an antipoverty strategy. People from the neighborhood sat on the CDC's boards, taking part in the planning and development of their neighborhoods for the benefit of the people who lived there. The idea was that this would empower residents to redesign and rebuild their own neighborhoods and to help create a healthier future.

Between 1979 and 1996, Franklin Thomas, an African American man, served as president of the Ford Foundation. Before him, all the Ford Foundation's presidents had been from the white elite. Thomas had grown up in a large low-income West Indian family in the Bedford-Stuyvesant neighborhood; he had done well in school and gone on to a distinguished career in law. Robert Kennedy had appointed him the first president of the Bedford-Stuyvesant Restoration Corporation. As president of the foundation, Thomas invested in a series of CDCs. Yet, by the 1990s, the CDC model came under sharp criticism for not being able to adequately address urban poverty. The argument was that while the population served by the CDC may have experienced growth and development and the economy of the larger metropolitan region had improved as a result, these economic opportunities did not extend to the many people of color living in urban areas. Inner-city poverty was a huge systemic problem that could not be adequately addressed by making grants to isolated CDCs. The Ford Foundation was ready to make a change. Their long tradition of working with CDCs was winding down, and my new position meant that I would have a say in how they would move forward.

The Need for a Smart and Equitable Regional Perspective

The idea of focusing on a metropolitan region rather than a single neighborhood, city, or suburb was emerging from various directions. Through my work at the Urban Habitat Program, I had come in contact with thought leaders like Bruce Katz, David Rusk, and Myron Orfield and their seminal works about regionalism and social justice.

From these thought leaders, I gleaned that the community development strategy didn't access metropolitan regions' most dynamic forces of growth and development, which were actually out in the suburbs. Suburban expansion and growth were generating new opportunities and wealth, including new economic institutions, industrial parks, commercial development, and schools. Inner-city people, even those who were part of a CDC, were not connected to the larger economy or the larger dynamics of the region. Bruce Katz and Amy Liu explored these conditions by founding the Metropolitan Policy Program at the Brookings Institution in 1996 to research and promote innovative strategies for metropolitan regions to foster sustainable economic growth while increasing opportunities for all residents. In order to attack the problems of poverty and the isolation of low-income communities trapped in the inner city, David Rusk (1999) suggested that we need a dual strategy of working locally where poor people live to generate jobs and wealth (he called this the "inside game") while fighting for larger policy reform ("outside game") that helps local efforts by influencing the centers of power at the regional level and reforming the metropolitan regions to create more opportunities for communities of color. David Rusk's ideas echoed some of the observations in the Kerner Commission report of 1968, particularly the need to connect urban communities to the kinds of opportunities that exist in the suburbs.

When I was working at the Urban Habitat Program, one of our most important resources for developing a regional approach was our relationship with Myron Orfield. Myron worked with us and other metropolitan regions, mapping the assets of the whole region and then moving on to assessment and planning. He also made an enormous contribution by documenting his work in the Twin Cities (Minneapolis and St. Paul, Minnesota) on the interdependence of cities and suburbs. He showed that the suburbs are not monolithic; some are wealthy and positioned to capture the spoils of growth while others are left behind. Orfield proposed that there was a basis for collaboration between the inner cities and the inner-ring suburbs where the poverty quotient was high. A revenue-sharing plan that had been successfully used in the Twin Cities, where he served in the Minnesota legislature, put 40 percent of each city and town in the region's tax receipts into a common pool and then redistributed funding based on need. In 1997's *Metropolitics: A Regional Agenda for Community and Stability,* Myron mapped the twenty-five largest metropolitan regions in the United States and demonstrated how the plan could benefit them. It was an amazing idea that caught on in a lot of places.

The regional equity policy recommendations proposed by Rusk, Katz, and Orfield made sense to me, but to be successful, they would require increased communication and collaboration among affected populations in the cities and suburbs. As a foundation executive, I could now influence public dialogue through grantmaking and the foundation's power to bring together different groups of people throughout society. In particular, the most marginalized, low-income communities of color need to be in the conversation because if they are not, the new policy direction will, at best, continue to be the same top-down decision making; at worst, it will be counterproductive and intensify racial polarization. I had the potential to mobilize people whose voices had not been heard and then engage them in communications about these new ideas. The environmental justice movement had inspired many marginalized communities to address issues of toxic pollution, but there were additional issues of racial, economic, and social equity that needed to be addressed at the regional level. While I was reflecting on the regional equity perspectives put forward by Rusk, Orfield, and Katz, I was also thinking about environmental sustainability from a regional perspective.

The Ford Foundation had tasked me to put together a portfolio on smart growth and regional equity. Existing patterns of metropolitan development were under attack from the environmental movement, which had a strong bias toward no growth, but the idea of smart growth had been taking shape since the 1970s when architect Peter Calthorpe started speaking and writing about designing walkable and transit-oriented cities and regions. The term smart growth now refers to a collection of principles for land use and development, including increased density for more efficient use of land and energy; opportunities for shopping, recreation, jobs, and transportation within comfortable walking distance of living spaces; safer access to public transit and travel by foot or bicycle; and preservation of the natural environment, including open space and agricultural lands.

I have known Peter Calthorpe for many years. In the late 1970s, when my friend and UC Berkeley colleague, Sim Van der Ryn, was appointed California's state architect, Peter served as deputy. Sim and Peter's work together focused on creating a new framework for architects and planners to address sustainability from a regional perspective, but they lacked a strong emphasis on social equity, a trend that continued in Peter's later work.

Although I advocated smart growth policies throughout the 1990s, I remained apprehensive that as societies moved toward smart growth and related policies, they would fail to include social equity or racial justice in their considerations. Smart growth represented a positive shift toward making the environment an important determinant in urban design, but too often, it was used to add a thin veneer of environmental concern to conventional real estate development.

A Culture of Collaboration at the Ford Foundation

All the program officers at the Ford Foundation were encouraged to hire a strategic communications consultant or consulting organization to create key messages from the unit to the outside world and to help with communication among the grantees. I selected Dr. Paloma Pavel, with whom I had worked on communications between the Social Equity Caucus and the Association of Bay Area Governments during the Plan Bay Area process. Early on, I invited her to work with me on an assessment of opportunities for innovation at the Ford Foundation. She helped me conduct a listening tour within the foundation—interviewing the leaders of various programs. We asked them about innovations they had made and ones they knew about in other programs. We discovered that there had not been a culture of collaboration. I was happy to bring to the Ford Foundation the spirit of celebrating, learning, and discovering together that I had enjoyed at the Urban Habitat Program.

During my tenure, the foundation had a worldwide meeting on communications, bringing representatives from all its global sites together with the New York headquarters. Foundation staff were working through many different communication challenges and looking for innovations. People in general were starting to use the Internet more, and the people at Ford were beginning to see the importance of communication on multiple levels. Their desire to build a culture where the program officers and the central administration were in the background was revealed in the expression, "Speak through your grantees." In other words, they wanted to move specific agendas, but through our grantees. I liked this notion; it was a great antidote to the tendency to lord over people when administering grants. When we were asked to present the work of our most progressive and innovative grantees at the foundation trustees meeting, we would bring the grantees to the central office and have them talk directly to the trustees. This was enlightening for the trustees and empowering for the grantees, and it helped keep the program officers in a supportive, coordinating, facilitating role.

Grantmaking for the Sustainable Metropolitan Communities Initiative

The Ford Foundation brought me in to head the Sustainable Metropolitan Communities Initiative (SMCI), an initiative to reduce patterns of concentrated poverty in the United States while promoting conservation of natural resources. I had eighteen months to study the existing program—to determine who it was serving and how it was funded—and make a proposal for how I would adapt and develop it. The central strategy was to take advantage of emerging new policies from the fields of smart growth and regional equity and find ways to connect them to communities who would act on, elaborate on, or reinvent them. SMCI funded the policy advocates whose ideas were found to be the most empowering. Chosen among these advocates were Orfield, Katz, and Rusk, who had enormously valuable ideas, but lacked strong community support. Together, we worked through SMCI to create a broad-based popular movement for regional equity.

Organizations that had a commitment to social and racial justice in society were becoming aware of environmental and sustainability issues. That new awareness worked to mobilize ordinary citizens in the cities and the suburbs, including members of faith-based organizing groups, labor groups, community development corporations, and other community-based organizations. Some groups based in the suburbs expanded their focus to include metropolitan areas while some academic and policy-oriented groups developed interest in supporting the convergence of social justice and sustainability.[3]

Through SMCI, we funded a variety of projects dealing with the different manifestations of poverty that we saw throughout metropolitan regions, funding policy organizations, organizing networks, and some individual projects that were clearly demonstration projects.[4] As we sought out potential grantee organizations throughout the country, we were concerned about three key issues: the displacement caused by gentrification; disinvestment and white flight in the older suburbs in response to increased diversity, which we called the suburbanization of poverty; and the need for continuing investment in new opportunities.

At the foundation, we were required to select suitable grantees who reflected the purpose of SMCI and to develop an expenditure plan for six years or for the extent of our contract. Each program officer started with four million dollars annually, or approximately twenty-four million dollars over six years (the length of a program officer contract), to be disbursed among the grantees we selected. We decided to invest in social justice organizations that were interested in working on environmental and sustainability issues and environmental and policy-making organizations interested in social justice—all of which had a regional perspective.

Our goal was not only to fund these organizations and projects, but also to develop a communication strategy that would link each to other activities in communities across the country. The idea was that we would be engaged in social movement building based on sustainability, as well as economic, environmental, and social justice. These were issues that had often been put in opposition to each other, but we sought to transform that, investigating through our grantees and the connections between them how, for example, jobs could be created that would improve the environment. By connecting our grantees in a collaborative environment, we strived to make the Ford Foundation into a community-based national learning network.

There are three hundred metropolitan regions in the country, each with unique characteristics. There are large cities, such as New York City, Chicago, and Los Angeles, and smaller cities, such as Camden in New Jersey and Charleston in South Carolina. There are cities that have been experiencing surges in economic growth, and there are weak-market cities being left behind. Cities differ widely in ethnic and racial composition—some have a strong African American presence while others have growing Latino, Asian, and Pacific Islander populations. Working at the Ford Foundation gave me the experience of working in a cross-section of diverse metropolitan regions and confirmed the idea that a regional equity strategy might work across the board.

Our organizing networks included the labor movement, civil rights groups, faith-based groups, transportation justice organizations, advocates of housing and good schools for low-income communities, and some CDCs. Each of these organizations was chosen for its long-standing commitment to social and racial justice, emerging focus on sustainability, and potential to expand its agenda to the metropolitan scale. Through this work, the SMCI could reach many constituencies that had a stake in regional processes, but had not been included in the process of defining the new metropolitan vision. To create a national movement, the SMCI brought together eight broad constituencies that were working on these issues and were ready to be mobilized: philanthropy, regional equity advocates, community organizing groups, community development corporations, civil rights groups, organized labor, urban farmers connecting to school districts, and cities facing severe abandonment.

Philanthropic Organizations The Ford Foundation is one of the largest foundations in the world. However, even if the foundation dedicated all its resources to addressing the issue of urban poverty, it would only be a drop in the bucket compared to what is needed. Under the auspices of the Funders' Network for Smart Growth and Livable Communities,[5] we reached out to other foundations that were interested in these ideas. We formed a working group focused on regional and neighborhood equity, and engaged many other funders to contribute to this effort. For example, some, like the Annie E. Casey Foundation, had been historically interested in supporting anti-poverty efforts while others, like the Robert Wood Johnson Foundation, were interested in addressing issues of public health. The results of this outreach were published 2005 in *Signs of Progress*, a report I coauthored with Funders' Network director, L. Benjamin Starrett.

Regional Equity Advocates In my work at the Ford Foundation, my goal was to nurture the growth of a national movement for regional equity and not simply to fund projects. I convened a gathering of regional equity advocates and activists from across the nation, which we came to call the Conversation on Regional Equity (CORE). Our intention was to amplify the growth in understanding and skill among our grantees and others interested in our work. This conversation brought together leaders of US policy groups and grassroots organizers to help lay the groundwork for the next few decades of building a national movement for regional equity.[6] A dozen thinkers and activists most closely involved in CORE met as a small group four times in four locations, with the first meeting held in New York in 2004.

In each place we met, our CORE group visited some of the vulnerable communities for whom we were advocating to ground the conversation in firsthand experience. In Los Angeles, one of our focuses was transportation of goods and the toxic effects of diesel exhaust from freight routes that frequently run right through low-income communities and communities of color. I will never forget seeing Bruce Katz blasted by rushing air and clanging noise as a giant freight train surged past only a few feet from the small houses of a predominantly African American and Latino community we were visiting in Los Angeles. Even though Bruce had published many influential books and reports on creating equity in urban regions, this was the first time he had stood in one of the many neighborhoods that suffer from near-constant toxic pollution and noise. Feeling the impact in his body for the first time, he was blown away.

African Americans and Other Communities of Color Many civil rights organizations had been focusing on helping inner-city African American neighborhoods. We wanted to support them in expanding their focus to the metropolitan region. In South Carolina, for example, we worked with the Center for Heirs' Property Preservation, helping to educate and empower low-income African American property owners to stand their ground against predatory developers and governmental pressures to give up land that had been in their families for generations. In the South, except for brief intervals during Reconstruction, African Americans had been denied access to the legal and other social infrastructures that protected whites.

Consequently, they developed their own ways of civil organization, such as passing land ownership from one generation to the next without a written title. In the late twentieth century, these rural lands were becoming desirable for suburban expansion or as tourist sites. Families were losing their land to developers and governments that used legal loopholes to claim the land or found an individual family member who was willing to sell and displace the rest of the family. The Center for Heirs' Property Preservation provides technical assistance to African American landowners navigating the property laws, helps them acquire written titles, and mobilizes them to protect their land and shape its future according to their own needs and priorities.

In Richmond, California, we funded the Richmond Equitable Development Initiative (REDI), which brought together several groups in the San Francisco Bay Area to collaborate on local issues and push for adding a climate action and a health section to the Richmond's General Plan. The mobilizing effort in Richmond began with a focus on the African American community and the effects of pollution from the Chevron refinery in Richmond. The West County Toxics Coalition and Citizens for a Better Environment (now known as Communities for a Better Environment to include those whose citizenship is unclear) initially led these efforts. The REDI collaborative was later joined by the Urban Habitat Program, East Bay Alliance for a Sustainable Economy, PolicyLink, and others.

It soon became evident that the stories of other communities needed to be included. The REDI collaborative has since been strengthened by the participation of the Asian Pacific Environmental Network (APEN). While APEN's initial focus was on environmental justice for the Laotian community, it has ended up playing a leadership role for not only the San Francisco Bay Area region but also the entire state of California. Environmental justice efforts in Richmond benefitted from the influx of youthful energy that came with support from Movement Generation, an organization dedicated to educating and mobilizing multiracial, working-class communities on ecological justice issues. What started as an African American campaign in Richmond has blossomed into a multiracial regional movement.

Regional Equity Demonstration Projects At the beginning of my work at the Ford Foundation, the six program officers in our department were operating in isolation from one another. Each funded organizations in their area of specialty only—forestry, community development corporations, technology, youth, etc. They had little or no exposure to other aspects of their grantees' programs and needs. Mil Duncan suggested that it might be interesting to select several metropolitan areas in which to develop a collaborative approach so that several program officers would be investing in each of these areas. I agreed. Eventually, we settled on five metropolitan regions as demonstration projects—Camden, New Jersey; Richmond, California; Atlanta, Georgia; Baltimore, Maryland; and Detroit, Michigan.

We invested most heavily in Camden since it was closest to Ford headquarters. Each component had its own program officer. We funded a community organizing network and an economic development organization. We also funded a redevelopment agency for the city of Camden. We funded a tree planting program, an environmental justice toxic clean-up site, a youth program, and a project on innovations in education. Our goal in this regional demonstration was to see if we could build collaborations among separate community interests.

Community Organizing Groups We funded several regional groups affiliated with the Gamaliel Foundation, which models its organizing approach on the ideas of Saul Alinsky, the Chicago community organizer about whom Manuel Castells wrote in *The City and the Grassroots* in 1983.

We put a huge amount of effort into our work in New Jersey. Camden had a reputation for violent crime. Our core efforts included organizing and economic development, and we invited other program officers to support forestry, community philanthropy, and youth development projects. We gained many ideas about the effectiveness of regional equity strategies with those investments.

A significant challenge in Camden was that there was no pattern of investment and we needed to figure out how to change that. We were promoting an organization called the New Jersey Regional

Coalition, which brought urban and suburban constituencies together around a new vision for the state. The New Jersey Supreme Court had created landmark legislation requiring every community to make its fair share of investment in affordable housing. The court's intention was to open up suburban neighborhoods with their better-funded schools and increased job opportunities to more of the region's economically disadvantaged citizens.

Of course, the wealthy communities didn't want affordable housing in their nice lily-white neighborhoods, so they got around the ruling by giving the money they would have spent on building the subsidized units—thirty to forty thousand dollars per unit—to the poor communities to build housing in their own communities. We understood that they were actually investing in keeping poor people away from opportunity—at thirty to forty thousand dollars a pop. These so-called Regional Contribution Agreements nullified the concept of opportunity-based housing, and a coalition of groups and individuals mounted a vigorous regional campaign to oppose them. Eventually, we had a major breakthrough: legislation was passed mandating that municipalities could no longer pay poor communities to keep their people away from housing opportunities elsewhere.

In the Detroit region, we worked with Metropolitan Organizing Strategies Enabling Strength (MOSES), a community-organizing group that began as a project of the Gamaliel Foundation and eventually led to collaboration with the Local Initiative Support Corporation.[7] MOSES staff and volunteers organized a meeting of various community-based groups from within Detroit and the surrounding suburban communities. On the agenda was what could be done with Detroit's ninety thousand vacant properties, about half of which were owned by the city. Over five thousand people showed up! They mapped all those properties and figured out which ones they could bring back and put into a new framework. Others would be transformed into urban farming communities. That was a major project.

Community Development Corporations (CDCs) The CDCs we worked with were atypical since they had developed regional organizing strategies. Bethel New Life, a Chicago-based community development corporation, was building new housing in West Garfield, a neighborhood on the West Side of Chicago. Bethel New Life was remarkable in its ability to reach out to organizations that were not traditional allies of inner-city neighborhoods. The Ford Board of Trustees made a site visit to our grantee Bethel New Life. They informed the board that they had engaged as consultants to the Argonne National Laboratory, the birthplace of the first nuclear bomb. The Argonne engineers were repurposing their skills to build non-toxic, energy-efficient housing.

Bethel New Life continuously exemplified some of the best thinking about CDCs. When the Chicago Transit Authority planned to take down the "L" train that went from the suburban neighborhoods, through this inner-city neighborhood, and then to downtown, the people from Bethel New Life took great issue; this line, the Green Line, was their best lifeline to the economy of the city. City authorities stood by the plan, so Bethel New Life organized inner-city residents, who began to go into the suburbs and organize alongside suburban residents in support of the Green Line, which still stands today. Bethel New Life's regional vision impressed me and my colleagues at the Ford Foundation: this CDC from a disadvantaged neighborhood had organized inner-city and suburban residents alike to keep a neighborhood asset, which was of great significance at the regional level, from being destroyed.

Bethel New Life continued to impress: a proposal was put forward by the city government to tear down the Garfield Park Conservatory located in West Garfield. The conservatory perennially struggled to attract visitors; there would be as few as ten or fifteen visitors in an entire year. Voices from West Garfield spoke up in support of keeping the conservatory open, but with such drastic underutilization, the significant cost of maintenance—heat, electricity, and staff—could not be balanced. Bethel New Life would need to make Garfield Park Conservatory's continued existence financially feasible.

The community reached out to Dale Chihuly, a world-famous glassblower. Chihuly designed an exhibition for the conservatory. The exhibition became a magnet for people from all over the Chicago metropolitan area—six or seven thousand people visited when it first opened. Since then, the participation rates at the conservatory, which had previously been threatened with closure, have remained remarkably high.

With people from all over the metropolitan region riding the Green Line into West Garfield to visit the conservatory, Bethel New Life proposed taking an old building that was located at the intersection of the Green Line stop and renovating it to have retail and other services on the first floor and training facilities for community use on the second floor. The building, which was called Bethel Center, included a green roof and direct connection to the train stop via a bridge. These features brought together some of the best in environmental and social sustainability and earned Bethel Center the first LEED certification in the state of Illinois. Imagine! A poor lower-income disadvantaged neighborhood creating a LEED-certified building and demonstrating more advanced techniques for the ways that we should be rehabilitating all our buildings throughout the metropolitan region.

Whether we were taking on projects in maximizing energy efficiency in housing in Chicago, transit-oriented development (TOD)[8] in Baltimore, or mixed-income suburban housing projects in Atlanta,[9] the Ford Foundation gave me the tremendous privilege of working with a number of other innovative and impactful CDCs.

Organized Labor We worked with the Los Angeles Alliance for a New Economy (LAANE), a labor organization in Los Angeles, to negotiate a community benefits agreement (CBA) around the expansion of the Los Angeles International Airport, or LAX. The large and diverse coalition they formed—the LAX Coalition for Economic, Environmental and Educational Justice—reminded me of the Social Equity Caucus we formed in the San Francisco Bay Area during my years at the Urban Habitat Program. The CBA was a legally binding agreement between the developers, cities, and communities that would define what benefits would actually be delivered to the community. To mitigate the huge problems that the noise and pollution from the airport expansion was creating for the neighboring communities, the LAX expansion developers shifted the landing patterns to reduce the negative stress from airport operations and agreed to provide more than 8.5 million dollars annually for the soundproofing of local schools, city buildings, places of worship, and homes. They also agreed to fund studies on air quality and community health, implement a number of other environmental controls, and provide jobs and educational and economic opportunities for the surrounding residents and the community organizations representing them. Such CBAs help ensure equitable development that benefits all members of the community. This contributes to stronger local economies, livable neighborhoods, and increased public participation in the planning process. The use of CBAs has spread throughout the country.

Farm and School Alliance A wonderful new opportunity was working with Robert Gottlieb and colleagues at Occidental College in Los Angeles to build an alliance between regional farmers and inner-city schools. The small family farmers needed to find markets for their produce while the schools wanted affordable healthy food for their lunch programs. We supported the collaboration between metropolitan farmers and schools in Southern California, strengthening the local farming economy, providing schoolchildren with farm-fresh food, and reinforcing connections between farms and schools via school field trips and other learning opportunities. These experiences helped students connect to the land and understand its role in sustaining our bodies and the economy of our regions.

Cities Facing Abandonment In addition to our work with MOSES in Detroit and our work in Camden, there were thousands and thousands of properties throughout the country that had been abandoned. We took on the question of abandoned properties not only as a social justice issue but also as an environmental concern—all these neighborhoods and cities were built using materials from the natural world. The buildings and their materials were being thrown away instead of being reused. Most of these cities were suffering because people were moving to the suburban fringes and abandoning the inner parts of the country in favor of coastal regions—East, West, and South. There were not only huge sections of each metropolitan region suffering from abandonment but also entire metro regions suffering as a whole, particularly in the Midwest with Cleveland, Ohio; Kansas City, Kansas; and St. Louis, Missouri. Up and down the country, urban suburban and rural areas were being abandoned. We looked at the pattern of abandoned buildings in these large metro regions and reached out to many stakeholders dealing with this issue. We brought together police departments, fire departments, and municipal jurisdictions to share ideas about how to bring those properties back into productive use.

Solidifying the Movement: Communications and the Learning Community

Throughout my work at the Ford Foundation, I realized that communications are an essential part of how a community learns and grows together. I had this insight during my work at the Urban Habitat Program, and it became more apparent as I collaborated with Paloma on Sustainable Metropolitan Communities Initiative (SMCI) communications.

The strategic communications plan Paloma designed for the SMCI—the Vision to Action Plan—consisted of seven strategies for creating a national movement:

1. Build the basic infrastructure
2. Brand the movement
3. Celebrate the victories
4. Build synergy across spokespeople
5. Develop capacity of grantees
6. Invest in model regions for grassroots advocacy grantees
7. Build a national campaign

The plan was very effective in getting publicity for our work and encouraging collaboration among grantee organizations.

Our ongoing work documenting the process of the SMCI culminated in a multiple-episode documentary series called *The New Metropolis*, produced by filmmaker Andrea Torrice (2009). It consisted of three episodes describing community-organizing efforts that resulted in breakthroughs in regional equity. Two of these episodes were approved for broadcast on PBS and were presented in 150 metropolitan regions across the country with a mobilizing strategy that included community dialogues. People gathered in their homes and in public places to have conversations about what they had seen and the implications for regional equity efforts in their own metropolitan regions.

While reviewing the projects I supported at the Ford Foundation in preparation for developing her book, *Breakthrough Communities*, Paloma observed the reoccurrence of a pattern or process, which she named the Compass for Transformative Leadership. This five-stage process begins with "Waking Up" to a new challenge or opportunity confronting the community. In the second stage, "Saying No," community members come together in opposition to something damaging the community. Common examples are sit-ins, boycotts, demonstrations, or litigation. In the third stage, "Getting Grounded," organizers and participants step back to assess the current situation and look at the social, economic, and political forces in their surroundings that are causing the problems. In the fourth stage, they are "Exploring New Horizons," or identifying nontraditional partners who can help develop solutions. This leads to the final stage, "Saying Yes," where groups commit to creative collaborations that produce long-term benefits for their communities (Pavel 2009, xxxviii–xxxix, 110–12). Upon reflection, I realized that our collective action was balanced between saying "no" to injustices and threats to our communities and putting forward a fully articulated vision of what we were saying "yes" to in the regional planning process. This holistic approach gave us the momentum and grounding to be effective as coalitions and create impact at the regional scale.

Our collaborative work at the Ford Foundation to build a movement for regional equity led to the publication of five books—the first two from Robert Bullard: *The Black Metropolis in the Twenty-First Century: Race, Power, and Politics of Place* (2007), an anthology he compiled and edited, and *Growing Smarter: Achieving Livable Communities, Environmental Justice, and Regional Equity* (2008). Manuel Pastor, Chris Benner, and Martha Matsuoka wrote *This Could Be the Start of Something Big: How Social Movements for*

Regional Equity Are Reshaping Metropolitan America (2009). Amy Dean and David Reynolds wrote *A New New Deal: How Regional Activism Will Reshape the American Labor Movement* (2009). Finally, there was *Breakthrough Communities: Sustainability and Justice in the Next American Metropolis* (2009), the collection of essays and reports that Paloma compiled and edited. Each of these publications grew directly out of the foundation's SMCI.

Urbanization as a Global Trend

Though my portfolio at SMCI was focused on cities in the United States, several events and experiences helped to give me a more global perspective. I was flown to Durban, South Africa, just a week after I moved into my new apartment in New York, to attend the 2001 World Conference against Racism, Racial Discrimination, Xenophobia and Related Intolerance[10]. The conference and the additional week I spent there were full of discoveries.

I was pleased to run into my friend Belvie Rooks, an amazing activist and networker, who, like me, is inspired by Thomas Berry's vision and its potential for healing and empowering African Americans, especially youth. A few years earlier, with partial funding from the Urban Habitat Program, she had developed a multimedia curriculum used as a pilot program with teenagers of South Central Los Angeles. It modeled a way that students could learn state-of-the-art multimedia technology while exploring critical social and environmental issues affecting their communities. In the course of creating an interactive CD, the students trace their personal timelines through family, community, bioregion, planet, solar system, and, ultimately, the universe. By identifying their heritage with the cosmic beginnings of our universe, they enlarge their perspectives and gain an ennobling and empowered sense of self.[11]

A decade later, Belvie and her partner, Dedan Gills, shared a transformative experience while visiting one of the slave castles in West Africa where chained captives had been held before being shipped from their homeland and sold into a lifetime of labor. Out of their grief, Belvie and Dedan were inspired by a vision of planting a million trees along the routes the enslaved were led to Atlantic port cities in Africa and along the Underground Railroad in the United States, routes to freedom. A desire to honor and remember the millions lost to the slave trade combined with intent to combat the effects of global warming and climate change. They named their project "Growing a Global Heart."

The conference had drawn many other delegates from the burgeoning environmental justice movement in the United States, including American Indians and native Hawaiians. Vernice Miller, cofounder of the West Harlem Environmental Action and an environmental justice program officer at the Ford Foundation, was also there with her staff.[12] I touched base with many activists and community leaders with whom I had worked at Earth Island Institute and the Urban Habitat Program. Environmental justice was clearly becoming an international movement, and that was very encouraging.

In South Africa, I enjoyed talking with the delegation from the Dalit (untouchables) community in India. I was struck by the similarities between their situation and the challenges faced by my ancestors and, to some extent, by contemporary African Americans. The Dalits were at the center of much discussion and dialogue at the conference. Not surprisingly, the Indian government tried to deflect accusations of racism by claiming that mistreatment of Dalits is a matter of caste and not race.

During the conference, Israel came under sharp criticism for its mistreatment of the Palestinian people. This was perceived as anti-Semitism by some politicians back in the US and resulted in a sharp reaction in Congress to what was happening at the Ford Foundation. A New York congressman introduced legislation to put the foundation under surveillance for its supposedly anti-Israel stance.

While in South Africa, our group of Ford program officers visited Khayelitsha, a neighborhood on the outskirts of Cape Town with housing developed by a group of impoverished and often homeless women. In 1992, they formed the Victoria Mxenge Housing Savings Scheme, named after the beloved anti-apartheid activist and lawyer assassinated in 1985. As apartheid was in effect and black people could not borrow credit from banks, they began saving. I was impressed by a chart showing each woman's contributions to the collective savings account—rarely exceeding one South African rand (less than ten cents) every day.

They built their first house in 1996. With their savings, help from non-governmental organizations (NGOs), and an initial gift of land from the Catholic Church, they designed and built a model sustainable community that now consists of over five thousand homes. They later became the Victoria Mxenge Housing Development Association and began sharing their skills and strategies with other needy communities.[13] I was deeply inspired by all they had accomplished.

I returned from South Africa and settled into my apartment in Midtown Manhattan, an area I had never lived in before. One September day while walking to work, I saw a bunch of people huddled around a TV set in a store, looking at what I thought was some science fiction show. On the screen, an airplane was flying into a building over and over. Bewildered, I wondered to myself, "Why aren't these people going to work? Don't they know it's nine o'clock and we're supposed to be at work?" Of course, that was September 11, 2001, and everyone was reeling from the shocking destruction of over three thousand lives and the entirety of the World Trade Center, including its iconic Twin Towers that had defined the skyline of Lower Manhattan. It struck me that I had almost rented an apartment near those towers.

The Ford Foundation was changed by September 11 in many ways. The xenophobia that emerged in reaction to the attacks created a different atmosphere. The foundation had spent a lot of money to provide scholarships for people to attend the conference against racism. In the wake of September 11, that expenditure came under criticism. We had to be more focused on our programs. Although this didn't undercut what I was doing, it did change it— everything tightened down. In a couple of months, the atmosphere shifted from one that was quite open to one where we had to be guarded about all our communications.

In the face of the enormous tragedy, I brought my best intentions and thinking to multiple meetings with architects, designers, and decision makers in New York City. I was heartened when my dear friend Max Bond received the contract to spearhead and oversee the National September 11 Memorial and Museum at the World Trade Center site.

My second trip to South Africa was in September of 2002 for the second World Summit on Sustainable Development (WSSD) in Johannesburg. The first WSSD took place in Rio de Janeiro in 1992, so this one was informally called Rio+10. I enjoyed the shared experience of traveling to and attending the summit with more than a dozen grantees of SMCI. We were all eager to participate in meetings and share best practices and challenges, feeling that increasing our knowledge of worldwide sustainability issues would make us more effective in our work in the United States. We were a diverse group— old and young, famous and unknown, and policy experts and community organizers: a microcosm of the communities I wanted to bring together. We camped at the Ford Foundation's Global Tent Village at the Rift Valley, the cradle of humankind where the first humans emerged in Africa millions of years ago. Anthropologists were excavating sites where the oldest hominid fossils had been found while we, in the same valley, were contemplating the possible collapse of conditions that support complex life on Earth.

We were housed in tents surrounded by zebras and giraffes that roamed around our canvas shelters in the night. Our tent village neighbors included activists from Ford Foundation projects around the world, and all were eager to learn directly from peer-to-peer contacts. By day, we rode in buses to the conference proceedings in Johannesburg, a short distance away. On our way, we passed the township of Soweto, home of Nelson Mandela and historic site in the struggle against apartheid. The settlement had grown up around gold mining, one of the largest extractive industries in South Africa. We learned that Soweto leaders and activists, in recovering from apartheid, were organizing their efforts around the same three Es to which we were committed: economics, environment, and equity. The Soweto residents we met were aware of and articulate about their environmental restoration path.

The Ford Foundation had funded sustainability projects for the Makuleke people, who had built an ecovillage inside of Kruger National Park, the largest game reserve in South Africa and one of the most celebrated wildlife sanctuaries in the world. I was invited to visit with a group of my grantees. The apartheid government had seized the traditional lands of the indigenous Makuleke in 1969 and enforced a whites-only policy. Specially trained forces had patrolled the perimeter and were notorious for killing black Africans. In 1998, after two years of complex negotiations, the Makuleke signed an agreement to manage the land as a Community Restoration Project (Steyn 2012, 72). We spoke with the Makuleke chief about restoring indigenous communities' relationship to their land and livelihoods and the relationship between black South Africans and nature. We asked him, "How will you learn sustainability and teach the younger ones?" His response came easily:

> It sounds very funny if they say black people cannot manage or conserve nature. We have been living here for many years. When I was growing up, we had indigenous trees from which we used to harvest fruits. We didn't cut down the trees; we sustained this wildlife, including biodiversity itself.
>
> We are now training some people as guides. We also have a study center where children are learning the way of conservation. We are learning Astro Tracking [tracking the stars] with computers. Another way of teaching is through our culture. People who are working here have established a choir. When they are home, they sing about this place. Through this, they show they are coming back to our life and connected to what they are doing. Some of the workers are in singing groups and dancing groups. So, you see, we have the power of our culture. We are quite equipped to face the challenge.

In 2004, I was appointed deputy director of the Ford Foundation's Community Resources Development Unit, and subsequently served as acting director for twenty months. Although I had been hired by the foundation to focus on our nation's cities, I realized when September 11 hit that our domestic issues are embedded in a larger global context. Now, I had responsibilities with the foundation's offices overseas, and I was looking for ways to increase our support of urban environmental programs in the underdeveloped world.

With a greater understanding of the international impact of the global economy, the Ford Foundation was rethinking its funding opportunities and challenges in the developing world. It had previously moved away from promoting large-scale urban development in the developing world and funding environmental projects unless they were grounded in a social context. Such investments had been criticized as reflecting an urban bias. Instead, the foundation shifted to investing in rural development and meeting the challenges to rural and wilderness programs in the developing world. Gradually, however, it became clear that all these dimensions were interconnected. As acting director, I raised the importance of exploring investment in initiatives in developing countries that encompass metropolitan regions and their surrounding rural and wilderness areas.

In Africa, we confronted a pattern of people all over the continent migrating en masse from rural areas to urban ones. Whole neighborhoods and communities were being displaced by the activities of large corporate industries, such as mining, agri-business, oil, and tourism, that were buying up or otherwise taking control of natural resources in lands previously defined by subsistence farming. Displaced and desperate for employment, migrants settled on the outskirts of cities in makeshift housing, eventually finding work in the cities and sending resources back to their families in the villages. To supplement their livelihood, many were growing food on the edge between urban and rural areas.

The top-down approach to urbanization looked at the vast urban areas settled by rural populations as "slums" and used a strategy of "slum clearance," which had consequences similar to those of US urban renewal strategies. Clearing slums and building new communities based on "modern" assumptions about development produced more dislocation than the new systems could absorb and inevitably resulted in even more displacement and dislocation. Clearly, we needed a bottom-up approach to urbanization.

Grassroots movements in Africa were demonstrating alternatives to slum clearance, improving the outer urban neighborhoods by strengthening their community institutions based on their identified needs and assets. A community savings movement that had started in India was seeing much better results. Like the women in

Khayelitsha, so-called slum dwellers would start a savings program, beginning with nickels and dimes, and eventually accumulate the capital to start improving their neighborhoods. Having seen the success of the Victoria Mxenge Housing Savings Scheme, I recommended that the foundation invest in supporting such asset-building programs.

We also made an initial investment in promoting grassroots participation in agriculture and food preparation in peri-urban areas—transition zones surrounding a city or town and its suburbs where urban and rural uses mix and sometimes clash. We also looked at similar programs in Brazil and in China and recommended investing in community savings programs and mobilizing communities to strengthen social institutions in areas perceived as slums.

Alongside this global trend toward urbanization, we were experiencing a growing pattern of climate disruption. Together, these forces are bringing about a new generation of challenges that require a grassroots response.

Global Climate Change Comes Home

On August 23, 2005, as I was coming toward the end of my contract with the Ford Foundation, a massive hurricane landed along the coast of the Gulf of Mexico, causing unprecedented damage to cities and towns in several states. New Orleans was the hardest hit due more to the failure of its inadequate levees rather than to Hurricane Katrina itself. People who depended on public transit were trapped as levees were breached and ocean waters poured into portions of the city that lay below sea level. As the storm subsided, the connection between protection of the environment and of vulnerable populations was manifest. It became clear that protection of the environment, particularly wetlands preservation and restoration, was a matter of both economics and social justice.

I was invited to join a response team that assessed the damage and made proposals to the governor's office about how to go forward. Peter Calthorpe conducted a planning process for the New Orleans region, and Angela Glover Blackwell developed a community organizing strategy.

The devastating impact of Hurricane Katrina underscored the interconnection between environmental preservation and social justice. The Central Wetlands in Louisiana could have shielded New Orleans and the Lower Ninth Ward from the worst of the hurricane had the wetlands not been decimated to make way for shipping channels that offered no clear benefits to the low-income people of color in the city. No longer could we say that protecting the wetlands was exclusively a white issue.

Hurricane Katrina also brought home the inescapable connections between our actions in the urban developed world and global environmental effects like climate change, which had seemed to only affect faraway places with melting arctic glaciers and polar bears on icebergs. But Katrina was a wake-up call from an angry Earth and a warning about the global effects of our extractive economy and its addiction to fossil fuels. It was a reminder to think not only about how our actions affect the changing temperature of the ocean but also about how these changes will affect people in the United States and around the world differently along race and class lines.

CHAPTER 15

Planning Healthy and Just Communities for All in the Age of Global Warming

R ETURNING HOME TO BERKELEY after seven years away at the Ford Foundation, I took a fresh look at the San Francisco Bay Area. After considering several places to live, I decided to move back to the house I had designed and created as my home on Carleton Street. I was surprised to see how much the neighborhood had changed; new neighbors were all around.

Although the changes surprised me, this was not the first time the neighborhood had undergone a major demographic shift. During the 1920s, houses in southwest Berkeley were owned primarily by Italian and Portuguese families. Japanese Americans began moving in during the 1930s, and by the 1940s, the Italians and Portuguese were all gone, leaving the block solidly Japanese. In the spring of 1942, a few months after the Imperial Japanese attack on Pearl Harbor, all the houses on my block had been evacuated. The Japanese American residents who hadn't gone into hiding were transported at gunpoint to internment camps. At the same time, African Americans who had been working in the sugarcane fields of Louisiana and Texas poured into Berkeley in search of job opportunities created by the war effort.

By the time we purchased our lot with its two small houses in 1972, the block was almost 100 percent African American. My son, Khalil, was born in that house on Carleton Street, and my grandson, Makai, was born there too, a generation later. Although we could

have purchased property anywhere in the city, we moved there because we wanted to live in a black neighborhood. But now, when I
returned and looked around at who my neighbors were, the block's
demographics had changed again: while there were still African
American neighbors on both sides of my property, the rest of the
block was completely white. I had grown accustomed to the elderly
African American woman two houses down who spent her retirement enjoying fresh air and the passing of neighbors from her front
stoop. Now, the director of sustainability for the City of Berkeley—a
white man—lived there with his family. In the forty years since I
had moved to Berkeley, the focus of my professional interests had
shifted from the neighborhood to the regional level, leaving me with
a deeper interest in where people moved to and why.

Shortly after my return to Berkeley, I celebrated my seventieth
birthday. Surrounded by lifelong friends and family who were wel-
coming me back to the changing Bay Area, I found myself reflecting
on my role and responsibilities as an elder. I felt a need to gather
what I had learned over my lifetime and pass it on to the next generation—not only looking back but also looking across a long horizon
to the future of our communities. I wanted to combine lessons I had
learned at the Ford Foundation with the inspiration I had felt from
the story of the universe and tie in the role the African American
community might play in protecting and restoring the health of the
environment on local and global scales. People of color, I reasoned,
had faced many challenges that have prepared them to model strategies of resilience in the face of global warming. I wanted to demonstrate how efforts to organize coalitions and develop leadership in
our communities are right in line with helping to preserve the life
support system of planet Earth.

Those of us who worked on the Sustainable Metropolitan Communities Initiative at the Ford Foundation learned many lessons.
One of the most powerful was that social justice advocates working
at the neighborhood and city levels can achieve greater collective
impact by collaborating at the scale of the metropolitan region. Such
collaboration allows groups to engage with sustainability issues that
can have a global impact, responding to the global environmental
imperative and to local community needs. It is clear to me that those

involved in this organizing and collaborating are participating in the great work of our time called for by Thomas Berry.

Having developed a deeper sense of regional and global interconnectedness while seeding the regional equity movement nationally, I wanted to bring the lessons I had learned back to California. I wondered what it would be like to work in these movements on the ground and in my own backyard. My movement-building efforts were strengthened by the opportunity to continue collaborating with Dr. Paloma Pavel, who had worked with me at the Ford Foundation.

Starting Breakthrough Communities

I was eager to see Paloma complete the book she had been developing, an anthology documenting the projects I had funded at the Ford Foundation, highlighting the accomplishments of grassroots organizers, labor groups, religious groups, and policy makers across the country as they scaled up from work in their neighborhoods and workplaces to the level of metropolitan policy. She had signed a contract with MIT Press to assemble and edit the book, which would be called *Breakthrough Communities: Sustainability and Justice in the Next American Metropolis*. I was certain that the book would be very useful and would take organizing and policy making to a new level. As she put the finishing touches on the manuscript, we agreed that I would write a foreword for the book.

Paloma had started the nonprofit Earth House Center in Oakland in 1990 to build healthy, just, and sustainable communities through education, leadership development, and multimedia. This work grew out of her background as an organizational and clinical psychologist, experience as a groundbreaking leader and educator in the field of organizational development and social change, and two decades of action as an environmental and antinuclear organizer in collaboration with activist-author Joanna Macy.

When MIT Press released the book in 2009, Paloma and I decided to form Breakthrough Communities as a project of Earth House Center to support the development of multiracial leadership for sustainable, socially just communities in California and the nation—complementing and reinforcing the successful regional work of the Urban Habitat Program. Both Paloma and I had been inspired by the work of Thomas Berry and his colleagues, Brian Thomas Swimme and Mary Evelyn Tucker. We wanted to help broaden their vision and make the universe story and the great work of healing and restoring the living systems of planet Earth relevant to a larger pool of readers, including marginalized communities that have historically been denied equal access to housing, jobs, transportation, education, and health care. We recognized the need to extend the work of healing and restoration to the socioeconomic landscape and to address human needs along with the needs of compromised ecosystems.

We agreed about the two areas missing in the new story Berry and Swimme were developing, and we were prepared to help fill in the gap. First, they had not said much about cities even though most of the human population lives in cities today. The second area was race; Berry and his colleagues make hardly any references to people of color and their role as underpaid laborers in the cause of industrial growth. Yet, low-income people of color are the majority worldwide, and the population of California, where we were aiming to directly inspire our communities, is estimated to be 61 percent people of color.[1]

Next Steps

I was ready to assess what I should be doing in the next period of my life. I saw signs that the work the Urban Habitat Program had done in the Bay Area over the past eighteen years was beginning to take root. Richmond—several miles north of Berkeley—was completing its general plan, which was part of its Regional Equitable Development Initiative, one of the demonstration projects I had helped implement while at the Ford Foundation. The Richmond General Plan was innovative in bringing together elements not previously seen in municipal plans, such as health equity and climate change.

All around the Bay Area, there were emerging signs of increased awareness of environmental issues. The Ella Baker Center for Human Rights had begun convening the Oakland Climate Action Coalition and made great strides between 2009 and 2011, working with over fifty organizational members and allies to engage members of low-income communities of color in guiding Oakland's policy on mitigating and adapting to the effects of climate change. In 2007, Ella Baker's cofounder and director, Van Jones, had teamed up with Majora Carter, founder of Sustainable South Bronx, to found Green for All, a national organization working to create more green jobs in the United States. In 2009, Van was tapped to serve as green jobs advisor to the Obama administration, and in 2011, he cofounded Rebuild the Dream (2016), a think tank for bottom-up, people-powered innovations that is "fighting for an economy that works for everyone—especially young people facing too few jobs, too much debt, and threats to survival from guns to climate change."[2]

By 2010, there were extensive efforts within Bay Area communities of color to grow food. Many of these had been nurtured by the People of Color Greening Network that Karl Linn and I and other community greening activists had established in the early 1990ss, including People's Grocery in Oakland and Urban Tilth in Richmond. The Environmental Justice Coalition in Richmond, which included the Just Transition Alliance,[3] Movement Generation, and others, added new dimensions to community organizing for sustainability and justice. The Urban Habitat Program was going strong, but the efforts of social justice advocates in communities of color were still fragmented. People were working hard on specific issues—such as public health or transportation justice—or in their own neighborhoods, but many were working in isolation from one another. I felt we all could benefit from sharing knowledge and experience and working together across disciplines and geographic boundaries. Seeing how our issues were interconnected, we could begin to build a movement on a regional scale.

I had learned a lot about social movements through my work at the Ford Foundation. My understanding was informed particularly by the work of sociologist Doug McAdam at Stanford University. He had studied the civil rights movement of the 1960s and compared it with other notable social movements around the world, observing that successful social movements begin with the presence of political opportunity. Success is enhanced by relatively autonomous mobilizing structures within the affected communities and movement leadership that frames issues so the mobilizing structures can take full advantage of the opportunity. He argued that successful social movements are based on three basic conditions: an emerging political opportunity, favorable conditions for community mobilization (for example, the existence of organizations like unions and churches with potential to mobilize large numbers of supporters), and the framing of issues by leaders and spokespersons in ways that inspire activism and commitment (McAdam, McCarthy, and Zald 1996).[4]

Organizing for Climate Justice in California

Since its beginning in the late 1980s, the environmental justice movement has grown from a preoccupation with the disproportionate siting of hazardous waste facilities in communities of color to the work of preserving and restoring sustainable and socially just communities everywhere. As a social movement, environmental justice is worldwide in scope, encompassing such issues as land use, energy policy, food security, forestry, water, human rights, population, cultural survival of indigenous communities, biodiversity, global warming, and intellectual property rights. I had been editing and publishing writings about many of these issues over the years with Luke Cole in the *Race, Poverty, and the Environment* journal.

When I realized that climate change was emerging as the number one environmental issue, I focused more and more on the opportunities it presents for changing the racial climate in this country, searching for political opportunities like those McAdam had described. Low-income neighborhoods and communities of color are typically more vulnerable to the floods and droughts brought on by climate change and to the effects of long subfreezing winters and excessively hot summers. In the fall of 2005, this became tragically clear when Hurricane Katrina flooded New Orleans and other Gulf Coast communities. These events also made me realize that in our local activism, we must commit to a strategy that takes global impact into account. To reduce carbon dioxide emissions and mitigate rising sea levels, we will need to reconfigure our economy and our cities. This gives us opportunities to correct built-in inequality in both systems.

In the absence of leadership at the national level, California established its own plan to reduce greenhouse gas (GHG) emissions. In 2006, the California State Assembly passed the Global Warming Solutions Act (AB 32), mandating that the state reduce its GHG emissions to 1990 levels by 2020. Then, in 2008, the State Senate passed the Sustainable Communities and Climate Protection Act (SB 375), calling for each of the eighteen metropolitan planning organizations in California to localize AB 32's goal by designing a new transportation plan.

According to the Air Resources Board (2014, 12), about 40 percent of GHG emissions in California come from automobile transportation.[5] SB 375 requires the reorganization of housing and transportation in California to reduce reliance on automobiles for commuting to work and neighborhood trips to meet daily needs. Implementation of AB 32 and SB 375 would mean reorganizing our regions to reduce sprawl, encouraging infill development for dense, walkable urban centers, and increasing public transportation infrastructure. Yet, concentrating on new development in existing urban neighborhoods risks displacing low-income inner-city communities, and many people from our communities recognized the devastating potential of these policies. Many also saw that implementing the legislation might be the political opportunity we needed.

The Metropolitan Transportation Commission (MTC) and the Association of Bay Area Governments (ABAG) were responsible for implementing SB 375 in the San Francisco Bay Area. This is a region of nine counties, ninety-eight municipal jurisdictions, and a population of over seven million (Bay Area Census 2017). Over a three-year period, from 2010 to 2013, MTC and ABAG were charged with drafting a Sustainable Community Strategy.

In the spring of 2010, MTC called the first meeting of the Regional Advisory Working Group (RAWG) to consider the best way to respond to the challenges presented by the new Sustainable Communities Act. Representatives from cities, counties, and other political institutions, interested parties from the private sector, and social justice activists attended. Immediately following the first meeting of the RAWG, twenty-six social equity groups, including Breakthrough Communities, met and shared their concerns that this legislation could have a negative impact on the most vulnerable populations in the region, but that it also had potential for significant positive impact.

Political Opportunity, Mobilizing Structures, and Framing the Issues

The groundbreaking enactment of legislation to address climate change inspired us, and we agreed that the legislative structures of AB 32 and SB 375 presented an opportunity to mobilize for social justice in the San Francisco Bay Area. We drafted a memo titled "Let's Work Together: Planning and Organizing for Regional Equity in the San Francisco Bay Area" and sent it to all the social equity groups that had participated in the first meeting of the RAWG. Without a firm commitment to reversing the longstanding social and economic inequities experienced by people of color, this legislation could have disastrous results in the lives of California's low-income communities, putting them at risk of increased isolation from employment and educational opportunities. Deeply rooted social inequity in transportation, housing, health, and economic opportunity would become more entrenched. At the same time, the legislation presented an opportunity for us to organize and empower spokespersons to represent the interests of low-income communities of color and to mobilize for greater inclusion of all communities in the planning process. As we say in our movement: If we are not at the table to make the decisions, we will be on the menu.

In his analyses of successful social movements, Doug McAdam uses the term "mobilizing structures" to describe organizations like churches and unions that can mobilize large numbers of supporters (McAdam, McCarthy, and Zald 1996). Such organizations already existed within our communities. The challenge, though, was bringing our new coalition's hard-won knowledge from these established movements to the new strategic opportunity presented by the Sustainable Communities Act. Our memo recommended that the social justice organizations, while maintaining their individual identities, take advantage of the opportunity to work together to achieve mutual goals and consider how best to create a region-wide living network to coordinate their activities. The memo was well received. As a result, representatives from many organizations began meeting regularly over the summer of 2010, both independently and, at times, with open-minded officials from ABAG and MTC.

Designing Healthy and Just Communities: The Six Wins for Social Equity Campaign

The formation of the coalition we call the Six Wins Network was the culmination of twenty-five years of effort laying the foundation for a regional equity movement in the San Francisco Bay Area—a movement that is intergenerational, multiracial, and inclusive. Our work on regional equity began with the Urban Habitat Program at the Earth Island Institute. It continued when Sunne McPeak and I formed the Social Equity Caucus in 1996, seeking to ensure that social justice considerations would not be overlooked in the work of the Bay Area Alliance for Sustainable Communities. The Bay Area Council (the voice of Bay Area business) and PolicyLink joined this effort soon thereafter.

After my work at the Ford Foundation, I was more convinced than ever of the importance of region-wide coalition building. I was encouraged by the coalition of community-based social advocacy groups that began to gel immediately after the first gathering of RAWG. As people shared their concerns and aspirations, we found that the goals of participating organizations fell into six general areas:

1. **healthy and safe communities** that have clean air, water, and soil, and provide safe walking and bicycling access between essential destinations;

2. **robust and affordable local transit service** that connects people to economic and educational opportunity, as well as free youth bus passes in communities where students depend on public transit to get to school;

3. **affordable housing** that is near jobs, reliable public transit, good schools, parks, and recreational facilities;

4. **investment without displacement**[6] through incentives that strengthen and stabilize communities vulnerable to gentrification and the displacement of low-income residents;

5. **economic opportunity** through more quality green- and transit-related jobs, as well as access to them and other economic opportunities for marginalized populations; and

6. **community power** for working-class people of color in local and regional decision-making.

Each of these goals was deeply rooted in our communities. Many people and organizations had worked on these issues, some for several decades. As we listened to one another, we began to see that our issues were deeply interconnected: access to quality jobs and housing is essential to health; investments in transportation benefit low-income communities only if they are accompanied by safeguards against displacement, like affordable housing; and affordable housing does no good in isolated communities without jobs or access to public transportation. Advocating together as a region-wide coalition was the only way to win. We agreed to form a coalition of Bay Area social justice organizations to advocate for these six key areas.

The Six Wins Network campaign brought together forty-five social justice advocacy groups led by a coordinating committee. Parisa Fatehi of Public Advocates and Lindsay Imai of the Urban Habitat Program performed the day-to-day administrative activities. Through Breakthrough Communities, Paloma and I drew on our national experience to build a strong political base for the coalition. We coached coalition members to work closely and effectively with elected officials and took part in statewide planning efforts to complement work in the Bay Area. Early on, we served as a bridge for the public health groups in our network to take part in transportation and land-use planning.

As participants worked together and built mutual respect and trust, we began to share knowledge and experience in cross-disciplinary trainings. Our coalition of organizers from vulnerable communities had deep-seated knowledge of what was making our region unsustainable and inequitable. We didn't want to dissipate our energy by opposing the bad parts of MTC and ABAG's scenarios in a piecemeal fashion. Instead, we wanted to fully articulate our vision for a Bay Area that would work for all.

To familiarize ourselves with the complex decision-making process MTC and ABAG were observing, our coalition began researching and analyzing the political orientation of each MTC and ABAG member. It was empowering to understand who cared about which issues. Coalition members began meeting with open-minded commissioners, and to their delight, they found themselves functioning as grassroots lobbyists.

Our Six Wins Network partners at Public Advocates reached out to the Center for Regional Change, an interdisciplinary department at the University of California at Davis. The department worked collaboratively with our social justice advocates and community organizations to translate our vision of a just and sustainable Bay Area into the language of land-use and transportation modeling. After many letter-writing campaigns, small group meetings, and large public meetings throughout the summer of 2010, we celebrated finalizing and ratifying our proposal at a well-attended community meeting in October. Introducing the Equity, Environment, and Jobs (EEJ) scenario into the regional planning debate was a major accomplishment. The EEJ scenario called for greater investment in operating local transit services, increased allocation of affordable housing in transit-connected suburban communities with educational and employment opportunities, and a regional grant program to create incentives for local cities to zone for affordable housing and implement protections against displacement. Social justice advocates had never before created a unified transportation and land-use plan for achieving equity throughout the nine-county region.

MTC and ABAG were moving forward in the SB 375 process by developing six hypothetical regional land-use and transportation scenarios for the Bay Area. They would then analyze these scenarios through an environmental impact report (EIR) and, based on the results, would choose one of the scenarios to become the Bay Area's Sustainable Community Strategy. At first, ABAG and MTC did not want to accept our plan, but our advocacy in public meetings, letter-writing campaigns, and communications with sympathetic members of their planning team resulted in their decision to include

the EEJ scenario in the EIR and the draft plan (the tentative proposal for Plan Bay Area). The EEJ scenario provided an alternative
to a plan that emphasized the priorities of powerful and entrenched
suburban constituencies.

Richard Marcantonio, our coalition partner from Public Advocates, and Alex Karner, our university ally who worked with CRC,
summarized our work and our policy wins in an article published in
Poverty & Race titled "Disadvantaged Communities Teach Regional
Planners a Lesson in Equitable and Sustainable Development." Marcantonio and Karner (2014, 12) explain that the network of organizations involved in the Six Wins Network campaign.

> demonstrated that a regional plan that leads with the needs
> of disadvantaged communities can better promote the gen-
> eral welfare. In doing so, the Network [of organizations]
> also won some tangible victories. For one, the agencies ad-
> opted a regional One Bay Area Grant (OBAG) program that
> conditions grants to local jurisdictions for planning activi-
> ties and infrastructure on the completion of state-certified
> affordable housing plans.[7]

The review of the EIR and draft plan by the consulting firm
hired by MTC and ABAG concluded that the EEJ alternative would
best achieve the region's performance standards adopted by ABAG
and MTC at the start of the process. These standards related to
public health, air quality, displacement, and traffic. In fact, the report identified the EEJ scenario as the "environmentally superior
alternative" (Dyett & Bhatia 2013, 3.1-146–48).[8] The consulting
firm's review determined that our community-generated plan that
prioritizes the most pressing needs of disadvantaged communities
could serve the entire region better than a plan that privileges more
powerful constituents.

In the end, however, the plan that favored entrenched suburban
interests was adopted, but only after being modified to include three
substantial amendments that Six Wins Network members drafted
and brought to their champions on the ABAG and MTC boards.
The amendments included commitment to funding improved levels

of transit service, allocation of at least 25 percent of the anticipated three billion dollars from cap and trade[9] to benefit disadvantaged communities, and stronger measures to prevent displacement. When the dust settled after three long years of organizing and citizen engagement, the effect of these final amendments was summarized in two words in a memo from Bob Allen of the Urban Habitat Program to the Six Wins Network coalition members: "We won."

The Six Wins Network demonstrated the power of a new model of coalition building that brought together urban planners, academics, community organizers, labor unions, public health experts, affordable housing advocates, transportation justice advocates, public interest attorneys, and environmentalists—all dedicated to social justice and the empowerment of disadvantaged communities. Finally, by creating the EEJ and advocating fiercely for its inclusion in the EIR, we demonstrated the effectiveness of leading with the demand for social equity firmly embedded in the sustainability planning process. Along with our policy victories, these bigger cultural shifts will give us the power to expand and continue the movement in the Bay Area, thus providing models for metropolitan regions everywhere.

When reflecting on the success of the Six Wins Network campaign, I came to understand the tremendous potential of collaborating with university partners. Developing collaborations like the one we had with CRC will prove valuable in our movements going forward. Universities that are deeply engaged with community needs can be a hub for sharing strategies and building bridges to political and business leaders to meet real community needs while helping to reduce the impact of metropolitan regional development on the life support systems of the planet. When community-based organizations set priorities and define the issues to be addressed and university partners provide support and technical assistance to projects, everyone benefits. Universities can draw on community experience and feedback to develop their course material. The Climate Readiness Institute, a collaborative of the Universities of California at Berkeley and Davis, Lawrence Berkeley Labs, and Stanford University, could benefit from a community partnership to develop climate change adaptation and mitigation processes.

Although policy is usually the purview of so-called elite academia, it seems equally important to explore ways in which the entire educational system, including K–12 and the community college system, can provide institutional resources for developing responses to climate change. The lives of this next generation will be indelibly shaped and altered by its impacts. An engaged education system is central to developing responsible and responsive leadership. Our educational systems have a huge influence on the kind of future we are creating.

Ending Suburban Poverty

While the Six Wins Network campaign had great impact and helped focus attention on regional equity, we had some blind spots. About three quarters of the way through the Plan Bay Area process, I attended a meeting hosted by the Federal Reserve Bank of San Francisco, where they shared *Suburbanization of Poverty in the Bay Area*, a 2012 report by Matthew Soursourian that revealed that in 2005, for the first time, more poor people lived in the suburbs of major US metropolitan areas than in central cities. Confirmation of this demographic shift soon came from another report for the Brookings Institution by Elizabeth Kneebone and Alan Berube (2013, xxx), which cited data from the 2005 American Community Survey and determined that from 2000 to 2014, the population of the suburban poor had grown 64 percent.[10]

The increasing numbers of suburban poor was an unsettling revelation. It represented a major shift in our understanding of how our metropolitan regions were shaping up. While I was aware of the phenomenon—addressing the suburbanization of poverty was a priority during my time at the Ford Foundation—data were not yet available to describe the extent to which this was happening. Our Six Wins Network coalition had been very effective in planning sustainable metropolitan communities that would discourage suburban sprawl, but it was now confronted with the fact that affluent white people were not the only ones sprawling into the suburbs; low-income people of color were moving to the suburbs as well. This meant that while we were working to make the inner cities more livable and walkable and working to protect inner-city residents from being displaced to the suburbs, a large percentage of our vulnerable populations had already been displaced and scattered to low-income suburbs. While housing may be more affordable there, residents often have little or no access to good jobs, schools, or public-transit infrastructure. Cut off from family and neighborhood support systems and from the networks of social services and nonprofits that serve inner-city populations, those displaced to low-income suburbs are often worse off there than in inner-city neighborhoods.

Compounding these challenges, communities displaced to the periphery of a metropolitan region are less likely to have a chance to participate in public planning processes to discuss and determine infrastructure planning. Unfortunately, investing all our region's development funds on building concentrated housing and mixed-use development near urban transportation hubs in order to reduce greenhouse gases leaves the suburban population on the sidelines. The policies we were advocating would do nothing for folks already living in suburban poverty.

Analysts like Myron Orfield (2006) had long predicted that we would have to address the problem of increasing poverty in the older suburbs.[11] We have experienced the ground shifting beneath us in our movements before. The African American community achieved great successes in the 1960s when we channeled our energy toward integration and black power. As a result, quite a few African American mayors were elected during the 1970s. But as the century came to a close, we were confronted with the fact that the base we had worked hard to build in the inner cities in the 1960s and 1970s had evaporated. We are now confronted with a resurgence of these challenges. How should we think about our access to urban and metropolitan regional planning now that many of our populations have moved to older, inner-ring suburbs and are even more marginalized to the spatial and social periphery?

When I first heard about suburban expansion and the exploding metropolis back in the 1950s, I saw that our nation was investing in highways and sprawling suburban communities that were creating more segregation. More than fifty years after the 1954 enactment of *Brown v. Board of Education*, which declared segregation in schools unconstitutional, a 2013 study by Richard Rothstein for the Economic Policy Institute found that our public schools were more segregated in the 1990s and in the year 2000 than they were in the 1950s. There are no longer signs that say "whites only" as there were in the 1950s, so this was a shocking revelation. The segregation of rich from poor and white people from people of color in the United States had been proceeding through processes that seemed racially neutral and so had continued under the radar. We need to learn from this revelation and remember to look closely at conditions and think deeply about how best to respond.

The next step toward equity in our metropolitan regions in the early twenty-first century is to focus on helping not only urban communities but also suburban low-income communities. While the work of the Six Wins Network demonstrated the value and effectiveness of collective input at a regional scale, it was only a beginning. There is much more work ahead. Although our contributions to Plan Bay Area were groundbreaking, they did not take into consideration the reality of the suburbanization of poverty. That will be a major challenge for our movement and for public officials in upcoming advocacy work.

Community Resilience and Adaptation to Climate Change

Climate change is with us now. As global climate systems destabilize, our world is wracked with record-breaking high and low temperatures. Devastating storms and tornadoes are occurring with greater frequency. Droughts, wildfires, floods, and rising sea levels threaten to destroy homes and businesses and make traditional community lands uninhabitable. While we must continue working to mitigate climate change by reducing our greenhouse gas emissions, we must also face the reality that Earth has already been pushed past the point where we might have avoided negative climate effects. As a result, we must work simultaneously toward mitigating the effects and helping our most vulnerable populations and climate refugees adapt.

Building resilience to climate change in vulnerable communities often entails technical responses: bolstering shoreline communities against flooding and sea level rise, training and equipping communities for emergency preparedness, and strengthening relief programs to deal with chronic stressors such as rising energy and food costs, heat island effect, and drought, as well as sudden disasters like flooding, hurricanes, tornados, and other extreme weather events that can cause massive destruction and displacement. Considering what we learned from working on the Six Wins Network, it is clear that creating sustainable and resilient communities in the face of climate change also provides opportunities for gaining greater social equity and justice.

Increasingly, African Americans and other people of color are emerging as leaders and activists in urban agriculture and permaculture projects. One such leader is Will Allen. Born in 1949 to South Carolina sharecroppers who eventually bought a small farm in Maryland, Allen's childhood was rooted in farming. Following a basketball career in which he was the first African American on the University of Miami basketball team that was life-altering (for himself and innumerable others), he returned to his roots and bought a nursery in foreclosure in the Milwaukee, Wisconsin, region and began urban farming, eventually starting the nonprofit Growing Power, Inc. His leading-edge agricultural techniques include greenhouse farming, worm composting, and aquaponics (raising fish and produce together in a mutually nourishing, no-waste system). He has become a teacher to many, locally and internationally. Growing Power, Inc. is but one of many examples of organizations and projects aimed at enhancing resilience and empowering members of vulnerable communities (Bybee 2009).

Building community resilience also means supporting and strengthening community infrastructure such as neighborhood associations, churches, schools, day cares, senior centers, community gardens, small local businesses, local health clinics, community centers, recreation programs, art studios, museums, galleries, and local performing arts troupes. I have often heard it said that the number one factor in surviving a catastrophic event is whether or not you know your neighbors. Such community power not only fosters re-silience when facing climate challenges but also enhances the experience of day-to-day living.[12] While we advocate against processes and policies that break communities apart, such as gentrification, displacement of long-time residents and businesses, and discriminatory schooling, policing, and sentencing practices that decimate communities of color, we also build community resilience to face major climate challenges as they arise and improve conditions for vulnerable communities here and now.

Metropolitan planning organizations have attempted to treat planning for climate change and planning for regional equity as separate and unrelated, but there is no reason for social justice advocates to follow their lead. There are good reasons for aligning risk reduction and development of resilience in the face of global warming with the goals of regional equity. Public policies that respond to the need for adaptation continue to offer opportunities for low-income communities to participate in regional planning processes. We need to build multidisciplinary coalitions across geographic and social divides and look at our metropolitan regions as an interconnected system.

The challenge of global warming requires that we support the development of non-extractive and nonpolluting transportation choices, such as public transit and safe bicycle and pedestrian paths. A great deal of public attention has been focused on alternate energy sources. While this attention is important, equally significant is how we live together as extended families and viable communities. New community design strategies can reduce demand for energy while maintaining and improving the quality of life for everyone. An old drama of human achievement celebrated the rugged individualist who triumphs by extracting riches from nature and from the labor of workers. That myth is losing its appeal. An emerging new story recognizes the dignity and worth of all beings and celebrates the power of collaborative effort to solve challenging problems. Communities of color can be powerful models of sharing and intergenerational support.

The Power of Cultural Work

In our work building just and resilient communities, we need diverse ways of communicating across our differences. To make lasting impact, we must not only speak the language of policy and climate science but also be able to communicate psychological and spiritual realities. I have come to understand that artistic and cultural expressions have power to cause people to think about situations and issues in new ways and bring people together across divides. Beginning in 1999 with *Voices from the Community* and continuing with *The New Metropolis* in 2009, I supported Paloma in developing a series of film and community dialogue events devoted to environmental justice.

In 2013, we created a day-long event centered on screening the climate change film, *Rising Waters: Global Warming and the Fate of the Pacific Islands*, to coincide with the public comment and community response period for the Plan Bay Area process. The event brought together community members, elected officials, and renowned local artists. It was cosponsored by the Environmental Quality Committee of the City of El Cerrito and the League of Women Voters, with support from the Six Wins Network coalition, the Resilient Communities Initiative, and others. The event opened with a stunning jazz vocal piece by Jennifer Johns, a Green for All "artivist" for climate justice.[13] Artist Carter Philips created a dynamic climate justice installation: cherished daily artifacts (a watch, eyeglasses, a child's toy, and more) embedded in an ice sculpture that melted throughout the event—a potent reminder of the urgency of our situation.

The film provided stunning visual documentation of climate impacts already decimating island nations. The opening scene took my breath away: a Kiribati island leader walking through the ceremonial grounds of his ancestors that are now under two feet of water. The filmmaker, Andrea Torrice, one of my Ford Foundation grantees and the producer of *The New Metropolis*, joined us from Ohio and brought personal footage from Superstorm Sandy, amplifying the immediacy and impact of our climate crises. I knew that Andrea had grown up in the neighborhood she was filming, which made the devastation even more poignant. The film was followed by brief remarks from a panel that included Paloma, elected officials, community leaders, and me. Afterwards, we heard from people in the audience, considered their questions and concerns, and took time for everyone to share their grief at the possibility of major weather events occurring in our own backyards.

Next, we moved next door to a Vietnamese restaurant for a shared meal where community leaders and elected officials co-facilitated the formation of multiracial thematic working groups to respond to current legislative plans for the Bay Area. Will Travis, executive director of the Bay Area Conservation and Development Commission, added depth to our dialogue by showing maps of the San Francisco Bay Area indicating the communities that will be underwater as sea levels rise. Each of the working group sessions was opened by a community member sharing personal experiences and concerns. At the end of the day, each group delivered recommendations for Plan Bay Area to representatives of ABAG and MTC.

After speaking, each community leader stood with their partnered elected official and each took a cup of water from the melting ice sculpture and watered a young potted tree that someone had borrowed from the large collection of plants in the Vietnamese restaurant. The gesture of watering the tree symbolized a shared commitment to grow a new future that includes us all, and the boat symbolized navigating our course toward that future.

Finally, we circled around the wooden boat, the new tree, and the ice sculpture for the closing ceremony. Two Tongan sisters, Fuifui and Loa Niumeitolu, taught us the contemporary Tongan chant, translated as "We Are Building the Boat," written by Pacific Islander climate justice activists and community members as they watched the sea rise and swallow their former home. The song moved us to tears. Linking to the larger global reality, we felt the vulnerability of our local communities in the Bay Area. This song was a call to preserve a displaced culture, a diaspora of elders and young people seeking a new homeland. A handout gave the lyrics in Tongan with this rough translation: "A song is a boat that can keep people together. We can create a shared place to keep our culture as we move to safe ground." It seemed that throughout the day we had been, like the Tongans, building a boat. By learning, communicating, and sharing food and ritual, we were creating a vessel, a shared space for our aspirations. I will always remember standing in that circle, looking at this multiracial, intergenerational, cross-cultural gathering of activists, elected officials, and ordinary residents from many walks of life, representing the diversity of our Bay Area region and coming together in pursuit of collaborative climate justice solutions.

The Rising Waters event deepened and broadened our understanding of climate justice issues and brought firsthand experience from our most vulnerable communities into our activism. Months later, we were still receiving comments from elected officials and community leaders about the power of this event. It gave us a taste of the new culture we are all yearning for.

Inspiring the Black Community

Since 1989, I had thrown myself into the work of uniting environmentalists and social justice activists through the Urban Habitat Program and then laid foundations for the regional equity movement through my work at the Ford Foundation and my organizing and educational efforts with Breakthrough Communities and the Six Wins Network. While I was sometimes discouraged by how few African Americans got involved and was often puzzled as to why, I recognized that everyone needs to be included in the new story I was envisioning, and I valued the opportunities to get to know the cultures and stories of other ethnic minorities involved with me in these organizations and movements.

When Michelle Alexander was promoting her groundbreaking 2010 book *The New Jim Crow: Mass Incarceration in the Age of Colorblindness*, I attended one of her presentations and was amazed to find myself in a hall packed with black people. As I reflected, I realized that people respond most strongly to life-and-death situations. The black community is facing an emergency scenario, and people are responding. Outrageously high numbers of black and brown youth are being shunted off to prison—the majority for minor drug crimes that are not equally enforced against white youth. Increasing numbers of our youth are being criminalized, stripped of rights, and shot down in the streets. Black families are being shattered by bureaucratic and austere policies. As Michelle Alexander (2010) points out, mass incarceration today serves to maintain a racial caste system every bit as disempowering as the post–Civil War Black Codes and the Jim Crow restrictions that we once thought had been overturned by the victories of the civil rights movement.

For decades, I have been following Angela Davis, another powerful black woman, in her role as a social critic, denouncing the mushrooming prison-industrial complex and the way that failing schools and racist attitudes and policies have created a school-to-prison pipeline.[14] It is clear to me that the school system is failing our most vulnerable populations. African American kids and other children of color are more likely to live in low-income districts and attend schools that fail to engage them and prepare them for success in the mainstream educational and economic system. African American students are more likely to be criminalized at a young age—reprimanded more harshly than their white counterparts and given more suspensions and expulsions (US Department of Education Office of Civil Rights 2014).[15] Suspended kids tend to fall behind in their coursework, increasing the likelihood of dropping out (American Civil Liberties Union 2015).[16]

The regional equity movement is tackling these problems by breaking down the forces in our regions that create inequities. As the Kerner Commission made clear in 1968, some areas of each metropolitan region thrive while others are plagued by unemployment and limited opportunity for economic and social advancement. In order to build just and sustainable regions in response to climate change, we need everyone on board, making the change together. This cannot happen when a segment of our population is being targeted by state-sponsored police violence or when our most vulnerable communities are being decimated by skyrocketing rates of incarceration.

Some black activists and allies are addressing these injustices by an approach known as restorative justice.[17] It is modeled on traditional practices of tribal people, and its most well-known application was the Truth and Reconciliation process in South Africa that helped heal wounds and resentments lingering after the apartheid regime had crumbled.[18]

Attorney Fania Davis, Angela's sister and my friend, founded Restorative Justice for Oakland Youth (RJOY) in 2005. Their pilot project at West Oakland Middle School eliminated violence and expulsions and reduced suspension rates by 87 percent (RJOY 2017). At another of their school sites, referrals for violence fell 77 percent after one year while graduation rates and test scores increased (Davis 2014). Other cities, including Boston, are seeing remarkable results using restorative justice approaches (Encarnacao 2013).[19]

In 2014, longtime social activist Alicia Garza branded a movement by tweeting under the hashtag #BlackLivesMatter.[20] The hashtag went viral, and Alicia and her friends and fellow organizers decided to use its popularity to stimulate discussion of the way black lives are devalued in America and what people can do to change that. Since then, the slogan has been a rallying cry for justice in response to the deaths of dozens of unarmed black people at the hands of police officers. These passionate demands for respect and justice have energized and encouraged me.

At the heart of Black Lives Matter is the conviction that we matter to ourselves and to the larger community. Our concern cannot be limited to racial profiling and being incarcerated or assassinated. Our whole lives matter. The black people I have been talking with are deeply concerned that their lives are being cut short because the social system in which they are engaged violates the very essence of their being. For the time being, the immediate concern of staying alive takes a front seat in relation to the equity concerns that I've been talking about, but achieving equity in our metropolitan regions will go a long way toward ending the racist attitudes and policies that are oppressing and killing members of our community.

When I say that we need to fashion a new story for the African American community, I don't mean to imply that we have outgrown the old story—the one that begins with enslavement and exploitation and continues to the oppressive situations that afflict our communities today. The old story is still relevant, but we need to refashion it and make it deeper, broader, more inclusive, and geared toward our vision of the future.

Concluding Thoughts

Alternate energy sources and other technical innovations are important elements in building a sustainable world, but we cannot expect technology to solve all our problems. We need to understand and acknowledge the unsustainable burdens that industrial civilization has placed on Earth's natural resources and the effect those burdens have on ecological balance. The challenge of global warming requires that we move away from the global love affair with the automobile. Instead, we need to support the development of non-extractive and nonpolluting transportation and housing choices; we need to create diverse neighborhoods with housing near jobs and public transit with safe conditions for walking and bicycling. These opportunities will manifest differently in each region, depending on local environmental, geographic, economic, and political factors. But as the urgency of climate change continues to press decision makers into action in our states, regions, counties, and municipalities, disadvantaged communities and their allies must continue to step forward, collaborate, and make our voices heard in planning, designing, and building equitable and sustainable regions.

The innovations proposed to get us through the climate change crisis will require strong social consensus and local-to-global community building—elements usually left out of proposals. The strong sense of community we need in order to cope with climate change is undermined by growing racial disparities, both within the United States and between the global North and South. These racial disparities are exacerbated by the ongoing spatial division of the wealthy from the disadvantaged. Spatial apartheid limits access of low-income people of color to education, good jobs, housing, nontoxic environments, transportation, healthy food, and green spaces, resulting in alarming disparities in health, life expectancy, and economic well-being.

Climate change confronts us with many giant challenges—reducing greenhouse gas emissions, building community resilience to extreme weather, confronting poverty in our regions, and restoring and protecting the web of life on which our own lives depend. We each have a role to play in facing these challenges. Some of us will get involved in political processes, set up cooperative businesses or nonprofits, and find new ways of sharing space and resources. Others will create art, music, gardens, schools, and networks of mutual aid. The needs and the possibilities are endless. The voices of elders are joining with those of young people around the world who are expressing their care for the planet, their passion for justice, and their hope for a livable future. They must be acknowledged and encouraged. We must come together as one human family to care for Earth and for one another—working together, listening to each other's stories, and appreciating and celebrating our diversity.

Discovering New Foundations for the Great Work of Our Time

> History is governed by those overarching movements that give shape and meaning to life by relating the human venture to the larger destiny of the universe. Creating such a movement might be called the Great Work of a people. . . . The historical mission of our times is to reinvent the human—at the species level, with critical reflection, within the community of life-systems.
> —Thomas Berry, *The Great Work* (1999)

THESE WORDS ELECTRIFIED ME when I first encountered them more than twenty-five years ago, and I still hold them dear. Civilization as we know it is in urgent need of a great shift in how we participate in the life of this planet. In order to thrive and even survive at this moment in our development as a species, we must learn to understand ourselves and to behave as what we are and not as what we have been acculturated to believe we are. As our scientists and technologists have learned more and more about our world and how to manipulate its various elements, we have gradually come to assume that using and discarding their inventions is somehow what makes life worth living. In the process, most of us have been trained out of our capacity to experience awe and wonder in the world and have lost the crucial knowledge that we are interdependent living beings in the ecosystem of planet Earth.

Many voices, especially those of peoples who traditionally live close to the land, have been sounding the alarm for generations now.

They warn us that it is time to wake up from our almost complete human-centeredness and mature into social responsibility within the community of life. I don't need to spend a lot of time going over the kinds and the levels of danger we face—from the rapid profusion of human-generated chemical pollution to habitat loss and species extinction, from climate disruption to global warming, and from severe depletion of water tables worldwide to nuclear weapons on a hair trigger. If we do not grow up in a hurry, the consequences will be dire for life on Earth as we know it—on a scale unequalled in sixty-five million years.

Although my central concerns were originally with creating social and racial equity in the context of urban and regional development, I came to enthusiastically embrace the new paradigm of human identity within the universe that was being articulated by thinkers like Thomas Berry, Brian Swimme, and Mary Evelyn Tucker. Reading Berry reawakened parts of myself that had been dormant since childhood. I began to recover a sense of my birthright and forge a new identity to replace the sense of inferiority I had taken on as a man of African ancestry in white America.

In 1963, when my brother, Lewie, took Harlem Education Project students to Maine to see the solar eclipse, he was deeply engaged at Princeton in studying the evolution of stars and wanted to share his excitement with these young black people. I was experiencing a similar excitement about advances in the civil rights movement, such as sit-ins, boycotts, and the powerful oratory of Martin Luther King Jr. I was also deeply engaged in working with Karl Linn and neighborhood residents in designing and building the Harlem Neighborhood Commons.

As I began my formal studies in architecture and urban planning at Columbia University, I became increasingly aware of the relationships between the shape of our cities and patterns of segregation and exploitation. For example, Columbia was a bastion of whiteness at the top of Morningside Heights. It looked down on Harlem's half million African American residents. In April of 1968, the year before I graduated, Martin Luther King Jr. was killed and inner cities across the nation erupted in rage. At Columbia, protesting students shut down the school for a month. While classes were cancelled, teach-ins and student-led projects flourished. It was a fertile period—very upsetting to the status quo but inspiring to me. The intense conflicts that swept through US inner cities inspired me to dedicate my future career to challenging the inequities that underlay the rage.

I was excited by innovations in the field designed to make cities work for people, such as advocacy planning, community development corporations, and the ideas of Jane Jacobs (1961) in *The Death and Life of Great American Cities*. I was disappointed at how few other African Americans there were in these movements, and I worked hard to recruit black students at Columbia and, later, both students and faculty at the University of California at Berkeley.

Years after I moved to California, when I became involved in the environmental justice movement and connected more closely with the Universe Story, I drew closer to Lewie, years after his passing. As I began to reexperience my connection to the cosmos, I recognized the need for a new story about race and place in American cities. This was a major factor in my work building the Urban Habitat Program, and it continued to inspire me when I directed the Sustainable Metropolitan Communities Initiative at the Ford Foundation and in my subsequent work.

Gradually, I came to recognize the evolutionary moment we now face as human beings, where we must reinvent ourselves as a species within the community of life. The story of the Big Bang and the formation of galaxies, stars, the solar system, and, eventually, us offers deeper meaning to our lives and has the potential to lead humanity away from our unjust and irresponsible planet-destroying ways. This perspective inspired me to break out of the claustrophobic identity box in which the culture of white America confined me. Learning about the birth of the universe and the fascinating development of life on Earth gave me a brand new sense of wonder, pleasure, and gratitude at being alive. I experienced myself as stardust come to living form in an amazing, self-organizing universe.

I have found that the perspective of deep time, when applied to the last five hundred years, has enabled me to free myself from the shame and horror of my ancestors being caught in the net of one of the most traumatic events in human history: the trans-Atlantic slave trade. My history not only goes back to the time in which some of my ancestors were overpowered, kidnapped, and transported across the Atlantic to be slaves of Europeans. It goes much further back to about two hundred thousand years ago when humanity was born in Mother Africa and beyond that to the Big Bang, or, as Berry called it, the primordial Flaring Forth. We are not latecomers. Our family has been here all along. Nobody can kick us out.

Understanding our place in the immense drama of the Universe Story can help us heal the trauma of the Middle Passage and confront the challenge of changing our perspective and behavior to recognize and care for all our fellow human beings as one family (especially across racial and cultural boundaries). The dedicated activists on the front lines of the environmental justice movement are leading the way for all of us to break out of the hypnotic trance of technological development with its many racist overtones. People of color have a unique ability to lead a multiracial movement for environmental health and social justice. We are accountable to one another. As I walk around my neighborhood in south Berkeley, I experience myself as on a journey through the universe, encompassing the emergence of our galaxy and the evolution of our species.

Where will we be in another fifty years? Will we reconnect with the support system of the planet and begin to develop new habits? The truth about climate change is now widely known, and denial will not magically create the world in which the privileged among us would like to believe we live. As a species, we must learn to live sustainably and conduct ourselves in a way that will encourage the flourishing of all life and not just a privileged subset of the human species. If we ignore this challenge, we will contribute to the most rapid collapse in Earth's community of life since the dinosaurs went extinct sixty-five million years ago. The good news is that the awesome story of cosmic beginnings and the evolution of life on Earth gives us new tools for personal and social transformation.

A great deal has happened since I left the Ford Foundation. My colleague Paloma Pavel, who served as a communications specialist supporting my work at Ford, edited *Breakthrough Communities: Sustainability and Justice in the Next American Metropolis*, which was published by MIT Press. The 2009 book includes analyses and case studies, highlighting ways that social and racial justice interface with care for people and the environment and provide economic opportunity for disenfranchised urban residents. We decided to create a project based on the ideas in the book, and we named it Breakthrough Communities. It has been gratifying to see new communities, individuals, and organizations discover this perspective and become inspired by new possibilities for action and community mobilization even in the face of overwhelming obstacles. As our work evolved, we developed a variety of resources for building multiracial leadership at the metropolitan scale, including the All In: Learning Action Guide, which offers an intergenerational framework for deep social innovation.

The primordial Flaring Forth of the universe was an enormous energy event that has been replicated over and over again at different scales from the birth of the stars and the galaxies to the development and multiplication of our cities. We belong in the universe. We are an expression of the unlimited creativity that lay hidden in its depths before time and space. That creativity is in each of us. Nobody can tell us how to see ourselves or what we can and cannot accomplish. So, I ask you, my readers, especially the youth among you: How will you contribute to this great adventure?

Our challenge is to refashion our social structures and our organization of space and infrastructure around the central ideal of maximizing justice and full-spectrum sustainability. The current era of development controlled by small groups of privileged elites seeking profit by using and discarding people and resources is nearing its end. We are cautioned by so many sources to grasp every opportunity to change course. We must commit to meeting our current needs while protecting the capacity of future generations to meet theirs. A key strategy for success is to analyze and solve social and environmental problems at the metropolitan and regional levels. We need to approach our regions as whole systems in order to dismantle the legacy of racism and environmental exploitation that currently afflicts them.

I am convinced that coming to terms with caring for our human family will guide us in the direction of care for the planet as a whole. Many of the sustainability driven projects I have seen or been involved with during my career have confirmed what I have sensed all along: that social and racial justice-making are integral and essential steps toward the protection and nurturing of the living systems of our planet. Colleagues recently made me aware that biodiversity is essential for environmental and human health. I think that racial diversity has a similarly positive effect.

We are at a cusp in human history—not textbook, Eurocentric history, but the hundred-millennia-long history of our species spreading out to inhabit the planet. Americans of color have indispensable leadership gifts to contribute to the reinvention of human habitat. We understand the necessity of coming together to preserve and protect our most vulnerable neighbors while working for the health and vitality of our bioregions.

As I write this, I think back to my elementary school years when, during Negro History Week, my father insisted I give presentations in my racially integrated classroom explaining the lives and legacies of Sojourner Truth, Frederick Douglass, Booker T. Washington, Ida B. Wells, W. E. B. Dubois, Mary McLeod Bethune, and other black luminaries. My classmates were mostly white, and I always felt that nobody really cared about what I was saying. As the years have passed, however, my continued attempts to honor people and communities of color have been more and more welcomed. At the same time, awareness of racial injustice has heightened.

The increase in mobile video recording in cell phones has sparked a growing movement to protest the abuse and killing of people of color by police. Paloma and I attended demonstrations in Ferguson, Missouri, to commemorate the one-year anniversary of the death of Michael Brown, a young man shot at least six times by a police officer based on a complaint that he was walking in the street. Protests over his killing were a major impetus for the Black Lives Matter movement that continues to grow. Then, in July of 2015, Sandra Bland, a Black Lives Matter activist, ended up injured and shortly thereafter dead in a jail cell after a daytime traffic stop for failing to signal a lane change. The list goes on.

Institutional violence against people of color in the United States is ever-present and unrelenting. The pain they experience continues to be acute. The trauma of a voracious cradle-to-prison pipeline that young activists have taken to calling the "criminal injustice system" is stressing our people and communities almost to the breaking point. I offer the learnings in this book to them and to all who have devoted themselves to the flourishing of life with the hope that they will go from fierce resistance and fierce resilience to fierce leadership and fierce public advocacy on behalf of the most vulnerable in our cities and metropolitan regions and on behalf of all our relatives in the network of life on Earth.

Notes

Introduction

1. Perhaps the generations of pent-up frustration caused by the racist assumption that African people have no roots accounts in some small part for the extraordinary popularity of the 1977 television miniseries *Roots*. Adapted from the 1976 novel by Alex Haley, which was based loosely on his family's history that he had gathered during twelve years of research, the story begins in the 1700s in Africa with an adolescent Kunta Kinte, who is captured and sold into slavery in the United States. The stories of the successive generations of his descendants fascinated the nation. It seemed like everyone was watching it.

   More recently, advances in genetic testing and in decoding DNA make it possible to discover your ancestral origins. The writings and documentary films by Henry Louis Gates Jr. are guiding many people to find their roots.

2. The first part of my essay, "The Big House and the Slave Quarter," was subtitled "Prelude to New World Architecture," while the second part was subtitled "African Contributions to the New World." They were published in 1976 in the spring and autumn issues of *Landscape*.

3. I was pleased to learn that the United Nations General Assembly (2013) proclaimed 2015 to 2024 as the International Decade for People of African Descent and committed to exploring the themes of recognition, justice, and development. In 2007, the United Nations General Assembly declared March 25 as the International Day of Remembrance for the Victims of Slavery and the Transatlantic Slave Trade.

4. Thomas Berry preferred to be called a "geologian" or "Earth scholar" rather than a theologian.

Origins

1. Stokely Carmichael was later renamed Kwame Touré and became well known as a fiery black power leader and Pan-African nationalist.
2. At the time of the field trip to Maine, I was preoccupied with civil rights struggles and failed to see the relevance of viewing a solar eclipse. I had lots of responsibilities and considered the trip "Lewie's thing." However, when I heard the details of the experience from Lewie and others, I was moved and wished I had seen it for myself.
3. One of many accounts of Greek and Roman star myths is *Legends of the Stars* by Sir Patrick Moore (2009), prestigious British astronomer and author.
4. To learn more about the growing field of archaeoastronomy and its discoveries, you might start by reading *The Power Of Stars: How Celestial Observations Have Shaped Civilization* by Bryan E. Penprase (2011), astronomy professor at Pomona College; *Stairways to the Stars: Skywatching in Three Great Ancient Cultures* and *People and the Sky: Our Ancestors and the Cosmos* by Anthony Aveni (1997, 2008), an academic researcher, author, and professor of anthropology and astronomy at Colgate University; or *Echoes of the Ancient Skies: The Astronomy of Lost Civilizations* and *Beyond the Blue Horizon: Myths and Legends of the Sun, Moon, Stars, and Planets* by Edwin C. Krupp (1983, 1991), astronomer and director of the Griffith Observatory in Los Angeles.
5. This condensed timeline of life on Earth was developed by J. Webb Mealy, a Biblical scholar I was consulting with as I worked on this chapter. He started with the timeline that appears at the end of Swimme and Berry's (1992) *The Universe Story* and, consulting numerous sources, chose mileposts that he found most striking and relevant to the book. He did his own calculations, checking to see if the scientific consensus had changed on the dates of any of the mileposts since *The Universe Story* was published. An updated version of the timeline appears as the appendix to Swimme and Tucker's (2011) *The Journey of the Universe.*

CHAPTER 1 Growing Up in a Dying City

1. Mother's maiden name became my middle name: Carl Cokine Anthony.
2. I was fascinated to learn more about my ancestor William Jervay and his descendants who remained in South Carolina, founded a printing company, and enjoyed careers in journalism (Herget 2015).
3. For a brief history of the remarkable Lincoln University, founded in 1854 in southeastern Pennsylvania, see Allison Marie O'Connor (2016).
4. My father later learned that Finnish immigrants were the pioneers of the co-operative movement in the United States.

5. Prominent black historian and educator Carter G. Woodson and his colleagues started Negro History Week in 1926, six years after they had developed the Association for the Study of Negro Life and History. In 1976, it was replaced by Black History Month, celebrated each February.

6. I later discovered that William Penn himself had slaves and that his father, Admiral Sir William Penn, had achieved his great wealth by participating in the Atlantic slave trade. The large land grant that King Charles II settled on the younger William Penn was in repayment of a large loan extended to the king by the admiral.

7. In 1968, after several years of litigation, Girard College finally ended its racial ban. The courts ruled that the school was "permanently enjoined from denying admission of poor male orphans on the sole ground that they are not white, provided they are otherwise qualified for admission." The first African American student was enrolled at Girard College in 1968; by 1984, more amendments to the admissions policy allowed women, as well as students who were not orphans, to attend the school (Schroeder 2016).

CHAPTER 2 Finding Mentors

1. For a collection of videos about Karl Linn's life and work, see Verona Fonte (2016).

2. A camping vacation would have been dangerous for an African American family then, judging from our car trip to Washington, DC (see Chapter 1: Growing Up in a Dying City) and stories I heard.

3. This letter is part of Karl Linn's archive at the University of California at Berkeley's College of Environmental Design and is quoted on the Tributes page under "Reflections from Karl's Mentors" on Karllinn.org (2016).

4. *Notes of a Native Son* was Baldwin's first nonfiction book. The volume collects ten of his essays, which had previously appeared in such magazines as *Harper's*, *Partisan Review*, and *New Leader*. The essays mostly tackle issues of racism in America and Europe.

5. Eventually, Mumford wrote over thirty books, including the great work for which he is best known, *The City in History*. In addition, he wrote about a thousand essays for *The New Yorker* magazine.

7. Much later, I learned that the Better Philadelphia Exhibition, which had inspired my passion for city planning, played an important role in the urban renewal efforts in the city, consequently displacing thousands of African Americans from their neighborhoods.

CHAPTER 3 Moving to New York

1. Lenox Avenue was renamed Malcolm X Boulevard in 1987. A portion of what was previously Seventh Avenue in Harlem was officially changed to Adam

Clayton Powell Jr. Boulevard in 1974 to honor the late African American pastor turned politician. A large portion of Eighth Avenue above Central Park was changed to Frederick Douglass Boulevard in 1977, and 125th Street was changed to Dr. Martin Luther King Jr. Boulevard in 1984. However, most street signs show the old names along with the new.

2. I include a brief account of that visit in Chapter 7: Teaching, Research, and Professional Practice.

3. Baldwin's "A Letter to My Nephew," was first published in the December 1962 issue of *The Progressive* magazine. He later adapted it in his essay collection, *The Fire Next Time*. Later still, he included it in *The Price of the Ticket*. It was republished in *The Progressive* on December 4, 2014.

4. Marcus Garvey led the Back to Africa movement and founded the United Negro Improvement Association in 1914. For more about this influential leader, watch 2001's *Marcus Garvey: Look for Me in the Whirlwind*, directed by Stanley Nelson. Another source is James G. Spady (1988).

5. The publication information on all the books I mention and many more is in the References and Additional Resources sections at the end of the book.

6. In *The Lost Cities of Africa*, Davidson (1970) also touched upon the civilization of Egypt and some of the controversies over the origins of its peoples.

7. While Connecticut College for Women had had black students in the past—a total of eight, the first of whom graduated in 1931—the classes of 1959–1967 were all white (Connecticut College 2016).

8. This reality is well documented in Vandana Shiva's 2002 book, *Water Wars: Privatization, Pollution, and Profit*, and in the 2008 documentary film, *Flow: For Love of Water*, directed by Irena Salina.

9. The Cooper Union for the Advancement of Science and Art is a privately funded (and, until recently, tuition free) college with outstanding academic programs in architecture, art, and engineering, along with a faculty of humanities and social sciences.

10. Much later, I heard stories about African American women who went to predominantly white universities and spent the whole time during their university years, usually a prime dating time, without any dates.

CHAPTER 4 Columbia's School of Architecture

1. Since 1989, architecture professors Dennis Alan Mann and Bradford Grant have been tracking the number of licensed African American architects and the colleges and universities where they received their degrees. The researchers have twice published a directory of African American architects and completed two professional surveys. They shared their findings in 2009 in *African American Architects and Their Education: A Demographic Study*, published by the University of Cincinnati.

2. The work of visionary inventor R. Buckminster Fuller included designing and promoting geodesic domes as a means of making shelter more comfortable, efficient, and affordable. The Buckminster Fuller Institute has lots of information on geodesic domes on their website, BFI.org.

3. Chester Hartman founded the Planners Network in 1975 to serve as a voice for social, economic, and environmental justice through planning. In 2002, its newsletter developed into *Progressive Planning*, a quarterly magazine. Around the same time that Karl Linn and I were starting the Urban Habitat Program in 1989–1990, Chester founded the Poverty and Race Research Action Council (PRRAC), a civil rights and social justice policy organization in Washington, DC. He is the author of many books, including *City for Sale: The Transformation of San Francisco.*

CHAPTER 5 Journey to West Africa

1. Founded during the tenth century, Timbuktu became an important trading center for the Mali and Songhai empires, as well as a repository for large collections of manuscripts. A university grew up in and around the spectacular pyramid-shaped Sankoré Mosque, which was primarily for study of the Koran but also of the sciences, law, history, and philosophy. Unfortunately, modern-day conflict has impeded multinational efforts to preserve and translate Timbuktu's precious records from the flourishing medieval African civilizations. In 2012, Tuareg Islamist rebels occupied the city and set fire to the library at the Ahmed Baba Institute of Higher Learning and Islamic Research. Journalist Joshua Hammer wrote about the efforts by individuals to preserve manuscripts in a 2014 *Smithsonian* magazine article and in a 2016 book that followed up on earlier films and articles about the manuscripts, including the 2009 BBC documentary, *The Lost Libraries of Timbuktu.*

2. Originally published in French in 1948 as *Dieu d'Eau* (God of Water), Marcel Griaule's work was translated to English in 1965 (nine years after his death) and published as *Conversations with Ogotemmêli: An Introduction to Dogon Religious Ideas.* Other anthropologists dispute some aspects of Griaule's work, alleging, for example, that he introduced the idea that ancient Dogon people knew about the two companion stars that orbit the star Sirius.

3. James Baldwin's essay on the meaning and experience of being an American, "The Discovery of What It Means to Be American," is included in *Nobody Knows My Name.*

4. This was a vessel of Ghana's national shipping company. Its name evoked the memory of the Black Star Line started by Pan-Africanist Marcus Garvey in 1919. When choosing the name, Garvey had been inspired by the British luxury steamship line called the White Star.

CHAPTER 6   **Unearthing the Hidden Narrative of Race**

1. As a corrective to this lopsided point of view, see Bill Freund (2007).

2. *White Over Black: American Attitudes Toward the Negro, 1550–1812* by Winthrop D. Jordan received the National Book Award in 1969.

3. If "treated like beasts" sounds like an exaggeration, note Frederick Douglass's (1845, 30–31) account of how he and the other children were fed at the plantation of Colonel Lloyd, where Douglass lived for two years before he turned eight: They devoured corn mush from a trough "like so many pigs." No spoons or bowls were provided. Likewise, they had no beds, hardly any clothing, even in winter (only a coarse linen shirt issued every six months), and no covers to protect them from the cold. Adults were given a coarse blanket, but, as Douglass suggests, it hardly mattered since they were so exhausted after the grueling day of work in the fields followed by their own washing, mending, and cooking.

4. To his credit, the second US president, John Adams, never owned slaves. For more information on slaveholding by US presidents, see the Hauenstein Center (2012).

5. Sally Hemings was an enslaved woman of mixed race who was owned by President Thomas Jefferson. After the early death of his wife, whose father had also fathered Sally, Jefferson seems to have begun a long-term relationship and fathered six or seven children with Sally. No evidence has been found thus far that Sally was ever freed.

6. Architectural historians Jean-Paul Bourdier and Dell Upton followed up on my investigations without acknowledging my main point—the prevalence of racism in shaping the built environment in America. John Michael Vlach (1993) wrote a very valuable, if sometimes controversial, book, *Back of the Big House: The Architecture of Plantation Slavery*, also based upon the themes of my essays but aimed at professional and popular readers of anthropology and folklore. In her insightful book, *Building the Dream: A Social History of Housing in America*, Gwendolyn Wright (1983) wrote a chapter called the "Big House and the Slave Quarter," borrowing heavily from my essay but interpreting this history as an element of American domestic architecture.

CHAPTER 7   **Teaching, Research, and Professional Practice**

1. Booker T. Washington, born a slave, went on to found the Tuskegee Normal and Industrial Institute, or Tuskegee Institute, as an agricultural and vocational college for African Americans in 1881. For much of his adult life, he was one of the most influential African American men in the United States. Tuskegee Institute is now Tuskegee University.

2. My mother loved to take Khalil for long walks in his stroller. Friends told us they had spotted them near the Claremont Hotel, around three miles from our house.

3. For more discussion on black towns, see Chapter 11: The Landscape of Freedom.

4. We borrowed the technique of equity sharing from Stanford University, which used it to assist new faculty in purchasing homes.

5. For more discussion on the Berkeley Waterfront Plan, see Chapter 8: Crisis and Turning Point and Chapter 13: Forging an Alliance between Environmentalists and Social Justice Activists.

CHAPTER 8 Crisis and Turning Point

1. The strait through which the waters of the Pacific Ocean flow into the San Francisco Bay is known as the Golden Gate. The strait and the bridge that spans it are often obscured by fog, but they both appear golden when the sun shines on them.

2. The process of filling the San Francisco Bay and its reversal thanks to the popular Save the Bay movement has been thoroughly explained in a 2009 film *Saving the Bay: The Story of the San Francisco Bay*, a four-hour documentary directed by Ron Blatman and narrated by Robert Redford. The film was originally aired on PBS stations and is often shown during fundraising drives. The Save the Bay movement was initiated in 1961 by three Berkeley housewives who started a grassroots organization they called Save San Francisco Bay Association. The women took to action after being appalled by an article in the *Oakland Tribune*, which reported that Berkeley officials were planning to fill in two thousand acres of the bay west of the city's shoreline and that the Army Corps of Engineers was floating plans that called for filling in most of the bay by 2020. The illustration that accompanied the article depicted San Francisco Bay as a narrow shipping channel. For more information, visit www.savesfbay.org.

3. For a brief history of the landfill-turned park, see the City of Berkeley's Parks Division (2017) website.

4. Many details of the decades-long campaign to preserve the most environmentally sensitive parts of the bay's shoreline as open space and parklands are chronicled in *Creating the Eastshore State Park: An Activist History*, a 2002 report by Sierra Club leader Norman La Force.

5. In 1980, Oakland's African American population was reported as 159,351. In 2010, it had fallen to 109,471, thus losing a third of its 1980 population. For more US census data on the city of Oakland, see Metropolitan Transportation Commission and the Association of Bay Area Governments (2017).

6. Karl Linn credited his decision to leave his tenured professorship at New Jersey Institute of Technology and work full time for peace to several long conversations with Lewis Mumford about nuclear proliferation and the threat of nuclear war.

7. The production of the book, *Places for Peace*, was sponsored by the International Architects, Designers, and Planners for the Prevention of Nuclear War and Architects/Designers/Planners for Social Responsibility.

8. Karl Linn and I assembled and edited *Places for Peace*, an 8.5 x 11 book intended primarily for distribution at the 1988 World Congress of the International Federation of Landscape Architects in Boston. Occasionally, a copy will turn up at an online bookseller, such as Alibris.

9. The Hindi word *chipko* means "to embrace" in the dialect of Uttarakhand, the state in northern India where the movement originated. Uttarakhand was carved out of the heavily populated state of Uttar Pradesh in 2000. The name Chipko refers to the practice by its adherents—local women—of hugging the trees being targeted for harvest, thus protecting them.

CHAPTER 9   Toward a New Story for African Americans

1. Karl Linn's *Urban Barnraising* VHS tapes (Parts 1 and 2) are viewable at a few university libraries and archives (Kent, Anthony, and Linn 1989a, 1989b). Many of the images and descriptions appear in Karl's 2007 book, *Building Commons and Community*.

2. In the Babylonian creation myth, Tiamat was the personification of the sea, also appearing in the form of a huge dragon. By Apsu, she gave birth to the first of the gods. Later, the god Marduk (her great-grandson) defeated her, cut her in half, and used the pieces of her body to make the earth and the sky (Mackenzie 1915, vii–viii, 143–7, 150–1; Jacobsen 1968).

3. There were many such disappointments. As a young boy, I was inspired to study architecture by Edmond Bacon's attractive urban design plans for downtown Philadelphia, which I saw at the Better Philadelphia Exhibition with my third-grade class. Decades later, I learned that the elegant plans had a hidden goal—to mobilize public approval for urban renewal, which is to say, the demolishing of buildings and removal of African Americans from the historic neighborhood of Society Hill, where they had made their homes as whites fled to the suburbs.

4. My essay "Why African Americans Should Be Environmentalists" first appeared in *Call to Action: Handbook for Ecology, Peace and Justice*, edited by Brad Erickson and published in 1990 by Sierra Club Books. The essay's popularity led to its inclusion in several other publications. In later versions, I changed the title to "Why People of Color Should Be Environmentalists."

CHAPTER 10 **Deep Time, Slavery, and the Making of the Modern Economic System**

1. For an impressive analysis and refutation of this mentality as exhibited by English-speaking historians and other thinkers from the nineteenth century into the latter years of the twentieth century, see *The Colonizer's Model of the World* by James M. Blaut (1993), particularly chapters "History Inside-Out" (1–49) and "The Myth of the European Miracle" (51–151). See also Blaut's (2000) *Eight Eurocentric Historians*.

2. M. Rohan Gani and Nahid D. S. Gani, researchers at the Energy and Geoscience Institute at the University of Utah in Salt Lake City, have made valuable contributions to our understanding of the saga of human evolution by focusing on the history of plate tectonics and the effects the resulting changes in topography and climate had on our ancient ancestors. For more information, see their January 2008 article "Tectonic Hypotheses of Human Evolution" published in *Geotimes: Earth, Energy and Environment News*.

3. Both *The Journey of Man: A Genetic Odyssey* by Spencer Wells and *The Real Eve: Modern Man's Journey Out of Africa* by Stephen Oppenheimer have been adapted as television documentaries. *The Journey of Man*, a 2002 PBS special, follows the author, Spencer Wells, as he looks for clues, genetic and archeological, while traveling the routes our ancestors seem to have taken as they left Africa and proceeded to people the earth. *The Real Eve*, a 2002 special produced by the Discovery Channel and narrated by Danny Glover, dramatizes the experiences of our ancient ancestors in a style similar to the historical reenactments seen on the History Channel.

4. A new classification system, taking into account the close relationship between humans and chimps, places orangutans, gorillas, and chimps together with humans and their ancestors in the family Hominidae (hominids); chimps and humans in the subfamily Homininae (hominines); and humans in the tribe Hominini (hominins). Thus, the term "hominins" is preferred over the traditional term "hominids." For more information, see *National Geographic Style Manual*, s.v. "hominid, hominin, hominoid, human."

5. Oppenheimer (2003, 67) suggests that the migration out of Africa took place 83,000 years ago while Wells (2002, 108) thinks it was more like 50,000 years ago.

6. BP stands for Before Present, a measurement used by archaeologists that is based on radiocarbon dating methods. The origin year for BP dates is 1950 CE, so 83,000 BP is the equivalent to 81,050 BCE.

7. *First Peoples*, a PBS series released in 2015, expands on the findings of Wells and Oppenheimer, adds a few migration routes, and presents DNA analysis indicating that Homo sapiens from Africa interbred with other early human species—Neanderthal, Denisovan, and possibly Homo erectus or a related species.

8. A 2012 analysis of artifacts from a cave in South Africa reveals that forty-four thousand years ago, its residents were carving bone tools, using pigments, making beads, and even using poison. For more information, see Stephanie Pappas's July 30, 2012 article "Start Date for Human Civilization Moved Back 20,000 Years or So," published in *The Christian Science Monitor*.

9. A March 2010 *Smithsonian Magazine* article by Ann Gibbons titled "The Human Family's Earliest Ancestors" provides a lot of interesting information about our ancient ancestors.

10. In *Big History: From the Big Bang to Present*, Cynthia Stokes Brown (2007, 90–93) develops an interesting interpretation of the epic of Gilgamesh and the Biblical story of Adam and Eve's expulsion from the Garden of Eden as laments of people who have lost their connection with the land.

11. The best-known rock art from this period is from the Tassili-n-Ajjer plateau in southeastern Algeria.

12. The Land of Punt disappeared from written records during the first millennium BCE.

13. The UNESCO website has images of and information about the amazing churches carved out of rock at Lalibela in a mountainous region in central Ethiopia.

14. Judging from the many editions of Ibn Battuta's travel narratives, his popularity does not seem to have been diminished by recent scholarship indicating that some of his writing was plagiarized from the accounts of other travelers.

15. In *How Europe Underdeveloped Africa*, the brilliant Guyanese historian and activist Walter Rodney (1972, 40–60) assembles an account of the high level of development throughout Africa that the first European explorers saw when they visited in the second half of the fifteenth century. Sadly, Rodney was assassinated in 1980 at the age of 38 because of his leftist political views.

16. The Library of Congress website has information about and photos of the ancient manuscripts in Timbuktu. See also the Global Gateway's 2007 article "Islamic Manuscripts from Mali: Timbuktu—an Islamic Cultural Center."

17. Iron ore must have been imported since there are no sources of it in the Niger floodplain around Djenné-Djenno. A few Roman and Hellenistic beads were discovered in the deepest levels of excavations, but they may have changed hands many times before reaching the Middle Niger River region. Roderick McIntosh and his wife, Susan Keech McIntosh, both anthropology professors at Rice University, share information about their work researching the Inland Niger Delta, "Jenne-jeno, an Ancient African City," on Rice University's anthropology department website.

18. In the chapter "Explaining 1492" in *The Colonizer's Model of the World: Geographical Diffusionism and Eurocentric History*, James M. Blaut (1993, 179–87) provides a historical account of the advantages and limitations of the soon-to-be colonial powers of the fifteenth century. He dismantles the

presumption that Europeans in 1492 held any particular advantage in terms of culture and technology over the Chinese, the Indians, and the East Africans in agriculture, shipbuilding, or navigation.

19. For an unvarnished account of this encounter and its aftermath, see Howard Zinn's (1980) *A People's History of the United States*.

20. For diverse—and complementary—perspectives on the role of slavery in the sugar economy, see Richard Sheridan's (1974) *Sugar and Slavery: An Economic History of the West Indies*; Andrea Stuart's (2013) *Sugar in the Blood: A Family's Story of Slavery and Empire*; and Jason W. Moore's (2000) paper "Sugar and the Expansion of the Early Modern World-Economy: Commodity Frontiers, Ecological Transformation, and Industrialization."

21. In 1996, UNESCO launched the Slave Route Project to shed light on the causes, issues, and consequences of slavery. The project worked with others to have slavery and the slave trade recognized as crimes against humanity at the 2001 World Conference against Racism, Racial Discrimination, Xenophobia and Related Intolerance in Durban, South Africa, which I attended shortly after I began working at the Ford Foundation. The United Nations declared 2004—the bicentennial of the Haitian Revolution—as the International Year to Commemorate the Struggle against Slavery and its Abolition. UNESCO produced a very informative 2004 report entitled "Struggles Against Slavery."

22. Many books in the References and Additional Resources sections shed light on this. For example, Eric Williams analyzes the Caribbean sugar industry and how it catapulted the English economy to global dominance in his 1944 book *Capitalism and Slavery*. Seventy years later, Edward Baptist (2014), in *The Half Was Never Told: Slavery and the Making of American Capitalism*, traces the development of the cotton industry in the American South and shows how a global economic empire was built literally on the backs of enslaved African Americans.

23. Moore (2000, 425) notes that Cristobal Colon's explanation of the effect of deforestation on climate was first quoted by Alfred Crosby (1986, 96–97) in *Ecological Imperialism: The Biological Expansion of Europe, 900–1900*.

24. In 1762, the Liverpool Town Council claimed, in a letter to one of the secretaries of state, that the "West-Indian and African trade is by far the largest branch of the great and extensive commerce of this town." This communication was quoted by Anthony Tibbles, director of the Merseyside Maritime Museum in Liverpool, in a lecture at Gresham College in London titled "Liverpool and the Slave Trade" on March 19, 2007.

25. The following Liverpool streets are named after well-known slave traders: Bold Street, Brooks Alley, Cuncliffe Street, Earl Road, Earl Street, Gladstone Road, Parr Street, Sir Thomas Street, and Tarleton Street. Goree and Jamaica Streets are named for islands important to the slave trade. For more information, see Laurence Westgaph's 2007 book *Read the Signs: Street Names with a Connection to the Transatlantic Slave Trade and Abolition in Liverpool*.

26. In his paper on "Ports of the Transatlantic Slave Trade" presented at the TextPorts Conference at Liverpool Hope University College in April 2000, Anthony Tibbles discusses many important aspects of the triangular trade.

27. Of course, a fortune could be lost in cases of shipwreck, piracy, rebellion, or outbreak of disease among the slaves. The practice of insuring the lives of slaves gave a big boost to the fledgling insurance industry (Grandin 2014, 79, 84).

28. I was fortunate to be living in Manhattan in 2005 when the New-York Historical Society mounted the first segment of a huge multimedia exhibition on "Slavery in New York," which continued until 2007. The companion book, *Slavery in New York*, edited by Ira Berlin, one of my favorite historians, and Leslie M. Harris is richly illustrated and beautifully put together.

29. In 1993, the African burial ground was declared a national historic landmark; in 2006, it was named a national monument. Since the 2007 dedication of the memorial, the National Parks Service has operated a visitor's center on the site. In 2009, Kutz Television released a four-part documentary titled *The African Burial Ground: An American Discovery*.

30. In *Black Men Built the Capitol: Discovering African American History in and around Washington, DC*, Jesse Holland (2007) provides a detailed account of the contributions of Africans, both enslaved and free, to the design and construction of the nation's capital. He employs a clever literary device, starting with a section titled "What Everyone Already Knows" followed by "The Rest of the Story."

CHAPTER 11   The Landscape of Freedom

1. The primary authors were Wells and Douglass, but journalist I. Garland Penn and Frederick L. Barnett (Wells's future husband) also contributed. Daphne Spain (2001, 220) recounts this story briefly in *How Women Saved the City*.

2. A page-by-page scan of *The Reason Why the Colored American Is Not in the World's Columbian Exposition* is available in the Library of Congress's *African-American Pamphlet Collection*. The collection contains 396 pamphlets published from 1822 through 1909 by African American authors and others who wrote about slavery, African colonization, emancipation, Reconstruction, and related topics.

3. Ida Wells planned to publish *The Reason Why the Colored American Is Not in the World's Columbian Exposition* in four languages, including French, German, and Spanish, but ran out of money before it could be printed in any language other than English. The pamphlet reproduced by the Library of Congress does contain a preface in French and German before the English version.

4. In a note following his statement about the market value of enslaved African Americans, Edward Baptist (2014, 479) cites his sources as Robert E. Gallman (1986, 165–214) and Richard H. Kilbourne (1995, 26–68).

5. Solomon Northup's memoir was adapted for the 2013 film of the same name.

6. The American Missionary Association was an abolitionist group that originally grew out of a committee organized in 1839 to defend and support the African slaves who had mutinied against their Spanish owners and brought their slave ship *Amistad* into New York waters in the hope of gaining protection and regaining their freedom.

7. The inspiring day-long event on May 1, 1865 was forgotten or ignored until historian David Blight (2011) had "some extraordinary luck in an archive at Harvard," where he found newspaper reports of what appears to be the earliest Memorial Day ceremony.

8. The year of 1877 is commonly cited as the end of Reconstruction. The defeat of Republican presidential candidate Rutherford Hayes to the Democrat Samuel Tilden in that year's election seemed likely. To avoid electoral defeat, Republicans agreed to remove federal troops who were protecting African Americans in the South in exchange for Democratic support in the forthcoming election. The result was a rise in lynchings and other types of violence, as well as countless episodes of injustice, against blacks throughout the South.

9. I was delighted when one of my assistants came across this information about my ancestor William Jervay in *The Wars of Reconstruction: The Brief, Violent History of America's Most Progressive Era* by Douglas Egerton (2014, 54).

10. Andrew Johnson was three when his father died and left the family in poverty. His mother, a seamstress, struggled to support Andrew and his brother, William, and when she remarried, both brothers became apprenticed to a tailor. Soon after, they ran away and worked as itinerant tailors. Andrew eventually established a successful tailoring business and acquired a few slaves, which he later freed. He became an advocate of the working class when he entered politics, but while he supported the preservation of the Union, he opposed the abolition of slavery.

11. "Peonage" refers to a condition of compulsory service based on the indebtedness of the laborer.

12. Douglas A. Blackmon's (2008) *Slavery by Another Name: The Re-Enslavement of Black Americans from the Civil War to World War II* won the 2009 Pulitzer Prize for General Nonfiction. The book documents debt peonage and convict leasing in the South through carefully researched case studies.

13. In a speech Booker T. Washington delivered to a predominantly white audience at the Cotton States and International Exposition in Atlanta on September 18, 1895, he assured listeners that blacks would not press for social equality but would concentrate on improving their condition by hard work and developing agricultural and industrial skills (Foner 2005, 211).

14. Norman L. Crockett's (1979) *The Black Towns* and William and Jane Pease's (1963) *Black Utopia: Negro Communal Experiments in America* are good sources on this important piece of history.

15. Another interesting and poignant article by DeNeen Brown (2015b) is "Black Towns, Established by Freed Slaves after the Civil War, Are Dying Out."

16. Another book with detailed historical accounts of white mob violence to defeat Reconstruction that I found compelling is Nicholas Lemann's (2006) *Redemption: The Last Battle of the Civil War*.

17. A companion to *Buried in the Bitter Waters* is sociologist James Loewen's (2005) *Sundown Towns: A Hidden Dimension of American Racism*. The term "sundown towns" refers to signs warning blacks to get out of town by sundown. Loewen discovers a huge number of these exclusionary towns and suburbs in the North and the Midwest—in fact, everywhere except in the South.

18. To each of the sixty paintings in his *Migration Series* (1940–41), painter Jacob Lawrence added a one-sentence caption. The works were later published as *The Great Migration: An American Story* in 1993. A more recent collection is *Jacob Lawrence: The Complete Prints, 1963–2000* (Nesbett 2001). The images and brief captions tell a powerful story.

CHAPTER 12   The City at a Crossroads

1. Willie Lee Rose was a student and protégé of C. Vann Woodward, author of *The Strange Career of Jim Crow* (1955) and other important works on the sociology and history of the South.

2. For more on segregation and the racialization of space, see Grace Elizabeth Hale's (1999) *Making Whiteness: The Culture of Segregation in the South, 1890–1940* and Howard Rabinowitz's (1996) *Race Relations in the Urban South, 1865–1890*.

3. The federal Home Owners' Loan Corporation map of Philadelphia in 1937 is reproduced in Gwen Sharp's (2012) "Philadelphia Redlining Maps."

4. Political economy professors Barry Bluestone and Bennett Harrison (1982) describe the process that has devastated so many American cities in *The Deindustrialization of America: Plant Closings, Community Abandonment, and the Dismantling of Basic Industry*. Sociology professor William Julius Wilson (1987; 1996) describes the effect this process has on urban populations in *The Truly Disadvantaged: The Inner City, the Underclass and Urban Policy* and *When Work Disappears: The World of the New Urban Poor*.

5. I thoroughly agree with Noliwe Rooks (2014), who suggests that to address racism and police violence, we revisit the Kerner Commission report since hardly any of its thoughtful recommendations were ever implemented.

6. For details about the spill and photos of the ugly mess, see National Oceanic and Atmospheric Association (2014).

7. Senator Gaylord Nelson modeled the environmental teach-in he proposed for the first Earth Day on the very successful teach-ins of the Vietnam War

protest movement, which, in turn, were inspired by and modeled on the civil rights Freedom School movement.

8. Photographer Dave Jordano grew up in Detroit and moved to Chicago in the 1970s to open a commercial studio. In 2010, he started revisiting his home town and documenting the everyday lives of its diverse population in a photo collection that he titled *Detroit: Unbroken Down* and published in 2015. Some of these images are featured in an article by Pete Brook (2013) in *Wired* magazine.

CHAPTER 13 Forging an Alliance between Environmentalists and Social Justice Activists

1. The environmental commitment of Daniel Ortega, who resumed presidency of Nicaragua in 2006, has come under suspicion due to his collaboration with Chinese businessmen to construct an unpopular canal through his country. The canal will be much wider, twice as deep, and three times as long as the Panama Canal.

2. Understanding of human dependence on trees is expressed in the popular Chipko slogan: "What do the forests bear? / Soil, water, and pure air." Tellingly, the response promoted by the forest industry was "What do the forests bear? / Profit on resin and timber."

3. A decade later, Pulitzer Prize–winning columnist Eugene Robinson (2010) gave an in-depth description of this situation, identifying four distinct black subcultures. He argued that each was going in a different direction with its set of wants and needs.

4. Later, I learned that Francis was a very influential community organizer and co-director of the Center for Third World Organizing.

5. A food desert is an area in which residents have no nearby markets from which they can buy healthy, fresh food.

6. In *The Environment and the People in American Cities, 1600s–1900s: Disorder, Inequality, and Social Change*, environmental sociologist Dorceta Taylor (2009) discusses the ways that race, class, and gender influenced the urban experience as American cities grew and industrialized. Her work is an important resource for racial and environmental justice organizing and for equitable and effective urban planning.

7. Luke Cole started the Center on Race, Poverty, and the Environment in collaboration with Ralph Abascal of California Rural Legal Assistance, providing legal and technical assistance to attorneys and community groups involved in environmental justice struggles nationwide. Abascal was a legendary lawyer for the poor, who argued hundreds of cases for farmworkers, immigrants, and welfare recipients, most notably the case that resulted in the ban on the use of DDT and other deadly pesticides in California's fields and orchards.

8. For more about Robert Bullard and his work, see Gregory Dicum's (2006) article in *Grist*: "Meet Robert Bullard, the Father of Environmental Justice."

9. Prior to redistricting by the California Citizens Redistricting Commission of 2011, the ninth district encompassed most of the East Bay of the San Francisco Bay Area with cities in the district including Oakland, Piedmont, and Berkeley. Much of the ninth district is now the thirteenth district, and the current ninth is largely the successor to the former eleventh district.

10. Ron Dellums served as a member of the US House of Representatives from California's ninth district from 1993 to 1998.

11. The article "Reintegrating the Flatlands: A Regional Framework for Military Base Conversion in the San Francisco Bay Area" was published as a fifty-six-page working paper by Urban Habitat Program in 1995 and appeared in *Capitalism, Nature, Socialism* in 1997.

12. Martha Matsuoka served as my alternate to the EBCRC and, later, headed the Urban Habitat Brownfield Program. She now teaches urban and environmental policy at Occidental College.

13. Sociologist and economist James O'Connor edited *Capitalism, Nature, Socialism: A Journal of Socialist Ecology* and authored *Natural Causes: Essays in Ecological Marxism*. He taught for many years at the University of California at Santa Cruz.

14. The term "brownfield" refers to an industrial or commercial site that has become idle or underused because of environmental pollution and has the potential to be reused once it is cleaned up.

15. After I left the Urban Habitat Program and went to work at the Ford Foundation, Sunne McPeak was appointed by Governor Schwarzenegger to head the California Business, Transportation and Housing Agency.

16. When the draft compact was finalized in 1999, it was published as a locally distributed newsletter by ABAG.

CHAPTER 14 **Laying the Groundwork
for a National Movement**

1. I became familiar with CDCs during my student days in New York as I worked to combine my commitment to civil rights with my passion for architectural design. See the section "Joining the Community Design Movement" in Chapter 3: Moving to New York.

2. G. William Domhoff (2005), research professor in psychology and sociology at the University of California at Santa Cruz, has written a very informative historical account of Ford Foundation's efforts to support solutions to inner-city problems.

3. One such group interested in helping to bridge the gap between environment and social justice was the Civil Rights Project at Harvard University Graduate

School of Education. The Project ended when the founders moved to the West Coast.

4. The work of many of the projects funded by the Ford Foundation's Sustainable Metropolitan Communities Initiative is documented in *Breakthrough Communities: Sustainability and Justice in the Next American Metropolis*, edited by Paloma Pavel (2009).

5. The Funders' Network for Smart Growth and Livable Communities was formed in the spring of 1999 by thirty philanthropic organizations after exploratory conversations among a few funders the previous year. It has grown into a substantial network of grantmaking organizations that are committed—individually and collectively—to supporting the development of communities that are economically prosperous, environmentally sustainable, and socially equitable.

6. The report, *Edging Toward Equity: Creating Shared Opportunity in America's Regions*, by Manuel Pastor, Chris Benner, and Rachel Rosner (2006) grew out of the Conversation on Regional Equity (CORE) and was published by the Center for Justice, Tolerance, and Community at the University of California at Santa Cruz with support from the Ford Foundation.

7. The Local Initiatives Support Corporation connects local organizations and community leaders with resources to revitalize neighborhoods and improve quality of life.

8. Transit-oriented development (TOD) is a regional strategy for developing housing, education, commerce, and public services near transit stops.

9. Hattie Dorsey, founder and executive director of the Atlanta Neighborhood Development Partnership (ANDP), partnered with several CDCs in the Atlanta area to develop new ways to reach out to the entire metropolitan region and unite the populations across geography. This charismatic five-foot-tall African American woman invented a new approach to mixed-income housing projects that became a national model and inspiration for how cities can grow to challenge segregation by race and class. ANDP took on the challenge of siting new affordable housing in suburban places, choosing locations outside the areas in which CDCs normally operate to create affordable housing in places with economic and educational opportunities.

10. This was the third of a series of conferences organized by UNESCO, the United Nations Educational, Scientific, and Cultural Organization. The first two were held in Geneva, Switzerland, one of the United Nation's four headquarters, along with New York City, Vienna, and Nairobi.

11. For more detail about Belvie Rooks and the Hey, Listen Up! curriculum, see Rooks (2001a, 2001b).

12. There must have been three or four hundred Ford Foundation workers attending the conference in Durban.

13. For more about this project that has become a social movement, read *The Victoria Mxenge Housing Project* by Salma Ismail (2015).

CHAPTER 15   **Planning Healthy and Just Communities for All in the Age of Global Warming**

1. The estimate of 61 percent people of color in California is derived by subtracting the percentage of whites reported by Edmund G. Brown, Jr. (2014, 150–51)—38.8 percent—from 100 percent.

2. Rebuild the Dream uses its website, rebuildthedream.com, as an organizing tool.

3. The Just Transition Alliance is a coalition of labor, economic justice, and environmental justice activists, indigenous people, and working-class people of color focused on contaminated sites that should be cleaned up and on the transition to clean production and sustainable economies.

4. In developing strategies for movement building, I was delighted to discover *Comparative Perspectives on Social Movements: Political Opportunities, Mobilizing Structures, and Cultural Framings*, edited by Doug McAdam, John McCarthy, and Mayer Zaid (1996). Their recommendations perfectly matched what I had been doing instinctively.

5. The Air Resources Board is a division of the California Environmental Protection Agency.

6. "Investment without displacement" refers to strategies to avoid the displacement of longtime neighborhood residents caused by gentrification, which, by improving conditions in run-down neighborhoods, raises property values and rents so that developers and investors profit, but low-income residents can no longer afford the higher rents or property taxes. This approach, also known as "development without displacement," focuses on improving living conditions and preserving cultural diversity.

7. "Disadvantaged Communities Teach Regional Planners a Lesson in Equitable and Sustainable Development," an article by Richard Marcantonio and Alex Karner (2014), appeared in *Poverty & Race*, the newsletter of the nonprofit Poverty & Race Research Action Council (PRRAC), cofounded by my longtime friend and colleague Chester Hartman, who serves as its research director.

8. You can read the relevant portion of the *Plan Bay Area Draft Environmental Impact Report* and get a sense of our Equity, Environment, and Jobs scenario and the other scenarios being considered at http://onebayarea.org/sites/default/files/pdf/Draft_Plan_Bay_Area/Draft_EIR.pdf.

9. Cap and trade is a way of putting a price on carbon emissions. Governments impose a limit on the amount of carbon dioxide industries are allowed to release and decrease the amount every year. They issue and distribute a finite number of permits for emissions and auction additional permits, which generates income for the state. At the end of each compliance period, every regulated emitter must surrender enough permits to cover its actual emissions.

California is the first state with a comprehensive cap-and-trade system, which began at the start of 2013.

10. An earlier and shorter study on rising suburban poverty, "Two Steps Back: City and Suburban Poverty Trends 1999–2005" by Alan Berube and Elizabeth Kneebone (2006), was part of the Brookings Institution's Living Cities Census Series.

11. Myron Orfield's (2006) extremely well-documented report titled *Minority Suburbanization, Stable Integration, and Economic Opportunity in Fifteen Metropolitan Regions* provides a starting point for understanding the suburbanization of poverty and what to do about it.

12. In *Building Resilience: Social Capital in Post-Disaster Recovery*, sociologist Daniel P. Aldrich (2012) examines the post-disaster responses of four distinct communities—Tokyo following the 1923 earthquake, Kobe after the 1995 earthquake, Tamil Nadu after the 2004 Indian Ocean tsunami, and New Orleans post-Hurricane Katrina. He finds that those with robust social networks were better able to coordinate recovery from disaster. See also Amy Patterson Neubert's (2011) article about Aldrich's research on the social impacts of the 2011 earthquake and tsunami in Japan.

13. Green for All is a project of Dream Corps Unlimited, which were both co-founded by civil rights leader Van Jones, along with Rebuild the Dream, Ella Baker Center for Human Rights, and others. Green for All (2016) "works to build an inclusive green economy strong enough to lift people out of poverty. Our goal is to make sure people of color have a place and a voice in the climate movement. That our neighborhoods are strong, resilient, and healthy. That, as the clean energy economy grows, it brings jobs and opportunity to our communities."

14. Angela Davis's three books on the prison-industrial complex and the school-to-prison pipeline—*The Prison Industrial Complex* (2000), *Are Prisons Obsolete?* (2003), and *Abolition Democracy: Beyond Prisons, Torture, and Empire* (2005)—are sadly still relevant.

15. The 2014 data snapshot on school discipline, restraint, and seclusion by the US Department of Education Office of Civil Rights provides statistics that establish racial bias in administering school discipline.

16. The fact sheet from the American Civil Liberties Union (2015) sheds light on the school-to-prison pipeline phenomenon.

17. Restorative justice has been known in academic circles as "victim-offender mediation." For some background and history, see Christopher Bright (2016).

18. The award-winning documentary film *Long Night's Journey into Day*, directed by Frances Reid and Deborah Hoffman (2000), is a powerful study of South Africa's Truth and Reconciliation Commission at work.

19. In the September 3, 2013 issue of the *Boston Herald*, Jack Encarnacao describes the "staggering drop in drug- and violence-related suspensions in

Boston schools since the district amended its discipline policies to allow 're-storative justice' measures in lieu of suspensions, including written apologies, conferences between offenders and victims, and anger management courses."

20. Alicia Garza worked for the National Domestic Workers Alliance as special project director. When she tweeted the slogan "Black Lives Matter," she was expressing her outrage over the acquittal of police officer George Zimmerman, who had shot to death unarmed, black, seventeen-year-old Trayvon Martin in a suburban city in the Miami-Dade County region.

References

Air Resources Board. 2014. *California Greenhouse Gas Emission Inventory: 2000–2012.* Sacramento, CA: California Environmental Protection Agency. https://www.arb.ca.gov/cc/inventory/pubs/reports/ghg_inventory_00-12_report.pdf.

Aldrich, Daniel P. 2012. *Building Resilience: Social Capital in Post-Disaster Recovery.* Chicago: University of Chicago Press.

Alexander, Christopher. 1979. *The Timeless Way of Building.* New York: Oxford University Press.

Alexander, Christopher, Sara Ishikawa, and Murray Silverstein. 1968. *A Pattern Language Which Generates Multi-Service Centers.* Berkeley, CA: Center for Environmental Structure.

———. 1977. *A Pattern Language: Towns, Buildings, and Construction.* New York: Oxford University Press.

Alexander, Michelle. 2010. *The New Jim Crow: Mass Incarceration in the Age of Colorblindness.* New York: The New Press.

American Civil Liberties Union. 2015. "School-to-Prison Pipeline." American Civil Liberties Union. Accessed August 7. https://www.aclu.org/fact-sheet/what-school-prison-pipeline.

Anthony, Carl. 1976a. "The Big House and the Slave Quarter: Prelude to New World Architecture, Part 1." *Landscape* 20 (3): 8–19.

———. 1976b. "The Big House and the Slave Quarter: African Contributions to the New World, Part 2." *Landscape* 21 (1): 9–15.

———. 1990a. "Why African Americans Should Be Environmentalists." In *Call to Action: Handbook for Ecology, Peace and Justice*, edited by Brad Erickson, 143–49. San Francisco: Sierra Club Books.

———. 1990b. "Why People of Color Should Be Environmentalists." *Race, Poverty, and the Environment* 1 (1): 5–6.

———. 1995. "Ecopsychology and the Deconstruction of Whiteness." In *Ecopsychology: Restoring the Earth, Healing the Mind*, edited by Theodore Roszak, 263–78. Berkeley, CA: Counterpoint Press.

Anthony, Carl, and Benjamin Starrett. 2005. *Signs of Progress: Stories of Philanthropic Leadership in Advancing Regional and Neighborhood Equity*. Coral Gables, FL: Funders' Network for Smart Growth and Livable Communities. http://www.fundersnetwork.org/files/learn/Sings_of_Promise_Final2.pdf.

Association of Bay Area Governments. 1999. "The Compact for a Sustainable Bay Area." *Service Matters* 4 (May/June). http://abag.ca.gov/pubs/newsletter/SrvMtrsMay-June99.pdf.

Aveni, Anthony. 1997. *Stairways to the Stars: Skywatching in Three Great Ancient Cultures*. San Francisco: John Wiley & Sons, Inc.

———. 2008. *People and the Sky: Our Ancestors and the Cosmos*. London: Thames & Hudson.

Baldwin, James. 1955. *Notes of a Native Son*. New York: Beacon Press.

———. 1961. *Nobody Knows My Name*. New York: Dell Publishing Company.

———. 1962. "A Letter to My Nephew." *The Progressive*, January 1. http://progressive.org/magazine/letter-nephew/.

Baptist, Edward E. 2014. *The Half Has Never Been Told: Slavery and the Making of American Capitalism*. New York: Perseus Basic Books.

Bay Area Census. 2017. "San Francisco Bay Area." Bay Area Census. Accessed April 15. http://www.bayareacensus.ca.gov/bayarea.htm.

Beamish, Jennifer, Clive Maltby, and Spencer Wells. 2002. *Journey of Man*. DVD. Alexandria, VA: PBS Home Video.

Beauregard, Robert A. 2006. *When America Became Suburban*. Minneapolis, MN: University of Minnesota Press.

Beckert, Sven. 2014. *The Empire of Cotton: A Global History*. New York: Knopf.

Berlin, Ira, and Leslie M. Harris, ed. 2005. *Slavery in New York*. New York: New Press.

Berry, Thomas. 1988. *The Dream of the Earth*. San Francisco: Sierra Club Books.

———. 1999. *The Great Work: Our Way into the Future*. New York: Bell Tower.

Berube, Alan, and Elizabeth Kneebone. 2006. "Two Steps Back: City and Suburban Poverty Trends 1999–2005." *Brookings*, December 1. https://www.brookings.edu/research/two-steps-back-city-and-suburban-poverty-trends-1999-2005/.

Blackmon, Douglas A. 2008. *Slavery by Another Name: The Re-Enslavement of Black Americans from the Civil War to World War II*. New York: Doubleday.

Blatman, Ron, Miles Saunders, and Robert Redford. 2009. *Saving the Bay: The Story of San Francisco Bay*. DVD. San Francisco: Ronald M. Blatman, Inc., and KQED/KTEH Public Television.

Blaut, James M. 1993. *The Colonizer's Model of the World: Geographical Diffusionism and Eurocentric History*. New York: Guilford Press.

———. 2000. *Eight Eurocentric Historians*. New York: Guilford Press.

Blight, David. 2011. "Forgetting Why We Remember." *New York Times*, May 29. http://www.nytimes.com/2011/05/30/opinion/30blight.html.

Bluestone, Barry, and Bennett Harrison. 1982. *The Deindustrialization of America: Plant Closings, Community Abandonment, and the Dismantling of Basic Industry*. New York: Basic Books.

Bradford, Sarah Hopkins. 1886. *Harriet: The Moses of Her People*. New York: Geo. R. Lockwood and Son. https://archive.org/details/harrietmosesofhebrad.

Bright, Christopher. 2016. "Lesson 3: Programs: Victim-Offender Mediation." Centre for Justice & Reconciliation. Accessed June 6. http://www.restorative justice.org/university-classroom/01introduction/tutorial-introduction-to -restorative-justice/processes/vom.

Brook, Pete. 2013. "Captivating Photos of Detroit Delve Deep to Reveal a Beautiful, Struggling City." *Wired*, January 29. http://www.wired.com/2013/01 /detroit-dave-jordano.

Brown, Cynthia Stokes. 2007. *Big History: From the Big Bang to the Present*. New York: New Press.

Brown, DeNeen L. 2015a. "All-Black Towns Across America: Life Was Hard but Full of Promise." *Washington Post*, March 27. http://www.washingtonpost .com/lifestyle/style/a-list-of-well-known-black-towns/2015/03/27/9f21ca42 -cdc4-11e4-a2a7-9517a3a70506_story.html.

———. 2015b. "Black Towns, Established by Freed Slaves After the Civil War, Are Dying Out." *Washington Post*, March 27. http://www.washingtonpost .com/local/black-towns-established-by-freed-slaves-after-civil-war-are-dying -out/2015/03/26/25872e5c-c608-11e4-a199-6cb5e63819d2_story.html.

Brown, Edmund G., Jr. 2014. *Governor's Budget Summary 2014–15*. Sacramento, CA: State of California. http://www.ebudget.ca.gov/2014-15/pdf/Budget Summary/FullBudgetSummary.pdf.

Bullard, Robert D. 1990. *Dumping in Dixie: Race, Class, and Environmental Quality*. Boulder, CO: Westview Press.

———. 2007. *The Black Metropolis in the Twenty-First Century: Race, Power, and Politics of Place*. Lanham, MD: Rowman & Littlefield.

———. 2008. *Growing Smarter: Achieving Livable Communities, Regional Equity and Environmental Justice*. Cambridge, MA: MIT Press.

Bullard, Robert D., Glenn Johnson, and Angel Torres, ed. 2004. *Highway Robbery: Transportation Racism and New Routes to Equity*. Cambridge, MA: South End Press.

Burton, LeVar, John Amos, Ben Vereen, Cicely Tyson, Thalmus Rasulala, Edward Asner, Ralph Waite, et al. 2011. *Roots: The Complete Collection*. Burbank, CA: Warner Brothers Entertainment.

Bybee, Roger. 2009. "Growing Power in an Urban Food Desert." *YES! Magazine*, February 13. http://www.yesmagazine.org/issues/food-for-everyone/growing -power-in-an-urban-food-desert.

Carson, Rachel. 1962. *Silent Spring*. Boston: Houghton Mifflin.

Castells, Manuel. 1983. *The City and the Grassroots: A Cross-Cultural Theory of Urban Social Movements*. Berkeley, CA: University of California Press.

Catton, Theodore. 1997. *Inhabited Wilderness: Indians, Eskimos, and National Parks in Alaska*. Albuquerque, NM: University of New Mexico Press.

Cerami, Charles. 2002. *Benjamin Banneker: Surveyor, Astronomer*. New York: J. Wiley.

Coates, Ta-Nehisi. 2014. "The Case for Reparations." *The Atlantic Monthly*, June 23. http://www.theatlantic.com/features/archive/2014/05/the-case-for -reparations/361631/.

Commission for Racial Justice. 1987. *Toxic Waste and Race in the United States: A National Report on the Racial and Socio-Economic Characteristics of Communities with Hazardous Waste Sites*. New York: United Church of Christ. http://d3n8a8pro7vhmx.cloudfront.net/unitedchurchofchrist/legacy_url /13567/toxwrace87.pdf

Comp, T. Allan. 1989. *Blueprint for the Environment: A Plan for Federal Action and Advice to President Bush from America's Environmental Community*. Salt Lake City, UT: Howe Brothers.

Connecticut College. 2016. "Unity House History." Connecticut College. Accessed May 26. https://www.conncoll.edu/campus-life/unity-house/unity-house -history/.

Crosby, Alfred W. (1972) 2003. *The Columbian Exchange: Biological and Cultural Consequences of 1492*. Westport, CT: Praeger.

———. (1986) 2004. *Ecological Imperialism: The Biological Expansion of Europe, 900–1900*. Cambridge, UK: Cambridge University Press.

Cruse, Harold W. 1967. *The Crisis of the Negro Intellectual: A Historical Analysis of the Failure of Black Leadership*. New York: New York Review Books.

Davidoff, Paul. 1965. "Advocacy and Pluralism in Planning." *Journal of the American Institute of Planners* 31 (4): 331–38.

Davidson, Basil. 1961. *Black Mother: The Years of the African Slave Trade*. Boston: Little, Brown and Company.

———. 1964. *The African Past: Chronicles from Antiquity to Modern Times*. London: Longman.

———. 1966. *Africa in History: Themes and Outlines*. New York City: Simon and Schuster.

———. 1970. *The Lost Cities of Africa*. Boston: Little, Brown and Company.

Davis, Angela Y. 2000. *Prison Industrial Complex*. Oakland, CA: AK Press.

———. 2003. *Are Prisons Obsolete?* New York: Seven Stories Press.

———. 2005. *Abolition Democracy: Beyond Prisons, Torture, and Empire*. New York: Seven Stories Press.

Davis, David Brion. 2006. *Inhuman Bondage: The Rise and Fall of Slavery in the New World*. Oxford, UK: Oxford University Press.

Davis, Fania. 2014. "Discipline with Dignity: Oakland Classrooms Try Healing Instead of Punishment." *YES! Magazine*, February 19. http://www.yesmagazine.org/issues/education-uprising/where-dignity-is-part-of-the-school-day.

Dean, Amy B., and David B. Reynolds. 2009. *A New New Deal: How Regional Activism Will Reshape the American Labor Movement*. Ithaca, NY: Cornell University Press.

DeGruy, Joy. 2005. *Post Traumatic Slave Syndrome: America's Legacy of Enduring Injury and Healing*. Portland, OR: Uptone Press.

Delegates to the First National People of Color Environmental Leadership Summit. 1991. *Principles of Environmental Justice*. Washington, DC: First National People of Color Environmental Leadership Summit. http://www.ejnet.org/ej/principles.html.

Dicum, Gregory. 2006. "Meet Robert Bullard, the Father of Environmental Justice." *Grist*, March 15. http://grist.org/article/dicum/.

Domhoff, G. William. 2005. "The Ford Foundation in the Inner City: Forging an Alliance with Neighborhood Activists." University of California at Santa Cruz. http://www2.ucsc.edu/whorulesamerica/local/ford_foundation.html.

Douglass, Frederick. 1845. *Narrative of the Life of Frederick Douglass, An American Slave, Written by Himself*. Boston: Anti-Slavery Office.

Du Bois, W. E. B. 1899. *The Philadelphia Negro: A Social Study*. Philadelphia: University of Pennsylvania Press.

———. (1903) 2007. *The Souls of Black Folk*. New York: Oxford World's Classics.

Duncan, Cynthia. 1999. *Worlds Apart: Why Poverty Persists in Rural America*. New Haven, CT: Yale University Press.

Dunn, Ross E. 1986. *The Adventures of Ibn Battuta: A Muslim Traveler of the 14th Century*. Berkeley, CA: University of California Press.

Dyett & Bhatia. 2013. *Plan Bay Area: Draft Environmental Impact Report, State Clearinghouse No. 2012062029*. San Francisco, CA: Association of Bay Area Governments and Metropolitan Transportation Commission.

East Bay Conversion and Reinvestment Commission. 1996. *Defense Conversion: A Road Map for Communities*. Oakland, CA: East Bay Conversion and Reinvestment Commission.

Egerton, Douglas R. 2014. *The Wars of Reconstruction: The Brief, Violent History of America's Most Progressive Era*. New York: Bloomsbury Press.

Ellsworth, Scott. 1982. *Death in a Promised Lad: The Tulsa Race Riot of 1921*. Baton Rouge, LA: Louisiana State University Press.

Encarnacao, Jack. 2013. "Sharp Drop in Suspensions as Boston Schools Try 'Restorative' Approach." *Boston Herald*, September 3. http://www.bostonherald.com/news_opinion/local_coverage/2013/09/sharp_drop_in_suspensions_as_boston_schools_try_restorative.

Engerman, Stanley L., and Kenneth L. Sokoloff. 2011. "Once Upon a Time in the Americas: Land and Immigration Policies in the New World." In *Understanding Long-Run Economic Growth: Geography, Institutions, and the*

Knowledge Economy, edited by Dora L. Costa and Naomi R. Lamoreaux, 13–48. Chicago: University of Chicago Press.

Fletcher, Sir Banister. (1896) 1996. *Sir Banister Fletcher's A History of Architecture*. 20th edition. Edited by Dan Cruickshank. Boston: Architectural Press.

Foner, Eric. 1988. *Reconstruction: America's Unfinished Revolution, 1863–1877*. New York: Harper & Row.

———. 2005. *Forever Free: The Story of Emancipation and Reconstruction*. New York: Alfred A. Knopf.

Fonte, Verona. 2016. "Digital Media Biography of Karl Linn." Karllinn.org. Accessed May 26. http://www.karllinn.org/media-library/digital-media-biography/.

Forna, Aminatta, Richard Trayler-Smith, Adrian Davies, and Tim Short. 2009. *The Lost Libraries of Timbuktu*. DVD. London: BBC Television.

Fraknoi, Andrew. 2016. "Unheard Voices, Part 1: The Astronomy of Many Cultures." Multiverse. Last updated August. http://multiverse.ssl.berkeley.edu/multicultural.

Freund, Bill. 2007. *The African City: A History*. Cambridge, UK: Cambridge University Press.

Friedman, John. 1979. *A Good Society*. Cambridge, MA: MIT Press.

———. 1987. *Planning in the Public Domain: From Knowledge to Action*. Princeton, NJ: Princeton University Press.

Gallman, Robert E. 1986. "The United States Capital Stock in the Nineteenth Century." In *Long-Term Factors in American Economic Growth*, edited by Stanley L. Engerman and Robert E. Gallman, 165–214. Chicago: University of Chicago Press.

Games, Alison. 2008. "Migrations and Frontiers." In *The Atlantic World 1450–2000*, edited by Toyin Falola and Kevin D. Roberts, 48–66. Bloomington, IN: University of Indiana Press.

Gani, M. Rohan, and Nahid D. S. Gani. 2008. "Tectonic Hypotheses of Human Evolution." *Geotimes: Earth, Energy and Environment News*, January. http://www.geotimes.org/jan08/article.html?id=feature_evolution.html.

Gibbons, Ann. 2010. "The Human Family's Earliest Ancestors." *Smithsonian Magazine*, March. http://www.smithsonianmag.com/science-nature/the-human-familys-earliest-ancestors-7372974/.

Global Gateway. 2007. "Islamic Manuscripts from Mali: Timbuktu—an Islamic Cultural Center." The Library of Congress. November 19. http://international.loc.gov/intldl/malihtml/islam.html.

Goodman, Paul, and Percival Goodman. 1960. *Communitas: Means of Livelihood and Ways of Life*. 2nd edition. New York: Vintage Books.

Gotham, Kevin Fox. 2002. *Race, Real Estate, and Uneven Development: The Kansas City Experience, 1900–2000*. Albany, NY: State University of New York Press.

Grandin, Greg. 2014. *The Empire of Necessity: Slavery, Freedom, and Deception in the New World*. New York: Henry Holt and Company.

Green for All. 2016. "About Us." Dream Corps Unlimited. Accessed on June 6. http://www.greenforall.org/about_us.

Griaule, Marcel. 1965. *Conversations with Ogotemmêli: An Introduction to Dogon Religious Ideas.* London: Oxford University Press.

Grove, Richard H. 1995. *Green Imperialism: Colonial Expansion, Tropical Island Edens and the Origins of Environmentalism, 1600–1860.* Cambridge, UK: Cambridge University Press.

Hale, Grace Elizabeth. 1999. *Making Whiteness: The Culture of Segregation in the South, 1890–1940.* New York: Vintage Books.

Haley, Alex. 1976. *Roots: The Saga of an American Family.* Bronx, NY: Ishi Press International.

Hamdun, Said, and Noël King. 1995. *Ibn Battuta in Black Africa.* Princeton, NJ: Marcus Wiener.

Hammer, Joshua. 2014. "The Race to Save Mali's Priceless Artifacts." *Smithsonian*, January 4. http://www.smithsonianmag.com/history/Race-Save-Mali -Artifacts-180947965/.

———. 2016. *The Bad-Ass Librarians of Timbuktu: And Their Race to Save the World's Most Precious Manuscripts.* New York: Simon & Schuster.

Hartman, Chester. 2002. *City for Sale: The Transformation of San Francisco.* Revised edition. Berkeley, CA: University of California Press.

Harvey, David. 1973. *Social Justice in the City.* Athens, GA: University of Georgia Press.

Hauenstein Center. 2012. "Slaveholding Presidents." Grand Valley State University. May 29. http://hauensteincenter.org/slaveholding/.

Herget, J. Barlow. 2015. "The Jervay Family." *The Carolinian.* Accessed April 27. http://www.caroliniannews.com/#!history/cbga.

Herman, Judith. 1992. *Trauma and Recovery: The Aftermath of Violence: From Domestic Abuse to Political Terror.* New York: Basic Books.

Holland, Jesse. 2007. *Black Men Built the Capitol: Discovering African-American History in and Around Washington, DC.* Guilford, CT: Globe Pequot Press.

International Slavery Museum. 2017. "About the International Slavery Museum." International Slavery Museum. Accessed June 1. http://www.liverpoolmuseums .org.uk/ism/about/.

Ismail, Salma. 2015. *The Victoria Mxenge Housing Project: Women Building Communities through Social Activism and Informal Learning.* Cape Town, South Africa: University of Cape Town Press.

Jacobs, Jane. 1961. *The Death and Life of Great American Cities.* New York: Random House.

Jacobsen, Thorkild. 1968. "The Battle Between Marduk and Tiamat." *Journal of the American Oriental Society* 88 (1): 104–8. doi:10.2307/597902.

James, George G. M. (1954) 2001. *Stolen Legacy: Greek Philosophy Is Stolen Egyptian Philosophy.* Chicago: African American Images.

Jaspin, Elliot. 2008. *Buried in the Bitter Waters: The Hidden History of Racial Cleansing in America*. New York: Basic Books.

Jenness, Mary. 1969. *Twelve Negro Americans*. New York: Books for Libraries Press.

Jones, E. Michael. 2004. *The Slaughter of Cities: Urban Renewal as Ethnic Cleansing*. South Bend, IN: St. Augustine's Press.

Jones, LeRoi. 1963. *The Blues People: Negro Music in White America*. New York: Harper Perennial.

Jordan, Winthrop. 1968. *White Over Black: American Attitudes Toward the Negro, 1550–1812*. Chapel Hill, NC: University of North Carolina Press.

Jordano, Dave, Nancy Barr, Sharon Zukin, and Dawoud Bey. 2015. *Detroit: Unbroken Down*. Brooklyn, NY: powerHouse Books.

Karllinn.org. 2016. "Reflections from Karl's Mentors." Karllinn.org. Accessed May 26. http://www.karllinn.org/about-1/tributes/.

Kent, Bruce R., Carl Anthony, and Karl Linn. 1989a. *Urban Barnraising. Part 1: Restoring Community through Building Neighborhood Commons*. VHS. San Francisco: Earth Island Institute and Urban Habitat Program.

———. 1989b. *Urban Barnraising. Part 2: Education for Service and Transformation*. VHS. San Francisco: Earth Island Institute and Urban Habitat Program.

Kilbourne, Richard H. 1995. *Debt, Investment, and Slaves: Credit Relations in East Feliciana Parish, Louisiana, 1825–1885*. Tuscaloosa, AL: University of Alabama Press.

King, Martin Luther, Jr. (1964) 2000. *Why We Can't Wait*. New York: Signet Classics.

Kneebone, Elizabeth, and Alan Berube. 2013. *Confronting Suburban Poverty in America*. Washington, DC: Brookings Institution Press.

Kouzes, James, and Barry Posner. 1987. *The Leadership Challenge: How to Make Extraordinary Things Happen in Organizations*. San Francisco: Jossey-Bass.

Krupp, Edwin C. 1983. *Echoes of the Ancient Skies: The Astronomy of Lost Civilizations*. New York: Harper.

———. 1991. *Beyond the Blue Horizon: Myths and Legends of the Sun, Moon, Stars, and Planets*. Oxford, UK: Oxford University Press.

Kutz, David, and Christopher Moore. 2009. *The African Burial Ground: An American Discovery*. DVD. Brooklyn, NY: Kutz Television.

La Force, Norman. 2002. *Creating the Eastshore State Park: An Activist History*. Berkeley, CA: Duplex Press.

Lambert, Tim, and Jonathan Hewes. 2015. *First Peoples*. DVD. Arlington, VA: PBS Distribution.

Lawrence, Jacob. 1993. *The Great Migration: An American Story*. New York: Harper Collins.

Lemann, Nicholas. 1991. *The Promised Land: The Great Black Migration and How It Changed America*. New York: Vintage Books.

Lifchez, Ray. 1987. *Rethinking Architecture: Design Students and Physically Disabled People*. Berkeley, CA: University of California Press.

Lifchez, Ray, and Barbara Winslow. 1979. *Design for Independent Living: The Environment and Physically Disabled People*. Berkeley, CA: University of California Press.

Linn, Karl. 2007. *Building Commons and Community*. Oakland, CA: New Village Press.

Linn, Karl, and Carl Anthony, ed. 1988. *Places for Peace*. Prepared for the 1988 World Congress of the International Federation of Landscape Architects. Boston: International Architects, Designers, and Planners for the Prevention of Nuclear War.

Loewen, James W. 2005. *Sundown Towns: A Hidden Dimension of American Racism*. New York: Touchstone Books.

Lynch, Kevin. 1981. *A Theory of Good City Form*. Cambridge, MA: MIT Press.

Mackenzie, Donald A. 1915. *Myths of Babylonia and Assyria*. London: Gresham Publishing Company.

Mann, Charles C. 2006. *1491: New Revelations of the Americas Before Columbus*. New York: Vintage Books.

Mann, Dennis Alan, and Bradford Grant. 2009. *African American Architects and Their Education: A Demographic Study*. Cincinnati, OH: University of Cincinnati.

Mann, Eric. 1991. *L.A.'s Lethal Air*. Los Angeles: Frontline Press.

Marcantonio, Richard A., and Alex Karner. 2014. "Disadvantaged Communities Teach Regional Planners a Lesson in Equitable and Sustainable Development." *Poverty & Race* 23 (1): 5–7, 12.

Matsuoka, Martha. 1997. "Reintegrating the Flatlands: A Regional Framework for Military Base Conversion in the San Francisco Bay Area." *Capitalism, Nature, Socialism* 8 (1): 109–24.

Matsuoka, Martha, and James O'Connor. 1995. "Reintegrating the Flatlands: A Regional Framework for Military Base Conversion in the San Francisco Bay Area." Working paper #1. *Assessing the Impact of Civilian Workforce Layoffs from Base Closures in Alameda and Solano Counties*. San Francisco: Urban Habitat Program.

McAdam, Doug, John D. McCarthy, and Mayer Zald. 1996. *Comparative Perspectives on Social Movements: Political Opportunities, Mobilizing Structures, and Cultural Framings*. Cambridge, UK: Cambridge University Press.

McIntosh, Roderick J. 2005. *Ancient Middle Niger: Urbanism and the Self-Organizing Landscape*. Cambridge, UK: Cambridge University Press.

McIntosh, Susan Keech, and Roderick J. McIntosh. 2014. "Jenne-Jeno, an Ancient African City." Rice University Department of Anthropology. http://anthropology.rice.edu/Content.aspx?id=500.

Meadows, Donella H., Dennis Meadows, Jørgen Randers, and William W. Behrens III. 1972. *The Limits to Growth: A Report for the Club of Rome's Project on the Predicament of Mankind*. Washington, DC: Potomac Associates. http:// donellameadows.org/wp-content/userfiles/Limits-to-Growth-digital-scan -version.pdf.

Merchant, Carolyn. 2002. *The Columbia Guide to American Environmental History*. New York: Columbia University Press.

Metropolitan Transportation Commission and the Association of Bay Area Governments. 2017. "Bay Area Census: City of Oakland." Metropolitan Transportation Commission and the Association of Bay Area Governments. Accessed May 28. http://www.bayareacensus.ca.gov/cities/Oakland.htm.

Moholy-Nagy, Sibyl. 1957. *Native Genius in Anonymous Architecture*. New York: Horizon Press.

Moore, Jason W. 2000. "Sugar and the Expansion of the Early Modern World-Economy: Commodity Frontiers, Ecological Transformation, and Industrialization." *Review: A Journal of the Fernand Braudel Center* 23 (3): 409–33.

Moore, Sir Patrick. 2009. *Legends of the Stars*. Stroud, UK: The History Press.

Movement Generation. 2017. "Mission and History." Movement Generation Justice & Ecology Project. Accessed April 2. http://movementgeneration.org /about/mission-and-history/.

Mumford, Lewis. (1922) 1962. *The Story of Utopias*. New York: Viking Press.

———. (1924) 1955. *Sticks and Stones: A Study of American Architecture and Civilization*. New York: Dover.

———. (1926) 1957. *The Golden Day: A Study in American Experience and Culture*. 2nd edition. Boston: Beacon Press.

———. 1944. *The Condition of Man*. New York: Harcourt, Brace and Company.

———. 1961. *The City in History: Its Origins, Its Transformations, and Its Prospects*. New York: Houghton Mifflin Harcourt Press.

National Advisory Commission on Civil Disorders. 1968. *Report of the National Advisory Commission on Civil Disorders*. Washington, DC: US Department of Justice.

National Oceanic and Atmospheric Association. 2014. "45 Years After the Santa Barbara Oil Spill, Looking at a Historic Disaster through Technology." Office of Response and Restoration. January 28. http://response.restoration.noaa.gov /about/media/45-years-after-santa-barbara-oil-spill-looking-historic-disaster -through-technology.html.

Nelson, Stanley. 2001. *Marcus Garvey: Look for Me in the Whirlwind*. DVD. Alexandria, VA: PBS Home Video.

Nesbett, Peter T. 2001. *Jacob Lawrence: The Complete Prints, 1963–2000*. Seattle, WA: University of Washington Press.

Neubert, Amy Patterson. 2011. "Lessons Learned from Japan's Earthquake Applicable for Hurricanes, Other Natural Disasters." *Purdue University News Service*, August 25. http://www.purdue.edu/newsroom/research/2011/110825T -AldrichJapan.html.

New-York Historical Society. 2016. "History of Slavery in New York." New-York Historical Society. Accessed May 26. http://www.slaveryinnewyork.org /history.htm.

Northup, Solomon. 1853. *12 Years A Slave*. Edited by David Wilson. Auburn, NY: Derby & Miller.

Nriagu, Jerome O. 1994. "Mercury Pollution from the Past Mining of Gold and Silver in the Americas." *The Science of the Total Environment* 149: 167–81.

O'Connor, Allison Marie. 2016. "Lincoln University [Pennsylvania] (1854–)." Black-Past.org. Accessed May 26. http://www.blackpast.org/aah/lincoln-university -1854.

O'Connor, James. 1997. *Natural Causes: Essays in Ecological Marxism*. New York: Guilford Press.

Oliver, Melvin L., and Thomas M. Shapiro. 1995. *Black Wealth / White Wealth: A New Perspective on Racial Equality*. New York: Routledge.

Oppenheimer, Stephen. 2003. *The Real Eve: Modern Man's Journey Out of Africa*. New York: Carroll & Graf.

Orfield, Myron. 1997. *Metropolitics: A Regional Agenda for Community and Stability*. Washington, DC: Brookings Institution Press.

———. 1998. *San Francisco Bay Area Metropolitics: A Regional Agenda for Community and Stability*. San Francisco: Urban Habitat Program.

———. 2006. *Minority Suburbanization, Stable Integration, and Economic Opportunity in Fifteen Metropolitan Regions: A Report by the Institute on Race and Poverty to the Detroit Branch NAACP*. Minneapolis, MN: Institute on Race and Poverty.

Pappas, Stephanie. 2012. "Start Date for Human Civilization Moved Back 20,000 Years or So." *The Christian Science Monitor*, July 30. http://www.csmonitor .com/Science/2012/0730/Start-date-for-human-civilization-moved-back -20-000-years-or-so.

Parks Division. 2017. "César Chávez Park." City of Berkeley Parks, Recreation and Waterfront Department. Accessed May 28. www.ci.berkeley.ca.us/Parks _Rec_Waterfront/Trees_Parks/Cesar_Chavez_Park.aspx.

Pastor, Manuel, Chris Benner, and Martha Matsuoka. 2009. *This Could Be the Start of Something Big: How Social Movements for Regional Equity Are Reshaping Metropolitan America*. Ithaca, NY: Cornell University Press.

Pastor, Manuel, Chris Benner, and Rachel Rosner. 2006. *Edging Toward Equity: Creating Shared Opportunity in America's Regions*. Santa Cruz, CA: Center for Justice, Tolerance, and Community, UC Santa Cruz. http://cjtc.ucsc.edu /docs/r_CORE_Edging_Toward_Equity_summary.pdf.

Pavel, M. Paloma, ed. 2009. *Breakthrough Communities: Sustainability and Justice in the Next American Metropolis*. Cambridge, MA: MIT Press.

Pavel, Paloma, Rick Butler, and Carl Anthony. 2001. *Voices from the Community: Social Equity and Smart Growth*. DVD. San Francisco: Urban Habitat Program.

Penprase, Bryan E. *The Power of Stars: How Celestial Observations Have Shaped Civilization.* New York: Springer.

Perlin, John. 1989. *A Forest Journey: The Story of Wood and Civilization.* Woodstock, VT: Countryman Press.

Piddington, Andrew. 2007. *The Real Eve.* DVD. Bethesda, MD: Discovery Communications, Inc.

Pollard, Sam, Catherine Allan, and Douglas A. Blackmon. 2012. *Slavery by Another Name.* DVD. St. Paul, MN: Twin Cities Public Television, Inc.

Ponting, Clive. (1991) 2007. *A New Green History of the World: The Environment and the Collapse of Great Civilizations.* London: Penguin Books.

Pope, Alexander. 1982. *Essay on Man.* Edited by Maynard Mack. London: Methuen.

Population Reference Bureau. 2016. "Human Population: Urbanization." Population Reference Bureau. http://www.prb.org/Publications/Lesson-Plans/Human Population/Urbanization.aspx.

Pulido, Laura. 2006. *Black, Brown, Yellow, and Left: Radical Activism in Los Angeles.* Berkeley, CA: University of California Press.

Rabinowitz, Howard N. 1996. *Race Relations in the Urban South, 1865–1890.* Athens, GA: University of Georgia Press.

Rebuild the Dream. 2016. "Our Work." Dream Corps Unlimited. Accessed June 6. https://www.rebuildthedream.com/our_work.

Rediker, Marcus. 2007. *The Slave Ship: A Human History.* New York: Viking Press.

Register, Richard. 1987. *Ecocity Berkeley: Building Cities for a Healthy Future.* Berkeley, CA: North Atlantic Books.

Reid, Frances, and Deborah Hoffmann. 2000. *Long Night's Journey into Day.* DVD. San Francisco: Iris Films.

RJOY [Restorative Justice for Oakland Youth]. 2017. "About Us." RJOY. Accessed April 16. http://rjoyoakland.org/about/.

Robinson, Eugene. 2010. *Disintegration: The Splintering of Black America.* New York: Doubleday.

Rodney, Walter. 1981. *How Europe Underdeveloped Africa.* Washington, DC: Howard University Press.

Rogers, Joel A. 1934. *100 Amazing Facts about the Negro with Complete Proof: A Short Cut to the World History of the Negro.* Lebanon, NH: Helga M. Rogers.

Rooks, Belvie. 2001a. "Hey, Listen Up!" *Yes! Magazine*, September 30. http://www.yesmagazine.org/issues/technology-who-chooses/463.

———. 2001b. "How to Look at a Brownfield and See a Flower Garden." *Race, Poverty, and the Environment* Winter: 24–26. http://www.reimaginerpe.org /files/1-40.pdf.

Rooks, Noliwe M. 2014. "The Path Forward for Policing Reform May Be the Kerner Commission's Almost 50-Year-Old Report." *Beacon Broadside,*

December 12. http://www.beaconbroadside.com/broadside/2014/12/the-path -forward-for-policing-reform.html.

Rose, Willie Lee. 1964. *Rehearsal for Reconstruction: The Port Royal Experiment.* Athens, GA: University of Georgia Press.

Rothstein, Richard. 2013. *For Public Schools, Segregation Then, Segregation Since: Education and the Unfinished March.* Washington, DC: Economic Policy Institute. http://www.epi.org/files/2013/Unfinished-March-School-Segregation .pdf.

Rusk, David. 1999. *Inside Game/Outside Game: Winning Strategies for Saving Urban America.* Washington, DC: Brookings Institution Press.

Sagan, Carl. 1980. *Cosmos.* New York: Random House.

Schneider, Dorothy, and Carl J. Schneider. 2000. *Slavery in America: From Colonial Times to the Civil War.* New York: Facts on File.

Schroeder, Amira Rose. 2016. "Girard College." Temple University Libraries. Accessed May 26. http://northerncity.library.temple.edu/exhibits/show/civil -rights-in-a-northern-cit/people-and-places/girard-college.

Sharp, Gwen. 2012. "Philadelphia Redlining Maps." The Society Pages: Sociological Images. April 25. https://thesocietypages.org/socimages/2012/04/25 /1934-philadelphia-redlining-map/.

Sheridan, Richard B. (1974) 2012. *Sugar and Slavery: An Economic History of the West Indies.* Kingston, Jamaica: University of the West Indies Press.

Shiva, Vandana. 2002. *Water Wars: Privatization, Pollution, and Profit.* Delhi: India Research Press.

Sibley, David. 1995. *Geographies of Exclusion: Society and Difference in the West.* London: Routledge.

Slotegraaf, Auke. 2013. "Africa Star-Lore." *Monthly Notes of the Astronomical Society of Southern Africa* 72 (3 & 4): 62–71. http://www.mnassa.org.za /html/Apr2013/2013MNASSA..72..Apr.pdf.

Smith, Gar. 1990. "Freeways, Community and Environmental Racism." *Race, Poverty, and the Environment* 1 (1): 7.

Smith, Kimberly K. 2007. *African American Environmental Thought: Foundations.* Lawrence, KS: University Press of Kansas.

Soursourian, Matthew. 2012. *Community Development Research Brief: Suburbanization of Poverty in the Bay Area.* San Francisco: Federal Reserve Bank of San Francisco. http://www.frbsf.org/community-development/files/Suburbanization-of-Poverty-in-the-Bay-Area1.pdf.

Spady, James G. 1988. "Marcus Mosiah Garvey: Man of Nobility and Mass Action." In *Great Black Leaders: Ancient and Modern,* edited by Ivan Van Sertima, 370–408. Piscataway, NJ: Transaction Publishers.

Spain, Daphne. 2001. *How Women Saved the City.* Minneapolis, MN: University of Minnesota Press.

Spirn, Anne Whiston. 2000. *The Language of Landscape.* New Haven, CT: Yale University Press.

Starr, Steven, and Irena Salina. 2008. *Flow: For Love of Water*. DVD. New York: Oscilloscope Pictures.

Steyn, Lala. 2012. "South Africa: Creating Win-Win Solutions for Business, Local Community Development, and Conservation." In *Untying the Land Knot Making Equitable, Efficient, and Sustainable Use of Industrial and Commercial Land*, edited by Xiaofang Shen and Xiaolun Sun, 71–85. Washington, DC: The World Bank.

Stowe, Harriet Beecher. 1852. *Uncle Tom's Cabin: Life Among the Lowly*. London: J. Cassell.

Stuart, Andrea. 2013. *Sugar in the Blood: A Family's Story of Slavery and Empire*. New York: Vintage Books.

Studnicki-Gizbert, Daviken, and David Schecter. 2010. "The Environmental Dynamics of a Colonial Fuel-Rush: Silver Mining and Deforestation in New Spain, 1522 to 1810." *Environmental History* 15 (1): 94–119.

Swimme, Brian, and Thomas Berry. 1992. *The Universe Story: From the Primordial Flaring Forth to the Ecozoic Era: A Celebration of the Unfolding of the Cosmos*. New York: Harper San Francisco.

Swimme, Brian, and Mary Evelyn Tucker. 2011. *The Journey of the Universe*. New Haven, CT: Yale University Press.

Taylor, Dorceta E. 2009. *The Environment and the People in American Cities, 1600s–1900s: Disorder, Inequality, and Social Change*. Durham, NC: Duke University Press.

Tibbles, Anthony. 2000. "Ports of the Transatlantic Slave Trade." Paper presented at the TextPorts Conference, Liverpool Hope University College, April. http://www.liverpoolmuseums.org.uk/ism/resources/slave_trade_ports.aspx.

———. 2007. "Liverpool and the Slave Trade." Lecture, Gresham College, London, March 19. http://gresham.ac.uk/lectures-and-events/liverpool-and-the-slave-trade.

Torrice, Andrea. 2000. *Rising Waters: Global Warming and the Fate of the Pacific Islands*. DVD. Oley, PA: Bullfrog Films

———. 2009. *The New Metropolis*. DVD. Oley, PA: Bullfrog Films.

United Nations. 2014. "World's Population Increasingly Urban with More than Half Living in Urban Areas." United Nations. July 10. http://www.un.org/en/development/desa/news/population/world-urbanization-prospects-2014.html.

United Nations General Assembly. 2007. Resolution 62/122. "Permanent Memorial to and Remembrance of the Victims of Slavery and the Transatlantic Slave Trade." December 17. http://www.un.org/en/ga/search/view_doc.asp?symbol=A/RES/62/122.

———. 2013. Resolution 68/237. "Proclamation of the International Decade for People of African Descent." December 23. http://www.un.org/en/ga/search/view_doc.asp?symbol=A/RES/68/237.

UNESCO [United Nations Educational, Scientific and Cultural Organization]. 2004. *Struggles Against Slavery: International Year to Commemorate the*

Struggle Against Slavery and Its Abolition. Paris: UNESCO. http://unesdoc
.unesco.org/images/0013/001337/133738e.pdf

Urban Habitat Program. 1995. *Sustainability and Justice: A Message to the President's Council on Sustainable Development.* San Francisco: Urban Habitat Program.

———. 1998. *What If We Shared?* San Francisco: Urban Habitat Program. http://urbanhabitat.org/files/1998-05-01-what_if_we_shared.pdf.

US Census Bureau. 2015. "New Census Bureau Report Analyzes U.S. Population Projections." Press release. March 3. https://www.census.gov/newsroom/press-releases/2015/cb15-tps16.html.

US Department of Education Office for Civil Rights. 2014. "Data Snapshot: School Discipline." *Civil Rights Data Collection*, March 21. http://ocrdata.ed.gov/Downloads/CRDC-School-Discipline-Snapshot.pdf.

Van der Ryn, Sim. 2005. *Design for Life: The Architecture of Sim Van der Ryn.* Layton, UT: Gibbs Smith.

Vlach, John Michael. 1993. *Back of the Big House: The Architecture of Plantation Slavery.* Chapel Hill, NC: University of North Carolina Press.

Wells, Ida B. 1893. "Preface." In *The Reason Why the Colored American Is Not in the World's Columbian Exposition: The Afro-American's Contribution to Columbian Literature*, edited by Ida B. Wells, 1. Chicago: Ida B. Wells. http://www.loc.gov/item/mfd.25023/.

Wells, Spencer. 2002. *The Journey of Man: A Genetic Odyssey.* New York: Random House.

Westgaph, Laurence. 2007. *Read the Signs: Street Names with a Connection to the Transatlantic Slave Trade and Abolition in Liverpool.* Liverpool, UK: Liverpool City Council.

Wilkerson, Isabel. 2010. *The Warmth of Other Suns: The Epic Story of America's Great Migration.* New York: Vintage Books.

Williams, Eric. (1944) 1994. *Capitalism and Slavery.* Chapel Hill, NC: University of North Carolina Press.

Wilson, William Julius. 1987. *The Truly Disadvantaged: The Inner City, the Underclass, and Public Policy.* Chicago: University of Chicago Press.

———. 1996. *When Work Disappears: The World of the New Urban Poor.* New York: Vintage Books.

Woodson, Carter G. (1933) 2010. *The Mis-Education of the Negro.* Lexington, KY: Seven Treasures Publications.

Woodward, C. Vann. 1955. *The Strange Career of Jim Crow.* Oxford: Oxford University Press.

World Commission on Environment and Development. 1987. *Our Common Future.* New York: Oxford University Press.

Wright, Gwendolyn. 1983. *Building the Dream: A Social History of Housing in America.* Cambridge, MA: MIT Press.

Zinn, Howard. 1980. *A People's History of the United States.* New York: Harper & Row.

Additional
Resources

Allen, Theodore W. 1994. *The Invention of the White Race, Volume 1: Racial Oppression and Social Control.* New York: Verso Books.

———. 1997. *The Invention of the White Race, Volume 2: The Origin of Racial Oppression in Anglo-America.* New York: Verso Books.

Anthony, Carl. 2006. "Reflections on the Purposes and Meanings of African American Environmental History." In *To Love the Wind and Rain: African Americans and Environmental History,* edited by Dianne Glave and Mark Stoll, 200–10. Pittsburgh, PA: University of Pittsburgh Press.

Anthony, Carl, and Renée Soule. 2008. "A Multicultural Approach to Ecopsychology." In *American Earth: Environmental Writing Since Thoreau,* edited by Bill McKibben, 849–54. New York: Penguin Putnam. Originally published in 1998 in *The Humanistic Psychologist* 26 (1–3): 155–62.

Baldwin, James. 1963. *The Fire Next Time.* New York: Knopf Doubleday.

———. 1985. "The Harlem Ghetto." In *The Price of the Ticket: Collected Nonfiction, 1948–1985, 1-12.* New York: Macmillan. Originally published in February 1948 in *Commentary.*

Battle, Thomas C., and Donna Wells, ed. 2006. *Legacy: Treasures of Black History.* Washington, DC: National Geographic.

Beauregard, Robert A. 2003. *Voices of Decline: The Postwar Fate of US Cities.* New York: Routledge.

Berlin, Ira. 1993. *Cultivation and Culture: Labor and the Shaping of Slave Life in the Americas.* Charlottesville, VA: University Press of Virginia.

———. 1998. *Many Thousands Gone: The First Two Centuries of Slavery in North America.* Cambridge, MA: Harvard University Press.

———. 2010. *The Making of African America: The Four Great Migrations.* New York: Viking.

Bernal, Martin. 1987. *Black Athena: Afroasiatic Roots of Classical Civilization, Volume I: The Fabrication of Ancient Greece, 1785-1985.* New Brunswick, NJ: Rutgers University Press.

Berry, Thomas. 2009. *The Christian Future and the Fate of the Earth.* Ossining, NY: Orbis Books.

———. 2009 *The Sacred Universe: Earth, Spirituality, and Religion in the Twenty-First Century.* New York: Columbia University Press.

Berry, Wendell. 2010. *The Hidden Wound.* Boston: Houghton-Mifflin.

Boger, John Charles, and Judith Welch Wegner, ed. *Race, Poverty, and American Cities.* Chapel Hill: University of North Carolina Press, 1996.

Buckminster Fuller Institute. 2015. "Geodesic Domes." Buckminster Fuller Institute. Accessed May 25. https://bfi.org/about-fuller/big-ideas/geodesic-domes.

Bullard, Robert D. 2005. *The Quest for Environmental Justice: Human Rights and the Politics of Pollution.* San Francisco: Sierra Club Books.

Bullard, Robert D., ed. 1993. *Confronting Environmental Racism: Voices from the Grassroots.* Boston, MA: South End Press.

Calthorpe, Peter. 1993. *The Next American Metropolis: Ecology, Community, and the American Dream.* Princeton, NJ: Princeton Architectural Press.

———. 2013. *Urbanism in the Age of Climate Change.* Washington, DC: Island Press.

Calthorpe, Peter, and William Fulton. 2001. *The Regional City: Planning for the End of Sprawl.* Washington, DC: Island Press.

Carney, Judith A. 2001. *Black Rice: The African Origins of Rice Cultivation in the Americas.* Cambridge, MA: Harvard University Press.

Carney, Judith A., and Richard N. Rosomoff. 2011. *In the Shadow of Slavery: Africa's Botanical Legacy in the Atlantic World.* Berkeley, CA: University of California Press.

Cole, Luke, and Sheila Foster. 2001. *From the Ground Up: Environmental Racism and the Rise of the Environmental Justice Movement.* New York: New York University Press.

Coquery-Vidrovitch, Catherine. 2005. *The History of African Cities South of the Sahara: From Origins to Colonization.* Translated by Mary Baker. Princeton, NJ: Markus Wiener Publishers.

Crockett, Norman L. 1979. *The Black Towns.* Lawrence, KS: Regents Press of Kansas.

Davidson, Basil. 1991. *African Civilization Revisited.* Trenton, NJ: Africa World Press.

Diop, Cheikh Anta. 1974. *The African Origin of Civilization: Myth or Reality.* Edited and translated by Mercer Cook. Westport, CT: Lawrence Hill & Co.

———. 1987. *Precolonial Black Africa: A Comparative Study of the Political and Social Systems of Europe and Black Africa, from Antiquity to the Formation of Modern States.* Translated by Harold J. Salemson. Westport, CT: Lawrence Hill & Co.

Dixon, Melvin. 1987. *Ride Out the Wilderness: Geography and Identity in Afro-American Literature*. Champaign, IL: University of Illinois Press.

Drake, St. Clair, and Horace R. Cayton. (1945) 1993. *Black Metropolis: A Study of Negro Life in a Northern City*. Chicago: University of Chicago Press.

Du Bois, W. E. B. (1935) 1998. *Black Reconstruction in America: 1860–1880*. New York: Free Press.

Erickson, Brad. 1990. *Call to Action: Handbook for Ecology, Peace and Justice*. San Francisco: Sierra Club Books.

Finkelman, Paul. 1989. *Economics, Industrialization, Urbanization, and Slavery*. New York: Garland Publishing.

Finney, Carolyn. 2014. *Black Faces, White Spaces: Reimagining the Relationship of African Americans to the Great Outdoors*. Chapel Hill, NC: University of North Carolina Press.

Foner, Eric. 1990. *A Short History of Reconstruction: 1863–1877*. New York: Harper and Row.

———. 2015. *Gateway to Freedom: The Hidden History of the Underground Railroad*. New York: W. W. Norton.

Franklin, John Hope. (1961) 1994. *Reconstruction after the Civil War*. 2nd edition. Chicago: University of Chicago Press.

Gates, Henry Louis, Jr. 2013. *Life Upon These Shores: Looking at African American History, 1513–2008*. New York: Alfred A. Knopf.

Gates, Henry Louis, Jr., and Cornell West. 2000. *The African American Century: How Black Americans Have Shaped Our Country*. New York: Free Press.

Genovese, Eugene. 1976. *Roll, Jordan, Roll: The World the Slaves Made*. New York: Vintage Books.

Giddings, Paula. 1984. *When and Where I Enter: The Impact of Black Women on Race and Sex in America*. New York: Morrow.

Gilbert, Olive. (1850) 2014. *Narrative of Sojourner Truth, a Northern Slave, Emancipated from Bodily Servitude by the State of New York, in 1828*. Boston, MA: Heraklion Press.

Glave, Dianne D. 2010. *Rooted in the Earth: Reclaiming the African American Environmental Heritage*. Chicago: Chicago Review Press.

Glave, Dianne D., and Mark Stoll, ed. 2005. *To Love the Wind and the Rain: African Americans and Environmental History*. Pittsburgh, PA: University of Pittsburgh Press.

Goldfield, David R. 1989. *Cotton Fields and Skyscrapers: Southern City and Region*. Baltimore, MD: Johns Hopkins University Press.

Grimmond, Sue. 2007. "Urbanization and Global Environmental Change: Local Effects of Urban Warming." *The Geographical Journal* 173: 83–88.

Hahn, Steven. 2003. *A Nation under Our Feet: Black Political Struggles in the Rural South from Slavery to the Great Migration*. Cambridge, MA: Harvard University Press.

Harding, Sandra, ed. 1993. *The "Racial" Economy of Science: Toward a Democratic Future.* Bloomington, IN: Indiana University Press.

Harlan, Louis R., ed. 1974. *The Booker T. Washington Papers.* Volume 3. Urbana, IL: University of Illinois Press.

Heifetz, Ronald. 1998. *Leadership without Easy Answers.* Cambridge, MA: Harvard University Press.

Hochschild, Adam. 1998. *King Leopold's Ghost: A Story of Greed, Terror, and Heroism in Colonial Africa.* New York: Macmillan.

———. 2005. *Bury the Chains: Prophets and Rebels in the Fight to Free an Empire's Slaves.* Boston, MA: Houghton Mifflin.

Horton, James Oliver, and Lois E. Horton. 2004. *Slavery and the Making of America.* New York: Oxford University Press.

Houston, Jean. 1987. *The Search for the Beloved: Journeys in Sacred Psychology.* New York: Tarcher.

International Slavery Museum. 2010. *Transatlantic Slavery: An Introduction.* Liverpool, UK: Liverpool University Press.

Jackson, John Brinckerhoff. 1972. *American Space: The Centennial Years, 1865–1876.* New York: W. W. Norton.

Jackson, Kenneth. 1985. *Crabgrass Frontier: The Suburbanization of the United States.* New York: Oxford University Press.

Jacobs, Harriet. (1861) 2012. *Incidents in the Life of a Slave Girl.* Mineola, NY: Dover Publications.

James, C. L. R. 1938. *The Black Jacobins: Toussaint L'Ouverture and the San Domingo Revolution.* New York: Dial Press.

Katz, Bruce, ed. 2000. *Reflections on Regionalism.* Washington, DC: Brookings Institution Press.

Katz, Bruce, and Jennifer Bradley. 2013. *The Metropolitan Revolution: How Cities and Metros Are Fixing Our Broken Politics and Fragile Economy.* Washington, DC: Brookings Institution Press.

Lawrence, Jacob. 2006. *Redemption: The Last Battle of the Civil War.* New York: Farrar, Straus & Giroux.

Linebaugh, Peter, and Marcus Rediker. 2000. *The Many Headed Hydra: Sailors, Slaves, Commoners, and the Hidden History of the Revolutionary Atlantic.* Boston, MA: Beacon Press.

Litwack, Leon F. 1979. *Been in the Storm So Long: The Aftermath of Slavery.* New York: Alfred A. Knopf.

———. 1999. *Trouble in Mind: Black Southerners in the Age of Jim Crow.* New York: Vintage Books.

McAdam, Doug. 1990. *Freedom Summer.* Oxford, UK: Oxford University Press.

———. 1982. *Political Process and the Development of the Black Insurgency, 1930–1970.* Chicago: University of Chicago Press.

Macy, Joanna, and Chris Johnstone. 2012. *Active Hope: How to Face the Mess We're in without Going Crazy.* Novato, CA: New World Library.

Marable, Manning. 1999. *How Capitalism Underdeveloped Black America: Problems in Race, Political Economy, and Society.* Cambridge, MA: South End Press.

Massey, Douglas, and Nancy Denton. 1998. *American Apartheid: Segregation and the Making of the Underclass.* Cambridge, MA: Harvard University Press.

Muir, John. (1916) 1992. *A Thousand-Mile Walk to the Gulf.* New York: Penguin Books.

Olmsted, Frederick Law. (1861) 2008. *The Cotton Kingdom: A Traveler's Observations on Cotton and Slavery in the American Slave States, 1853–1861.* Carlisle, MA: Applewood Books.

Oppenheimer, Stephen. 2004. *Out of Eden: The Peopling of the World.* London: Robinson Publishing.

Orfield, Myron. 2002. *American Metropolitics: The New Suburban Reality.* Washington, DC: Brookings Institution Press.

Osofski, Gibert. 1967. *The Burden of Race: A Documentary History of Negro-White Relations in America.* New York: Harper and Row.

———. 1971. *Harlem: The Making of a Ghetto: Negro New York, 1890–1930.* Chicago: Ivan R. Dee.

Painter, Nell Irvin. (1989) 2008. *Standing at Armageddon: A Grassroots History of the Progressive Era.* New York: W. W. Norton.

———. 2010. *The History of White People.* New York: W. W. Norton.

Pease, William H., and Jane H. Pease. 1963. *Black Utopia: Negro Communal Experiments in America.* Madison, WI: State Historical Society of Wisconsin.

Popkin, Nathaniel. 2002. *Song of the City: An Intimate History of the American Urban Landscape.* New York: Perseus Basic Books.

———. 2008. *The Possible City: Exercises in Dreaming Philadelphia.* Philadelphia, PA: Camino Books.

Potts, Richard. 1996. *Humanity's Descent: The Consequences of Ecological Instability.* New York: Avon Books.

Rudofsky, Bernard. 1964. *Architecture without Architects: A Short Introduction to Non-Pedigreed Architecture.* New York: Museum of Modern Art.

Rusk, David. 1995. *Cities without Suburbs.* Washington, DC: Woodrow Wilson Center Press.

Sandercock, Leonie. 1998. *Making the Invisible Visible: A Multicultural Planning History.* Berkeley, CA: University of California Press.

———. 1998. *Towards Cosmopolis: Planning for Multicultural Cities.* London: John Wiley.

———. 2003. *Cosmopolis II: Mongrel Cities of the 21st Century.* New York: MacMillan.

Schein, Edgar. 1992. *Organizational Culture and Leadership.* San Francisco: Jossey-Bass.

Sen, Amartya. 1999. *Development as Freedom.* New York: Knopf.

Smail, Daniel Lord. 2008. *On Deep History and the Brain*. Berkeley, CA: University of California Press.

Smallwood, Stephanie. 2007. *Saltwater Slavery: A Middle Passage from Africa to American Diaspora*. Cambridge, MA: Harvard University Press.

Speth, James Gustave. 2004. *Global Environmental Challenges: Transitions to a Sustainable World*. Hyderabad, India: Orient Blackswan.

———. 2012. *America the Possible: Manifesto for a New Economy*. New Haven, CT: Yale University Press.

Tyson, Neil deGrasse, Charles Tsun-Chu Liu, and Robert Irion. 1999. *One Universe: At Home in the Cosmos*. Washington, DC: National Academy Press.

Tyson, Neil deGrasse, and Donald Goldsmith. 2004. *Origins: Fourteen Billion Years of Cosmic Evolution*. New York: W. W. Norton.

Van der Ryn, Sim, and Peter Calthorpe. 2008. *Sustainable Communities: A New Design Synthesis for Cities, Suburbs and Towns*. Gabriola Island, Canada: New Catalyst Books.

Van Sertima, Ivan, ed. 1988. "Great Black Leaders Ancient and Modern." *Journal of African Civilizations* 9.

Washington, Booker T. 1991. *Up from Slavery*. Garden City, NY: Doubleday & Company, Inc.

Watkins, Mary, and Helene Shulman. 2008. *Toward Psychologies of Liberation*. New York: Palgrave Macmillan.

———. 2015. "When Will the North Face Its Racism?" *New York Times*, January 11. http://www.nytimes.com/2015/01/11/opinion/sunday/when-will-the-north-face-its-racism.html.

The White House Historical Association. 2014. "African Americans in the White House Timeline." The White House Historical Association. Accessed January 27. https://www.whitehousehistory.org/african-americans-in-the-white-house-timeline.

X, Malcolm. 1965. *Malcolm X Speaks: Selected Speeches and Statements*. Edited by George Breitman. New York: Grove Press.

Acknowledgments

First, I would like to acknowledge Dr. M. Paloma Pavel, who has been my colleague and partner in this work since 1998. She is a visionary leader whose creativity and strategic thinking have been essential to this book and to our work in the field. With her education as an eco-psychologist addressing large-scale systems change and individual transformation, she has made an important contribution to my work and to our communities. When I was directing the Sustainable Metropolitan Communities Initiative at the Ford Foundation, Paloma's skills came together in creating a peer-learning experience for our grantees. Much of this experience was documented in her book, *Breakthrough Communities: Sustainability and Justice in the Next American Metropolis*. This book launched Breakthrough Communities, an urban think-and-do tank we cofounded in Oakland, California. Paloma has designed a Learning Action Guide to complement the book, and, together, we continue to develop the leadership resources and training for the next generation of emerging advocates and activists.

I would like to acknowledge those who gave this manuscript its final push. My personal editors, Diana Young and Jan Thomas, played key roles. Jan combed through my writings and shaped the raw material of my ideas and observations into an initial manuscript. Diana then collaborated with me to flesh out and polish that manuscript. As I was losing vision, both Jan and Diana generated text by interviewing me and transcribing my statements.

Several funders were crucial for the completion of this manuscript, including the Ford Foundation and its president Darren Walker, Surdna

Foundation, Nathan Cummings Foundation, San Francisco Foundation, California Endowment, East Bay Community Foundation, Akonadi Foundation, and California Health Care Foundation. I would like to express my special appreciation to Don Chen, the Ford Foundation's director of Equitable Development, who has been a source of guidance and inspiration.

Other people who played important roles as readers and reviewers include Rick Butler, Grace Gilliam, David Henderson, Dan Hofstadter, Esther Mealy, Webb Mealy, Louise Music, Richard Page, Dennis Rivers, and Belvie Rooks and her partner, the late Dedan Gills.

I am honored to be working with New Village Press, which began as the publishing arm of Architects Designers Planners for Social Responsibility (ADPSR), an organization I have been involved with since the early 1980s. New Village Press has been a voice for grassroots community building with books on advocacy and planning, as well as arts and culture, and the essential vision and values that make life worth living in our metropolitan regions. I am grateful to Lynne Elizabeth, New Village Press CEO and urban visionary, as well as her capable team, including editors Jourdan Sayers and Erasmia Gorla, who interviewed me extensively and helped me shape the manuscript, copy editor Laura Leone, who fine-tuned grammar, punctuation, style, accuracy of historical details, and citations, and Muneeba Raza, who steers publicity for this book.

As I acknowledge other guides on the journey of this work, I must begin by expressing appreciation for my parents, who provided the early experiences that shaped my view of the world, and for my brother, Lewie, sixteen months older than me, with whom I shared a rich childhood and ongoing intellectual dialogue as we became adults.

My third grade teacher, Mrs. Aikens, inspired my love for the natural world and my fascination with deep time and the universe. She influenced my choice of career and is a testament to the power of childhood educators.

As I prepared for a sojourn at Columbia University, I found early mentors in Lewis Mumford, James Baldwin, and Karl Linn. The student organizers and elders I met at a pivotal conference I attended at Sarah Lawrence College during my early days at Columbia provided my first sense of multiracial community.

I was inspired by both Dr. Martin Luther King Jr. and Malcolm X and by my fellow activists in the Northern Student Movement as we worked to bring justice and opportunity to Harlem residents. I appreciate the influential faculty members at Columbia School of Architecture and others in the field, such as Paul Davidoff, who developed the practice of advocacy planning, and Bernard Rudofsky, who mounted an exhibition at the Museum of Modern Art on "Architecture Without Architects." I am deeply grateful to my colleagues at the Architects Renewal Committee in Harlem, the first advocacy planning organization in the US, and to its executive director Max Bond, who became the first African American faculty member at Columbia after his return from designing and constructing buildings in Ghana.

I was grateful for the opportunity to travel to Cuba in 1968 with a group organized by urban planner, author, and tireless voice for housing rights, Chester Hartman.

On the journey to West Africa with my then-partner, Jean Doak, I was grateful for time spent among the Wolof, Fulani, Hausa, Dogon, Ashanti, and Pô communities, who shared so generously their culture and life.

Returning to the United States, Jean and I came to the University of California at Berkeley, where I was fortunate to work with and learn from some of the most innovative and creative designers and planners in the field. Notably, I am grateful to Sym Van der Ryn, who was later appointed California state architect by Jerry Brown, for inviting me to join him in teaching the first courses in energy conservation and developing a natural energy pavilion. This was a beginning to my engagement with environmental issues in architecture. We based our teaching on the principles articulated by E. F. Schumacher in *Small is Beautiful*. However, the primary focus of our early work was appropriate technology, and we were not yet able to focus our attention on serving the most vulnerable populations.

During this leg of my journey, many African American friends and allies nourished my cultural grounding: Sala Ajanaqu, Barbara Christian, Maria Rosa Grinwald, David Henderson, Arthur Monroe, Claremont Moore, Daphne Muse, Ishmael and Carla Reed, and Cathy Sloan, to name a few. However, I continued to experience a growing tension between the needs within our most vulnerable communities and the orientation of the academy.

Wanting to prioritize the need for community development, I eventually chose to leave the university and open my own planning and architecture firm with Virgus Streets, an African American colleague who had just received his PhD in planning. At the end of that partnership, I formed another partnership with architect Randall Fleming. I am grateful to Kevin Lynch, a student of Frank Lloyd Wright and well-known planner who collaborated with us on a proposal for Oakland's Central District Redevelopment Plan. Although we were not awarded the contract, our proposal was well received and positioned us to be engaged as consultants on the Berkeley Waterfront Plan, which led to increased visibility and opportunity for actual projects. The success, however, came with a price. It required me to move away from my focus on social justice and the needs of the African American community. I am immeasurably thankful to my mentor, Karl Linn, for helping me face the emotional crisis this brought on and introducing me to the work of Thomas Berry, Joanna Macy, Vandana Shiva, and others who expanded my vision. From collaboration with Karl, I saw the need and possibility of developing a new model of service that would prioritize the needs of communities of color. Karl also introduced me to David Brower and the board of Earth Island Institute, who offered me a platform to develop the Urban Habitat Program (UHP), which focused on growing multiracial environmental leadership and mobilizing at the regional scale to address environmental issues affecting communities of color. I appreciate the many emerging leaders who came into my life through UHP and its programs and projects, as well as its funders for providing not only resources but also a sounding board and communication link to many other emerging groups in the environmental justice movement.

Every issue of our UHP publication, *Race, Poverty, and the Environment,* focused on a different urban challenge and would not have been possible without the work of guest editors, writers, and activists, whose contributions helped this field to expand. I give thanks to Joe Brooks for chairing the UHP board during my transition from role of director and to Juliet Ellis, Allan Hernandez Smith, and Ellen Wu for their leadership as subsequent executive directors.

I appreciate the many allies throughout the Bay Area who partnered with us during those years in impacting public policy through innovative methods of community engagement and organizing, such as the first smart growth and social equity film, which shaped the Bay Area Sustainability Footprint Project. I am grateful to all those in our social justice community and beyond who participated in that valuable regional planning process.

Owing to the impact of these social innovations in the Bay Area, I was invited by the Ford Foundation to develop the Sustainable Metropolitan Communities Initiative (SMCI). I am grateful for my many colleagues in philanthropy and for the convening power of the Ford Foundation, which enabled us to gather the group we called CORE (Conversation On Regional Equity). I must acknowledge Ben Starrett, who provided significant leadership in organizing philanthropic partners through the Smart Growth and Livable Communities Network. I also extend enormous gratitude to the

SCMI grantees who helped to build the foundation for a national regional equity movement.

After leaving Ford, I had the opportunity to apply knowledge from this national equity movement to the growing crisis of climate change. Major new legislation in California provided fertile opportunities to build new networks of social justice organizations. Indeed, those most deeply affected by a problem have genius that can provide solutions for not only their own communities but also the whole of society, and I would like to acknowledge our partners from the nine counties of the Bay Area who worked to build the Six Wins for Social Equity Network. I would also like to express my heartfelt appreciation to the Resilient Communities Initiative for working with us at Breakthrough Communities in adaptation to climate change.

Over the years, the courageous work of building sustainability and resilience with justice has benefited from legislative champions. Some of those I have worked with directly include Ron Dellums, Barbara Lee, Jerry Brown, Loni Hancock, Mark DeSaulnier, Darrell Steinberg, Sunne Wright McPeak, Sandré Swanson, Nancy Skinner, Tony Thurmond, John Gioia, David Campos, Keith Carson, Sheila Jordan, Gus Newport, Tom Bates, Jean Quan, Gayle McLaughlin, Libby Schaaf, Janet Abelson, Mark Friedman, Ying Lee, Linda Maio, and Max Anderson.

I extend deep appreciation to Van Jones for his visionary leadership and for making time to write a foreword for this book.

My extended family deserves special acknowledgement, including my cousin Paula Campbell and her husband, Kabera Kiross, and my brother's widow, Gwen Anthony, and their daughter, Robin Anthony Koati, her husband, Ouslam, and their daughter, Jasmine, and son, Nfali.

I am deeply indebted to Jean Doak, my life partner for fourteen years in the 1960s and 1970s. Jean carefully read the first six chapters of this book and offered many improvements and clarifications. She is the mother of our son, Khalil Doak Anthony, a creative and talented musician who is following his own dreams, and we are grandparents to Makai, son of Khalil and Dr. Stacia Sloan. I treasure the close relationship that Jean and I began in 1962 and have continued to the present day.

Index

CPSIA information can be obtained
at www.ICGtesting.com
Printed in the USA
LVOW13s0258280218
568166LV00024B/1141/P